Kosovo's Refugees in the European Union

Kosovo's Refugees in the European Union

Edited by

Joanne van Selm

PINTER
London and New York

Pinter
A Continuum Imprint
Wellington House, 125 Strand, London WC2R 0BB
370 Lexington Avenue, New York, NY 10017-6503

First published 2000

British Library Cataloguing-in-Publication Data
A catalogue record for this book is available from the British Library.
ISBN 1-85567-640-0 (hardback)
      1-85567-641-9 (paperback)

Library of Congress Cataloging-in-Publication Data
Kosovo's refugees in the European Union / edited by Joanne van Selm.
      p. cm.
   Includes bibliographical references and index.
   ISBN 1-85567-640-0 – ISBN 1-85567-641-9
   1. European Union. 2. Political refugees–Yugoslavia–Kosovo. 3.
Albanians–Yugoslavia–Kosovo (Serbia)–History. 4. Yugoslavia–Ethnic
relations. 5. Europe–Ethnic relations. I. Selm. Joanne van.

D1065.K67 K66 2000
949.703–dc21   00-021789

Typeset by BookEns Ltd, Royston, Herts.
Printed and bound in Great Britain by
Biddles Ltd, Guildford and King's Lynn

Contents

CONTENTS

Tables

Contributors

Elisabeth Abiri is Lecturer and Researcher in International Relations at the Department of Peace and Development Research, University of Gothenburg, Sweden.

Elspeth Guild is a partner with Kingsley Napley solicitors, London, and Academic Co-ordinator at the Centre for Migration Law at the University of Nijmegen, The Netherlands.

Christopher Hein is Director of the Italian Refugee Council, Rome, Member of the Executive Committee of ECRE and Lecturer at the University of Rome, Italy and the University of Madrid, Spain.

Khalid Koser is Lecturer in Human Geography and a member of the Migration Research Unit at University College London, UK. He was carrying out research in Germany between March and May 1999.

Sandra Lavenex is Lecturer in International Relations at the University of Zurich, Switzerland.

Joanne van Selm is Lecturer in International Relations at the University of Amsterdam, The Netherlands, where she also carries out research at the Institute for Ethnic and Migration Studies and the Amsterdam School for Social Science Research.

Irene Stacher is Head of the Austrian Forum for Migration Studies at ICMPD in Vienna and is Lecturer at the Institute for African Studies at the University of Vienna, Austria.

Acknowledgements

As editor of this volume, I would like to express my gratitude to each of the contributors for their positive responses to the ideas behind this volume, and their willingness to act quickly to produce the work. I would also like to thank Caroline Wintersgill at Continuum for her enthusiasm and support throughout this project, as well as all those at Continuum who worked so hard on the production of the book. Acknowledgement for her role in inspiring this book is also due to Frederiek de Vlaming. Meindert Fennema gave valuable comments on the overall vision and the Introduction and Conclusion in particular. Finally, I would like to thank Jeroen Doomernik, Karen Waringo and Aninia Nadig for their assistance in collecting general information when my own time ran short.

Joanne van Selm
Amsterdam
December 1999

CHAPTER ONE

Introduction

JOANNE VAN SELM

Images

There are images of the situation in and around Kosovo between 24 March and 14 June 1999 which many Europeans will not quickly forget. For some people those memories will centre on the often-used pictures of children; for some they will focus on overcrowded camps in Albania and Macedonia. Others will recall haunting reminders of the Second World War: footage of trains filled with what the media term 'human misery' arriving close to the border between Kosovo and Macedonia, only to be turned around, their human 'cargo' for the most part still aboard. Some people will remember seeing vague TV pictures, shot at a distance, of Serb soldiers 'removing the identity' of their victims: piling up and burning not only the passports and driving licences of ethnic Albanians, but also the number plates from the cars in which they were travelling. Many will remember the outpouring of goodwill as telethons and other major events took place in Western Europe and around the world, raising money and collecting goods for the relief of the Kosovar 'refugees'. Many will recall the fine words of European Union (EU) and NATO leaders about securing peace and defeating Milošević, so the refugees would be able to go home.

Some will remember the vacillation of EU and NATO governments when it came to deciding on how best to handle the massive displacements of Kosovars. The few images of planeloads of Kosovar victims evacuated to EU states will be recalled, amid memories of governments citing numbers they would accept, and then changing their minds. Those memories will speak volumes, not only about the particular case surrounding the Kosovo crisis, but also about the steps the EU has made and seeks to make towards creating a European immigration and asylum policy, and about the links between immigration and security. The records of the EU member states' reception of Kosovars in their own territory will be an important subject of research for those interested in asylum policies and practices generally, European integration and notions of post-Cold War European security. Those records will be as important for what did not happen as for what did.

About this book

In this book a group of researchers from different disciplines have come together to describe and analyse the approaches which a selection of EU governments took towards the displaced of Kosovo. We place the approaches of those governments towards the displaced in the context of both domestic politics and European integration. Our concern here is twofold. We aim to examine the EU member states' approach to the protection of Kosovars as a step in the process of altered political thought on the need and means of refugee protection, and as a step on the way to an EU common approach to this subject.

This book will seek to describe and analyse the vacillations of EU member states concerning the management of this European refugee crisis. Seven of the member states will be addressed in detail (Austria, France, Germany, Italy, The Netherlands, Sweden and the UK). The reception of Kosovo's refugees in other member states and some non-EU European states will be described more briefly in a final 'case chapter'. The seven states reflect the range of EU state stances with regard to:

- reputations with regard to asylum and immigration policies generally;
- approaches to the matter of 'solidarity' or 'burden sharing' at the EU level as a tool for accomplishing a common approach;
- geographical spread with regard to proximity to the Balkan region;
- stances on NATO intervention and involvement in that intervention.

The intervention and NATO bombing campaign itself may well be pondered upon in future works and analysed in terms of the lessons learned from the previous chapter in the Balkan conflicts of the 1990s, that played out from 1992 to 1995 in Bosnia and Herzegovina. Matters of refugee protection, protection of the displaced and humanitarian assistance also need to be examined from the point of view of the lessons learned, both positive and negative, from the reception of Bosnians in the EU and other European states and the attempts at creating alternative havens for them within Bosnia itself.

The seven chapters in this book each develop four main themes:

1   the lessons of the reception and statuses accorded to Bosnians and drawn on in dealing with the displacements of Kosovars;

2 the national debates on asylum and immigration within which this crisis took place and which influence policy-making;
3 the wider theoretical issues;
4 the way EU integration (or not) on the subject is impacting policy-making in the different states.

In some chapters these themes represent distinct sections, in others they are informing features of the analysis.

This book does not present a history of Kosovo or of the complex mesh of conflicts which have marked the Balkan region throughout the 1990s.[1] Nor does it set out to present a history of the NATO intervention in spring 1999, or the build-up to that. Rather we focus exclusively on questions relating to how the displacement crisis as such was, could and perhaps should (from the perspective of the norms of refugee protection and human rights standards) have been handled by EU governments.

There is an almost implicit assumption behind each chapter of this book: that the EU member states have a duty to accept and protect refugees. This means we leave one of the biggest and most often handled questions relating to refugee protection largely untouched: why should any state accept refugees, the unprotected and outcasts from another state? While that question is indirectly handled in the discussions that follow, on both domestic and EU-level politics and on xenophobia and 'new' security issues, it is not at the heart of this volume. It is not an irrelevant question. However, to allow us to tackle in more depth the core themes described above, all the contributors set out from the under-standing and premise that the participation of the current EU member states in the development of refugee law, human rights norms, and the general history of their practice of refugee protection lends weight to the notion that the acceptance and protection of some refugees is to be expected.[2] In spite of this history, however, the bigger questions for the EU states appear now to have become how to protect, where to protect and, above all, how many to protect.

As an introduction to the case study chapters below, this Introduction will set out, briefly, the background of Kosovar migration to the EU states up to the NATO intervention. Three key linked areas which form the background to the chapter-by-chapter analyses will then be presented. These are: matters relating to European integration in the field of asylum and immigration policies; an understanding of a comprehensive approach to refugee protection issues; and notions of 'societal security' linked to matters of threat perception, identity and xenophobia.

Kosovo's displaced and the EU before March 1999

Displacements in and from Kosovo did not begin with the NATO bombing on 24 March 1999. The scale of displacement and exodus became enormous after that date, but the fact that displacements were already taking place, and that massacres of ethnic Albanians by Serbian military and police were being reported and observed by international press and Organization for Security and Cooperation in Europe (OSCE) monitors, was one of the most outspoken reasons given for embarking on the NATO intervention. Between 1995 and 1997 at least 114,430 asylum applications had been lodged in EU member states by people coming from the Federal Republic of Yugoslavia.[3] There were also many tens of thousands of Kosovars already in the EU, either those who had entered Germany (and Switzerland) in particular as 'guest-workers' in the 1960s or their descendants, or more recently (rejected) asylum seekers who could not be returned to Yugoslavia owing to the lack of cooperation of the Belgrade government, which suggested that many were 'confirmed criminals'.[4]

The 1997 'Background paper on refugees and asylum seekers from Kosovo' from the United Nations High Commissioner for Refugees (UNHCR) discusses, as does Noel Malcolm, the centuries-long population movements and displacements in what is now the Kosovo region.[5] During and after the Second World War Serbs had been forced out of Kosovo in large numbers. Some Serbian reports claim that as many as 220,000 Serbs and Montenegrins abandoned their homes in Kosovo between 1968 and 1988, and that 600,000 Serbs had been displaced from Kosovo between 1878 and 1988.[6] Those same Serbian sources claimed that some 100,000 ethnic Albanians moved into Serbia during and immediately after the Second World War. Malcolm dismisses these claims as 'pure fantasy'. He found no evidence of such massive movements inwards in any of the documents of the occupying powers. He does concur that many Serbs and Montenegrins left, calling the figure of 30,000 'over-modest' and 100,000 'exaggerated'.[7]

Since the break-up of former Yugoslavia the Serbian leadership has tried, largely unsuccessfully, to 'encourage' Serbs returning after a period of refugeehood, or those refugees from other republics, to settle in Kosovo. One incentive was interest-free credits for building and buying accommodation. The resettling of these Serbs in Kosovo caused outrage among the ethnic Albanians, and reluctance among the Serbs. Out of 500,000 refugees in the Federal Republic of Yugoslavia in early 1997, only some 4000 had in fact settled in Kosovo.[8] Malcolm describes how Belgrade planned for 20,000 of the Krajina Serbs displaced by Croat attacks in 1995 to move to Kosovo. In one incident, 'when a bus-load of refugees only discovered *en route* that they were being taken to Kosovo, they put a gun to the driver's head and forced him to turn back to Belgrade'.[9] Official statistics in 1996 reported that 19,000 Serb refugee-colonists were in Kosovo.[10]

By the time the parties were sitting around the table for the unsuccessful Rambouillet meetings, several hundred thousand Kosovar Albanians had been displaced, many within Kosovo, but several tens of thousands also to neighbouring states, or more distant European states and the US where they had relatives who had previously migrated. UNHCR statistics given in Table 1.1 show movements within and from Kosovo.[11]

On 22 March the UNHCR reported that at least 20,000 ethnic Albanians had fled their homes in north-west Kosovo during two days of intense attacks by Serb security forces. It was estimated that in the previous week 40,000 people had fled their homes. Clearly the potential for many thousands more displacements, should the situation in Kosovo go unchecked, was high, given both the ongoing situation and the experiences of 'ethnic cleansing' in Bosnia, Serbia and Croatia from 1991 to 1995. It remains unclear whether the policy-makers involved in the decision to undertake NATO action were ignorant of the potential for mass exodus should they bomb, or simply did not prioritize the possibility (or rather probability) to such a degree that they would risk the secrecy surrounding the build-up to the bombing by alerting the appropriate protection agencies and taking protection-related decisions together with home affairs colleagues. What is clear is that the exodus which did occur, starting on 24 March, and the displacements within Kosovo itself, were met by those international and national organs charged with the protection of the displaced and refugees with an outward show of unpreparedness and lack of coordination. The conflict

Table 1.1 Displacements within and from Kosovo to March 1999

State	Kosovar displaced to March 1999
Within Kosovo	260,000
Serbia	55,000
Montenegro	25,000
Macedonia	16,000
Albania	18,500
Bosnia and Herzegovina	10,000
Europe	100,000
Croatia	350
Total	459,850

Source: UNHCR, 'Kosovo Crisis Update'

and crisis in Kosovo and Yugoslavia (Serbia and Montenegro) as a whole resulted, according to many sources, in the displacement of almost the entire Kosovar Albanian population (estimated at 1.8 million people), with at least half of them crossing Kosovo's borders. It also resulted in the displacement of other Muslims elsewhere in Yugoslavia, and, from mid-June onwards, of some 170,000 Serbs from Kosovo fleeing the indiscriminate revenge of returning ethnic Albanians.

In the days and weeks following 24 March 1999, confusion appeared to reign over who had the upper hand in refugee protection on the ground: NATO or UNHCR. By 6 April some clarity was emerging as NATO took charge of food, relief supplies, medical aid and airlifts to camps, apparently at the request of the UNHCR.[12] Speculation soon mounted, however, as to whether or not the NATO presence under 'Operation Allied Harbour' in Albania might be a means of amassing ground troops in the vicinity ready for an eventual land offensive.[13] NGOs, meanwhile, accused the UNHCR of not taking the lead.[14] Neighbouring governments were forced into a generosity beyond their means.[15] Amid increasing concern about the use of those Kosovar Albanians still in Kosovo as 'human shields' and other atrocities, debate and discussion raged as to where was the best place for the displaced to be assisted and protected. The UNHCR preferred reception close to home, but with some evacuations within the European region. The EU states maintained that the reception of the refugees in their region of origin was the optimal solution. Region, in this instance, was not Europe, not the Balkans (for that would include Greece) but Albania, Macedonia and (internal displacement to) Montenegro. Paradoxically, while in military security terms the whole of a broad 'Europe' became the sphere of interest for NATO, the 'region' for Europe's refugees seems limited to the neighbouring states of the country in crisis – as long as they are not members of the EU – perhaps in the interests of other security concerns, as will be discussed below.

The first airlifts of 'refugees' seemed to be chain deportations rather than evacuations. On 6 April some 3500 people were removed to Turkey and Norway, many fearful and unaware of their destinations, many separated from family members in the confused rush.[16] That same day the EU member states had continued to show their lack of coordination, insisting they could collectively accept only up to 100,000 of the 1,000,000 or more displaced persons. They were to meet on 7 April to examine how to share the costs. The starting positions were reported as fixed, clear and divergent. The UK was fixed in indecision; France was reported as giving in to public pressure to accept some refugees, and had pledged $40m in aid to Kosovo's neighbouring states; Spain had pledged $56m and would accept 7000–10,000 refugees. Sweden and Greece both claimed already to have 30,000 refugees from Kosovo in their respective countries, and stated that they would accept 5000 more each.[17] Germany and The

Netherlands were both seeking 'burden sharing': Germany by putting an upper limit on its quota until other states had acted too; The Netherlands by refusing to act until partners showed their willingness to play a part. The continuing attempts of Kosovars to reach Germany via the Czech Republic, Hungary and Poland, which had been going on since long before March 1999, were still being met by a paper curtain, as the lack of documentation meant refusal of legal entry.[18] This highlighted the distinctions being made between quota refugees from Kosovo and spontaneous arrivals: the former were somehow legitimized by the so-called selection process, which reports suggested was often open to corruption, while the latter were still often equated with illegal immigrants in spite of the very obvious conflict in their place of origin. As Guild shows in Chapter 4, however, there was no conformity on administrative expression of this standpoint, as the UK appeared to privilege those who had arrived spontaneously prior to the bombing campaign ('our refugees') above potential new quota arrivals ('others').

For those who were to be protected within the EU, the Belgian Defence Minister, Jean-Pol Poncelet, argued for equal conditions, specifying the protection to be offered by Belgium and its neighbouring states (Germany, France, The Netherlands and Luxembourg). The Belgian Interior Minister, Luc van den Bossche, was said to be in contact with his counterparts in those states on this subject.[19] As the chapters that follow will demonstrate, no such common approach was achieved, either for quota refugees evacuated from Macedonia or for spontaneous arrivals. The process of European integration to March 1999 had not brought agreement on whom to protect or how to protect them: the emergency situation brought about by the escalation of conflict in Kosovo pushed matters no further in the short term.

European integration

Political attention during the NATO campaign focused on the 'justness' (morality, legality and efficacy) of the bombing and intervention as the means to prevent 'ethnic cleansing'. Public attention, as suggested in the imagery described above, focused on the misery and suffering of fellow Europeans in refugee camps. Descriptions of European unity centred on creating and maintaining unity, or the image of unity, within NATO, and (tacitly at least) in non-NATO EU states, for the continuing bombing campaign. EU Justice and Home Affairs Ministers meeting under the German presidency were far from unified on how to manage the growing displacement crisis.[20]

On the 39th day of the bombing campaign, 1 May 1999, the Amsterdam Treaty entered into force. This set in motion a five-year programme of work on the field of asylum and immigration aimed at bringing that policy area into the scope of community activity by May 2004 – part of the creation of 'an area of freedom, security and justice'.[21] Full community activity should mean that there will be a common asylum and immigration policy for the twelve participating EU member states (the UK and Ireland have an opt-in clause; Denmark has opted out of this area of collective action).[22] The twelve member states have committed themselves to consider, by 2004, *who* is deserving of protection, *how* and, in a spirit of solidarity, *where*. However, as displaced Kosovars trekked across the borders into Albania and the former Yugoslav republic of Macedonia, as well as into the neighbouring republic of Yugoslavia, Montenegro, the EU member states reacted with confusion and a distinct lack of unity. Perhaps the only unifying feature was confusion. Whether to accept Kosovars even as asylum seekers? How to go about transporting the limited numbers accepted as part of quotas? How big a quota to establish? Could the displaced and refugees best be protected close to Kosovo? How close was close enough, and how close might be too close? All the buzz words of asylum policies and politics of the previous two decades flew around political debate and media reports: 'reception in the region', 'safe areas', 'temporary protection', 'comprehensive approach' and particularly the synonymous triplet of 'burden sharing', 'responsibility sharing' and 'solidarity'.

Just four years after the displacements in Bosnia and Herzegovina, massive dislocation of human beings was taking place in Europe again. From 1992 to 1995 the EU member states had developed varied approaches towards those forced to flee by war and generalized violence aimed arbitrarily at members of particular ethnic or religious groups. Many had accepted significant numbers of Bosnian refugees – according them either a refugee status (under the Geneva Convention or *de facto*), temporary protection or at least a guarantee against return.[23] Only one EU state had seen the departure of large numbers of Bosnians – although it is not clear that those 'encouraged' to leave Germany had in fact returned to Bosnia. As Koser examines in Chapter 2 on Germany, it is also not clear exactly what the impact of these 'returns' was, in terms of the lessons Germany had learned from the Bosnian case, on its approach to the displaced persons from Kosovo.

During and immediately after the Bosnian displacements, several proposals on both a common approach to temporary protection and 'burden sharing', or 'solidarity', had been tabled in the European Council and Council of Ministers, without binding results, if indeed any results at all.[24] Both issues form part of the five-year work programme elaborated in the Treaty of Amsterdam. No decisions had been taken for common action in crisis situations, and so, just as in the early 1990s, this 1999 crisis saw the EU member states having to turn to unilateral approaches with regard to the type of protection to be offered and guaranteed, and the

8

links between the granting of status and the means of entry, via quota evacuations or spontaneous arrivals. Also as in 1993, the lack of a common approach forced EU member states to take unilateral action while embarking on a new phase of activity which is said to be intended to lead to collective policy-making.

Power

The EU states claimed unity in their intention to use military power via NATO (or, where the neutral EU states were concerned, tacitly supported that expression of power), and in the earliest days of the campaign were apparently indeed unified (on the intergovernmental, if not the domestic, level) in the conviction of their position of power, together with the USA, against Milošević's Serbia. However, they were clearly not convinced of the level of their power in the face of potential immigration. In immigration matters, power essentially means the ability to control admission to territory and either the integration of those admitted into society or the possible scenarios for their onward resettlement or return movement. One important question here, which links to the notion of power within the discussion of 'societal security', is whether the search for an EU-level approach is based primarily on a pragmatic conviction that there is more strength to be found in a collective effort to control the various facets of immigration, or based on an admission of impotence as individual states. (It can, of course, involve both.) Building on this, a further question must be whether the difference in stance of the member states on cooperation with respect to immigration and asylum is indeed due to the difference in 'problems' (with asylum, or with illegal immigration, with smuggling, etc. relative to the individual state), as is often suggested, or is due to a differing perception of the state's own power to control. Immigration could be conceived of as a threat only if the receiving state perceives itself as being impotent in relation to the immigrants, on the basis of either control over their entry, legitimisation of their stay, or the nature of their activities while they are in the country, whether they are included in or excluded from society.

A comprehensive approach to immigration and asylum policies[25]

Since 1989 and the re-emergence of civil war and ethnic conflict, unchecked by Cold War super-power balancing, as well as the apparent increase in economically motivated migration to the developed world, many thinkers have suggested notions of a more 'comprehensive approach' to migration and protection issues. The protection of those displaced by conflict and political turmoil has become enveloped in wider questions of migration. Understandings of security, and means of warfare, have developed in such a way that displaced persons can no longer be considered mere unavoidable consequences of conflict and persecution. They can now be either a contributing factor to the spread of unrest, or the deliberate result of highly determined policies of 'ethnic cleansing'. There is a need for holistic policies which recognize the complexity of the migration phenomenon and bring a perception of management and control to the potentially large-scale migrations of both the displaced and those seeking employment and opportunities (legally or illegally), while upholding the rights of all the people concerned. These policies need to acknowledge the interdependence of various policy areas and goals which coincide in the puzzle that migration generally has become. Thus, for example, policies which seek to promote economic growth by removing frontier controls on the movement of goods, capital and services must, as the EU has discovered, also remove controls on the movement of people, even though this brings new policy needs for controlling the movement of those people and goods whose presence is not legally sanctioned.

In the area of forced displacement, a comprehensive approach could be simplified into three areas: prevention, protection and durable solutions. Prevention would mean the controlling of flight: removing the causes forcing flight, or (from the perspective of the more distant states, reluctant to open their borders) preventing flight from becoming international or inter-regional. Protection overlaps with prevention policies in the setting up of 'safe areas' (as in Bosnia) or provision of facilities and assistance for 'reception in the region', whereby many displaced persons remain in states neighbouring their state of origin (as in the Kosovo case). However, protection also involves the granting of legal status for the presence of displaced persons and refugees in other states, and could include issues of solidarity, whereby the responsibility for such protection would not fall on some states more than others. States in the region of origin also often call for solidarity, as Croatia and Slovenia did during the Bosnian crisis.[26] Longer-term solutions involve the integration of the displaced and refugees in their host country, through indefinite residence permits and perhaps naturalization where desired. They also involve the possibility of return, more possible or likely if the period of protection has been short and the causes of the displacement resolved, or of resettlement to more distant states, as when the USA resettled some 20,000 Bosnians from Germany rather than see them returning prematurely to Bosnia. Resettlement could also be understood as a form of solidarity.

In the Kosovo case arguments were made for the use of NATO intervention as a means of stopping Milošević in his aim of forcing people to leave Kosovo and Serbia. (As we know, the displacement continued, and may have increased as a result of the intervention.[27]) A desire to prevent flight could also be understood as being based on states' 'right' not to have refugees thrust upon them. While the NATO intervention in Serbia could be characterized as part of a preventive, root causes approach, the attempt to prevent forced displacement is not enough: the need to protect remains.[28] Although other elements of the approach have clearly been part of the developing situation, including the question of return, which has taken place on a staggering scale since this book was commissioned, our aim is to give a broad overview of the protection element of the comprehensive approach. We are, above all, concerned with the protective solution of temporary protection, potentially in conjunction with 'solidarity', and the accordance or otherwise of asylum or refugee status. As such, we are telling just a part of the wider story, but a part which is pivotal in the approach as a whole.

Theoretical issues: 'societal security'

Since the early 1990s and the end of the Cold War-type or 'traditional' security paradigm, the search has been on to identify the primary 'new' security concerns affecting international relations. If one accepts the premise that a key function of a state's existence is its role as the protector of the territory and population which it represents, the state as such can continue only if it has a role as the guarantor of security. The question after the Cold War is what does the state now have to protect, and from what? While domestically the state still needs to protect the population from crime from within, for example, what does it need to protect against on the international level, if not primarily nuclear war and ideological confrontation with a known enemy bloc or state? In other words, if specific other states are not the threat to a given state on the international level, then what is? Also, if the extinction of the people within a state and the challenge to its territory through war or invasion is not the threat it faces, then what is? After all, if there were no threat from outside, then the state as such would have lost one of the primary reasons for its very existence as a unit of division in the world.

One suggestion among several in international relations literature is that the facet of the state which needs protecting is its identity, and that the threat to that identity is immigration. This branch of recent theorizing on security has been termed 'societal security' and has been most significantly advanced, within the context of wider deliberations on the post-Cold War European security framework, by the so-called 'Copenhagen School'.[29] The perception of a loss of identity or 'swamping of culture' is nothing new; but the spread of this understanding and perception and almost unquestioning widespread acceptance of the predominantly xenophobic 'story' of immigration seems to indicate a swing in vision compared to mainstream thought in recent decades.

Although one exponent of the Copenhagen School, Waever, posits an interesting notion of a non-state-associated society, he soon reverts to an equation of society with state. This equivalence of state and society has become established in the literature, meaning that when the identity of a society is perceived as being under threat, the matter becomes one of national interest.[30] A static identity appears in these circumstances to become the most precious commodity a state holds. With national interest central, as Shaw points out, this 'new' 'societal security' becomes, in fact, a re-expression of traditional realism.

'Societal security' is part of a 'problem-solving' theory, seeking a way of understanding what the problem is with our world and how to solve it.[31] If 'identity' is threatened, there seems to be a presupposition that identity is a static and easily recognizable, monotone feature of states and societies. Identities attached to states, nations or societies have surely developed over the past millennium, often when people from other parts of the world have travelled, invaded, colonized, moved to work, moved out of interest, as tourists or adventurers. Many people would call this dynamic of identity a positive feature of developments in the world, and would turn to words such as 'multicultural', 'cosmopolitan' and 'globalization' to describe the evolution in the characteristics attributed to identities, people and places.

Power

Questions of power are central to all realist thinking. The notion of a threat includes the implication of a perception on the part of the 'threatened' of being challenged by the perceived threat-maker, who may not be perceived as necessarily stronger, but is seen as at least having the potential to disturb the *status quo*. Perceiving immigration as a threat means perceiving immigrants (*en masse*) as a powerful challenge either to the state they are trying to enter or to the society into which they might integrate (or, if they really are a threat, the society which they may conquer). As important, if not more so, is that the response to a perceived threat is normally expressed through the exertion of power – or the attempt to create a perception of the power of the potential 'victim'.

If identity can be perceived as under threat, however, one would expect this to have been the case in the past. There are very few recent stark cases of actual, objectively identifiable generalized threats from immigrants which spring to mind, although the World Trade Center bombers in the USA, for example, were indeed 'asylum seekers', or at least (ab)using that entry category in order to be present in the USA. Perhaps the strongest examples of immigrants threatening whole societies are in fact those of the

European colonizers conquering indigenous peoples in centuries past. The many thousands of Hungarian refugees accepted by West European states in 1956 and the Czechs and Slovaks in 1967 were not rejected on the grounds that their presence would threaten societal security, but rather accepted with open arms as challengers to, and people threatened by, the Communist enemy, as Stacher portrays in Chapter 6 of this book. Kosovar Albanians are also challengers to, and threatened by, the indicted war criminal Milošević and his regime, but, as will be seen, governmental offers for their protection in the EU were relatively limited.

Perceiving immigrants as a threat to the identity of society requires a qualification of the nature of a threat. The originators of the 'societal security' concept offer other sectors of security beyond the societal (e.g. environmental, economic, military). These are lenses through which 'security' problems may be viewed and analysed.[32] Perhaps these lenses need also to be attached to the notion of threat (not just the sector within which the threat is perceived), and thus turned on each other. For example the Moluccans in The Netherlands or the Kurdish Workers' Party (PKK) in Germany may be perceived as having presented a *political* threat to identity or 'societal security'; but race rioters in the UK or the attackers of asylum seekers in Germany might likewise be perceived as threats to the wider identity of society. Unemployed immigrants may be seen as an *economic* threat to societal identity (although if barriers of legality of residence attach to their unemployability, more questions remain about the origin of the threat). Increasing population density, whether caused by 'natural increase' or by immigration, may be perceived as an *environmental* threat to identity if that is perceived as more associated with the countryside than with urban conglomerations, but the depopulation of cities might also be perceived as a *cultural* threat.

The threats intimated by fearful West Europeans are clearly more subtle than bomb-blasts or invasion. They are primarily associated with rising numbers of asylum applications (see Appendix 2, Table 7), and instinctive, rather than as a result of critically questioning the causes of increased (forced) migration. The question is, are the perceived threats in fact so subtle as to be unrealistic? Are they figments of the imagination which, by causing a feeling of insecurity, may in themselves create a threat to the peace and stability of Europe in the longer term, returning Europe to the type of racism present in the 1930s, and forcing fleeing masses to remain in states which are far from politically stable or far from being able to cope with them, such as Albania and Macedonia in the case of Kosovars?[33]

Xenophobia

A further problem one could identify in Western Europe at the end of the 1990s is the rise in racism and xenophobia. However the solution to this problem, inferred both from the international relations literature and from government policies as described in the chapters that follow, seems to be that immigration should be stopped. This logic suggests that if there are no immigrants, there will be no xenophobia or racism, so there should be no immigrants. This logic is severely, and obviously, flawed. Racism and xenophobia are caused not by immigrants, but by the attitudes of existing members of the society receiving those immigrants. Jews were not responsible for the phenomenon we call Nazism; immigrants are similarly not responsible for the phenomenon we label racism and xenophobia. What is more, those subscribing to this flawed logic appear to suggest that if there are no immigrants, identity will be unchallenged, as there will be no challenge either from the immigrants with their 'other' cultures, or from those racists and xenophobes who pose enormous questions about what exactly being British, French, German, Dutch or any other nationality means. However, racism and xenophobia surely form a serious threat and challenge to all societies which claim a humanitarian identity (as EU states generally do). Are the refugees and immigrants the ones who need to be excluded to solve that particular problem?

Linking security and refugee movements

The most frequently heard arguments for the reluctance to accept Kosovars in EU states were that this would only be encouraging ethnic cleansing, and that EU states already have too many immigrants, asylum seekers and refugees who will not go home. These arguments reflect various security concerns and the political nature of refugee protection at both the domestic and the international levels. While the nexus of refugee or displacement issues on the one hand, and security issues on the other, cannot be denied, the key question is where that link lies. In turn, the answer seems to depend very much on who is asking the question, and the interests which are at stake. This means that the displaced are sometimes perceived as the threat to security, not as people whose security has been threatened.[34] When outpourings of generosity and humanity as seen in West European states in the context of the Kosovo crisis are juxtaposed with longer-term political understandings of national identity and interest, questions about how the displacement–security conundrum fits together become increasingly complex.

The problem-solving described above misses the heart of the link between refugees and security. In the process it also lends support to xenophobic groups and ideas.[35] Waever *et al.* themselves point to potential abuse of their notion of societal security:[36]

> The closeness to fascist ideology is troubling: is it therefore inadvisable to raise this agenda of societal security? Isn't there a risk that the result is to

14

legitimise xenophobic and nationalist reactions against foreigners or against integration - 'We're just defending our societal security!'? This could be a risk, but it seems to us a risk we have to take. This danger has to be offset against the necessity to use the concept of societal security to try to understand what is actually happening: the social construction of societal insecurity. Our main interest is not whether this or that increases or decreases societal security, but what processes trigger the definition among specific groups of an issue as 'a threat to societal security'.

Realizing the potential abuse of such theorizing, one could choose to abandon it (as the Copenhagen School appear to have done in their 1998 book, where the discussion on migration as a threat is much more hesitant, and the 'spin' given to their previous conceptualization more positive (creating a sense of society could increase integration of immigrants) rather than risking being negative.[37] However, abandonment, or hesitant recognition of abuse, is not sufficient. One needs to go further, both by pursuing the question of where exactly the security issue lies in refugee movements, and by developing further the theoretical notion of society as a useful concept in security thinking. While this volume does not seek specifically to engage in theory building, it does seek to pursue the question, both directly and indirectly via case studies, of where the security threat lies, and thereby to provide a basis to future, more theoretically oriented research.[38]

A useful approach to the link between security and refugee issues would be to consider the sort of threats and violations of security the refugees face and faced, which (in realist terms) force them out from the protection of their state of origin, into the 'anarchical system'. In migration studies terms, this does not necessarily have to mean that we are back at the unresolved 'root causes' debate.[39] Rather we should be posing questions about the linkages between the causes of forced migration, the type of protection offered, and the locus of challenge to the protecting state in refugee situations.

States have duties towards their citizens; that is one basis upon which the modern system of governance is premised. They also, through the creation of alliances and agreements, have duties towards other states. Those states or governments which cause flight, through persecution or conflict, violate the rights of their citizens by forcing flight. They also encroach upon the rights of other states to which victims will flee – whether individual flight is intended by the state or is simply a by-product of other policies and actions. However, the states towards which refugees turn have also, since the Second World War, established certain standards with regard to the acceptance of immigrants and human rights. One element of this is related to the status of refugees, as set out in the 1951 Geneva Convention and 1967 Protocol. The development of refugee law created a legal status for people considered to have lost, or who could objectively not accept, the protection of their state of origin. The provision of that refugee protection has often been used in the host state's interest.[40] The matter of protection by the state of origin, referring back to the comprehensive approach, forms an essential difference between economic migrants and refugees: an economic migrant remains willing and able to avail him- or herself of the protection of his or her state of origin. A refugee is not willing to avail him- or herself of such protection, and, along with many displaced persons not recognized as refugees, does not enjoy such protection.[41] Those forced to flee or displaced therefore have the right to 'seek and enjoy asylum in countries other than their own'.[42] The type of views expressed in academic terms by the Copenhagen School, and politically by extreme right-wing parties and, increasingly, mainstream parties across the political spectrum, although they may be directed at immigrants generally, mean that in practice those displaced by conflicts such as that in Kosovo cannot achieve this right to seek asylum, or even forms of protection which accord them fewer entitlements, in countries other than their country of origin's neighbours. Calls to close borders, and uphold the sovereign right of the state, are often associated with right-wing, xenophobic attitudes, and shouted down by those with a more liberal or humanitarian standpoint. Pragmatically, one must acknowledge that in granting protection within a comprehensive approach, states, as the guarantors of security, have to be aware of the domestic impact of their protection policy decisions. The creation of a comprehensive approach recognizing the security and protection needs of both states (and societies) and refugees is a delicate balancing act which has yet to be perfected. But to support wider European security, the EU states cannot simply shift the entire refugee protection burden in European crises on to weak European states. This is a misuse of power by the stronger states, and in fact could signify a sense of lost power when faced with potential immigration.

Nothing new under the sun?

A frequent criticism of the terminology and notion of 'new security' is that there is nothing new about the issues raised as security threats. A reading of Noel Malcolm's *Short History of Kosovo*[43] shows how, in the very region from which the displaced people we are discussing originate, there is nothing new about migration, forced displacement, adapting identities, adoption of different (more convenient) religions, and so on. Perhaps the point is that rather than being new as such, it is the potential for higher prioritization of the sort of environmental and societal issues to which security thinkers are turning which gives an added value to their consideration as being potentially threatened, or sources of threats, in the post-Cold War world. After decades in which nuclear war and weapons (and the opposing bloc, which might use them or manipulate change by threatening to use them) posed the greatest threat to the object of security held most important (the 'nation'-state, and its territory and ideology in particular), the change of focus to other objects of security may have made other threats and everything surrounding them seem new to many thinkers emerging from the Cold War mind-set. Whether or not one can agree with the notion of newness of these issues, it is important not to dismiss significant elements of debate just because the adjective used is disturbing. In this volume we seek to go beyond the question of novelty and address the matter of where priorities lie in security concerns which involve human displacement within a given territory or across borders. Rather than taking the entirety of the comprehensive approach as described above, we focus on the protection elements without dismissing either the causes or solutions.

The analysis in this book

We address security and identity politics issues in the context of a specific critique based on reactions to the Kosovar displacements, and specifically seek to demonstrate the usefulness or otherwise of the 'societal security' approach in understanding the policy reactions of EU governments engaged simultaneously in developing political integration in the fields of asylum and immigration policies, the NATO bombing campaign (and propaganda surrounding it) and the satisfaction of various tendencies in domestic public opinion. The contributors demonstrate on a state-by-state basis how such a 'new security' approach may help in understanding the policy decisions taken, both of rejecting (in general) significant numbers of displaced persons as fully fledged refugees, and in seeking to allow and assist them to stay in and return to their state of origin. However, even if theoretical notions of 'societal security' can offer a basis to this particular line of understanding, they still leave open many other questions, not least about the political bases of such thought. In addition, other factors and other areas of theory are, needless to say, also of great importance and relevance in building up a complete picture of the approach to Kosovo's refugees. We have selected this theoretical approach in the hope of adding to academic debate as well as offering analysis of the cases presented.

The analysis of the cases extends also into the realms of the intentions of the EU member states for collective action on asylum matters, and the lessons they either have or could have learned from the experience of the earlier Balkan crisis, in Bosnia in particular, but also in Croatia.

Some words on the order of chapters

While any ordering of case chapters representing the 'story' from different EU states would have to be somewhat arbitrary in nature, a certain logic has been sought here. *Germany* is in many ways a leader on the asylum and immigration issue, as on other issues in European integration. It also held the presidency of the EU during the period in question. We therefore begin with the German case. The Benelux states often appear, at least, to be following Germany in policy reactions to changes in asylum arrivals: when German law changes, and numbers reduce, it is perceived that numbers of arrivals rise in The Netherlands – which then also changes its laws. The Dutch case is the only Benelux case included here, and the Dutch government, like the German, was very vocal on 'solidarity' and the need for an EU approach to the Kosovo exodus, even if it used a different strategy. *The Netherlands* therefore follows Germany in this volume. While Germany and The Netherlands discussed solidarity from the perspective of EU member states moving towards a communitarized approach under the Treaty of Amsterdam, the *UK*, with its opt-out/opt-in arrangement, has a somewhat different starting point on these issues generally. Like the UK, *Sweden* has been experiencing a rise of political restrictions on immigration with explicit 'security' motives, yet public opinion supported a more humanitarian approach in the Kosovo case. *Austria*, as another neighbour to Germany, has a long history as a transit state for asylum seekers on their way from the East toward the capitalist and democratic West European states. Its role as a transit state has changed, but its proximity to the Balkans has meant that it has remained a significant recipient of Europe's end-of-twentieth-century 'refugees'. *Italy*, as an EU state easily reachable from the Balkans, has been the entry point for many of Kosovo's spontaneous arrivals in the EU as a whole. Those spontaneous arrivals have a role to play in the 'stories' as presented on Germany, The Netherlands, the UK and Austria. Finally, and in a sense 'closing the circle', *France*'s immigration approach is often seen as being in stark contrast to that of its neighbour, Germany. These two countries therefore give form to a symbolic line dividing the asylum and immigration approaches of the EU states, even if there remain fifteeen, rather than two, approaches.

Notes

1. See N. Malcolm, *Kosovo: A Short History* (London: Macmillan, 1998) on the history of Kosovo; and, for example, M. Glenny, *The Fall of Yugoslavia* (London: Penguin, 1992), L. Cohen, *Broken Bonds: The Disintegration of Yugoslavia* (Oxford: Westview, 1993), D. Dyker, and I. Vejvoda, *Yugoslavia*

and After: A Study in Fragmentation, Despair and Rebirth (London: Longman, 1996) on the wider Yugoslav crises.

2. There is an extensive bibliography of literature examining these subjects. A very limited number of examples include G.S. Goodwin-Gill, *The Refugee in International Law* (Oxford: Clarendon, 1996 – 2nd edn); J.C. Hathaway, *The Law of Refugee Status* (Toronto: Butterworths, 1991); A. Grahl-Madsen, *The Status of Refugees in International Law*, vols 1 and 2 (Leiden: A.W. Sijthoff, 1966 and 1972 respectively).

3. UNHCR, 'Populations of concern to UNHCR – 1997 Statistical Overview': www.unhcr.ch/refworld/refbib/refstat/1998/98tab26.htm.

4. UNHCR, 'Background paper on refugees and asylum seekers from Kosovo' (February 1997): www.unhcr.ch/refworld/country/cdr/cdrkos.htm.

5. *Ibid.* and Malcolm, *Kosovo*.

6. Cited by WRITENET, 'Country Papers – Albanians in Kosovo: prospects for the future' (October 1994): www.unhcr.ch/refworld/country/writenet/wriyug.htm.

7. Malcolm, *Kosovo*, p. 313.

8. UNHCR, 'Background paper on refugees', section 5.

9. Malcolm, *Kosovo*, p. 353.

10. *Ibid.*, note 39.

11. UNHCR, 'Kosovo crisis update' (6 April 1999): www.unhcr.ch/news/media/kosovo.htm. Document for public information purposes, not official UN information.

12. 'With aid effort overwhelmed, NATO will take over coordination' and 'Faster aid for the refugees' (7 April 1999): www.nytimes.com. The independent evaluation carried out for UNHCR indicates that NATO took on a humanitarian role, while UNHCR was seemingly expected to be responsible for refugee *security* in the camps – see pp. vii and ix, A. Suhrke, M. Barutciski, P. Sandison and R. Garlock, *The Kosovo Crisis: an evaluation of UNHCR's emergency preparedness and response* (Feb. 2000): www.unhcr.ch.

13. *Guardian*, 'NATO builds up troop force' (9 April 1999): www.guardian.co.uk.

14. For example, criticism from Oxfam noted in *Independent*, 'War in the Balkans – briefing: day 56' (19 May 1999): www.independent.co.uk.

15. See Appendix 1.

16. Reuters, 'Macedonia's biggest refugee area clears' and 'Kosovo refugees bused out of Macedonia' (7 April 1999): www.reuters.com; *Washington Post*, '3,500 expelled from Macedonia' (7 April 1999): www.washingtonpost.com; *New York Times*, 'Many fear where they're going as well as where they've been' (7 April 1999): www.nytimes.com; *Guardian*, 'Split families hustled to flights out of Macedonia' (7 April 1999): www.guardian.co.uk.

17. *Guardian*, 'EU at loggerheads over growing refugee crisis' (7 April 1999): www.guardian.co.uk; Reuters, 'EU prefers to keep Kosovan refugees near home' (7 April 1999), www.reuters.com.

18. *International Herald Tribune*, ' "Paper curtain" snags Kosovo refugees' (7 April 1999): www.iht.com.

19. Reuters, 'Belgian minister urges Europe-wide refugee status' (13 April 1999): www.reuters.com.

20. This contrasts with the enforced unity of foreign policy (when Germany took the lead as the Treaty on European Union was concluded) and lack of unity on asylum policy in 1992-3. For a description of this, see J. van Selm Thorburn and B. Verbeek, 'The chance of a lifetime: the European Community's foreign and refugee policies towards the conflict in Yugoslavia, 1991-1995', in P. Gray and P. 't Hart (eds) *Public Policy Disasters in Western Europe* (London: Routledge, 1998).

21. Title IV of the consolidated version of the Treaty Establishing the European Community after the entry into force of the Amsterdam Treaty.

22. See J. van Selm-Thorburn, 'Asylum in the Amsterdam Treaty: a harmonious future?', *Journal of Ethnic and Migration Studies* 24 (4) (1998), 175-92.

23. See J. van Selm-Thorburn, *Refugee Protection in Europe: Lessons of the Yugoslav Crisis* (The Hague: Kluwer Law International, 1998) on the forms of protection developed in EU states for those fleeing Bosnia and Herzegovina.

24. European Commission, *Proposal to the Council for a Joint Action Based on Article K.3(2)(b) of the Treaty on European Union Concerning Temporary Protection of Displaced Persons*, COM(97) 93 final, 97/0081 (CNS) (Brussels, 5 March 1997); Council of Ministers, European Community, *Conclusions on People Displaced by the Conflict in the Former Yugoslavia of the Meeting of Ministers Responsible for Immigration* (London, 30 November-1 December 1992), European Union, *Council Resolution on Burden-Sharing with Regard to the Admission and Residence of Displaced Persons on a Temporary Basis*, Brussels, 25 September 1995 (*Official Journal* no. C262, 7 October 1995, p. 1).

25. See also van Selm-Thorburn, *Refugee Protection in Europe.*

26. Vice Prime Minister Mate Granic MD, PhD, *Report on Problems of Displaced Persons and Refugees in the Republic of Croatia* (18 November 1992); Ministry of Foreign Affairs, Office for Immigration and Refugees in Slovenia, *Information on the Refugee Problem in the Republic of Slovenia* (15 February 1993).

27. See *The Economist* of 3-9 April 1999, vol. 351, no. 8113, which ran the cover story 'Victim of Serbia or NATO?', asking 'Is the world's first war "to stop genocidal violence" merely promoting it?'.

28. See van Selm-Thorburn, *Refugee Protection in Europe.*

29. The key 'products' of the 'Copenhagen School' are the following: B. Buzan, M. Kelstrup, P. Lemaitre, E. Tromer and O. Waever, *The European Security Order Recast: Scenarios for the Post-Cold War Era* (London: Pinter, 1990); B. Buzan, *People, States and Fear: An Agenda for International Security Studies in the Post-Cold War Era* (2nd edn, Hemel Hempstead: Harvester Wheatsheaf, 1991) O. Waever, B. Buzan, M. Kelstrup and P. Lemaitre, *Identity, Migration and the New Security Agenda in Europe* (London: Pinter, 1993) and B. Buzan, O. Waever and J. de Wilde, *Security: A New Framework for Analysis* (London: Lynne Rienner, 1998).

30. Waever *et al.*, *Identity, Migration and the New Security Agenda*, p. 19. See also (for critique) M. Shaw, *Global Society and International Relations* (Cambridge: Polity, 1994), p. 101.

31. See R. Cox, 'Social forces, states and world orders: beyond international relations theory', *Millennium* 10 (2) (1981), 989-1012 on the distinction between problem-solving and critical theories.

32. Waever *et al., Identity, Migration and the New Security Agenda*, and Buzan *et al., Security*.
33. Robert Jervis wrote instructively on questions of perceptions and mispercep-tions in the context of the Cold War international security paradigm. It is illuminating to return to thoughts on the psychological nature of perceptions of threat in societal discourse and policy-making spheres. See R. Jervis, *Perception and Misperception in International Politics* (Princeton, NJ: Princeton University Press, 1976).
34. See C. Haerpfer, C. Milosinski and C. Wallace, 'Old and new security issues in post-communist Eastern Europe: results of an 11 nation study', *Europe–Asia Studies* 51 (6) (1999), 569–89 who describe dispassionately the Copenhagen School vision of 'the *threat* by immigrants and refugees arriving from outside of the countries' (p. 992, emphasis added), and show with statistical research that in spite of the small numbers of arrivals, both in absolute terms and as a proportion of arrivals in the EU states, the population of Central and East European states seem to view immigrants as 'a source of threat and insecurity' (p. 999).
35. See J. Huysmans, 'The question of the limit: desecuritisation and the aesthetics of horror in political realism', *Millennium*, 27 (3) (1998), 000–000.
36. Waever *et al., Identity, Migration and the New Security Agenda*, pp. 188–9.
37. Buzan, *et al., Security*, pp. 121, 132.
38. A start to critical security thinking has been made, for example in K. Krause and M. Williams (eds), *Critical Security Studies: Concepts and Cases* (London: UCL, 1997). However, where the migration issue is concerned, there remains a long way to go.
39. See, for example, A. Zolberg, A. Suhrke and S. Aguayo, *Escape from Violence: Conflict and the Refugee Crisis in the Developing World* (Oxford: Oxford University Press, 1989).
40. See, for example, G.S. Goodwin-Gill, *The Refugee in International Law*; Zolberg *et al., Escape from Violence*; Hathaway, *The Law of Refugee Status*; G. Loescher and L. Monahan (eds) *Refugees and International Relations* (Oxford: Oxford University Press, 1990).
41. There is no intention here to deny that categories can blur; rather, the aim is to try to offer a clear-cut difference for the purpose of the argument.
42. Article 14, Universal Declaration of Human Rights.
43. Malcolm, *Kosovo*.

Bibliography

Books and journal articles

Buzan, B., Kelstrup, M., Lemaitre, P., Tromer, E. and Waever, O., *The European Security Order Recast: Scenarios for the Post-Cold War Era* (London: Pinter, 1990).

Buzan, B., *People, States and Fear: An Agenda for International Security Studies in the Post-Cold War Era* (Hemel Hempstead: Harvester Wheatsheaf, 1991, 2nd edn).

Buzan, B., Waever, O. and de Wilde, J., *Security: A New Framework for Analysis* (London: Lynne Rienner, 1998).

Cohen, L., *Broken Bonds: The Disintegration of Yugoslavia* (Oxford: Westview, 1993).

Cox, R., 'Social forces, states and world orders: beyond international relations theory', *Millennium* 10 (2) (1981), 989–1012.

Dyker, D. and Vejvoda, I., *Yugoslavia and After: A Study in Fragmentation, Despair and Rebirth* (London: Longman, 1996).

Glenny, M., *The Fall of Yugoslavia* (London: Penguin, 1992).

Goodwin-Gill, G.S., *The Refugee in International Law* (Oxford: Clarendon, 1996, 2nd edn).

Grahl-Madsen, A., *The Status of Refugees in International Law*, vols 1 and 2 (Leiden: A.W. Sijthoff, 1966 and 1972 respectively).

Haerpfer, C., Milosinski, C. and Wallace, C., 'Old and new security issues in post-communist Eastern Europe: results of an 11 nation study', Europe–Asia Studies 51 (6) (1999), 569–89.

Hathaway, J.C., *The Law of Refugee Status* (Toronto: Butterworths, 1991).

Huysmans, J., 'The question of the limit: desecuritisation and the aesthetics of horror in political realism', *Millennium* 27 (3) (1998), 000–000.

Jervis, R., *Perception and Misperception in International Politics* (Princeton, NJ: Princeton University Press, 1976).

Krause, K. and Williams, M., (eds), *Critical Security Studies: Concepts and Cases* (London: UCL, 1997).

Loescher, G. and Monahan, L., (eds) *Refugees and International Relations* (Oxford: Oxford University Press, 1990)

Malcolm, N., *Kosovo: A Short History* (London: Macmillan, 1998).

Selm-Thorburn, J. van and Verbeek, B., 'The chance of a lifetime: the European Community's foreign and refugee policies towards the conflict in Yugoslavia, 1991–1995', in P. Gray, and P. 't Hart, *Public Policy Disasters in Western Europe* (London: Routledge, 1998).

Selm-Thorburn, J. van, 'Asylum in the Amsterdam Treaty: a harmonious future?', *Journal of Ethnic and Migration Studies* 24 (4) (1998), 175–92.

Selm-Thorburn, J. van, *Refugee Protection in Europe: Lessons of the Yugoslav crisis* (Dordrecht: Martinus Nijhoff, 1998).

Shaw, M., *Global Society and International Relations* (Cambridge: Polity, 1994).

Waever, O., Buzan, B., Kelstrup, M. and Lemaitre, P., *Identity, Migration and the New Security Agenda in Europe* (London: Pinter, 1993).

Zolberg, A., Suhrke, A. and Aguayo, S., *Escape from Violence: Conflict and the Refugee Crisis in the Developing World* (Oxford: Oxford University Press, 1989).

Reports

Suhrke, A., Barutciski, M., Sandison, P. and Garlock, R., *The Kosovo Crisis: an evaluation of UNHCR's emergency preparedness and response* (Feb. 2000): www.unhcr.ch.

UNHCR, 'Background paper on refugees and asylum seekers from Kosovo' (February 1997): www.unhcr.ch/refworld/country/cdr/cdrkos.htm.

WRITENET, 'Country papers – Albanians in Kosovo: prospects for the future' (October 1994): www.unhcr.ch/refworld/country/writenet/wriyug.htm.

Primary sources

Council of Ministers, European Community, *Conclusions on People Displaced by the Conflict in the Former Yugoslavia of the Meeting of Ministers Responsible for Immigration*, (London, 30 November–1 December 1992).

European Commission, *Proposal to the Council for a Joint Action Based on Article K.3(2)(b) of the Treaty on European Union concerning temporary protection of displaced persons*, COM(97) 93 final, 97/0081 (CNS) (Brussels, 5 March 1997).

European Union, *Council Resolution on Burden-Sharing with Regard to the Admission and Residence of Displaced Persons on a Temporary Basis*, Brussels, 25 September 1995 (Official Journal no. C262, 7 October 1995, p. 1).

Granic, M., *Report on Problems of Displaced Persons and Refugees in the Republic of Croatia* (18 November 1992).

Ministry of Foreign Affairs, Office for Immigration and Refugees in Slovenia, *Information on the Refugee Problem in the Republic of Slovenia* (15 February 1993).

Web sites

Guardian: www.guardian.co.uk
Independent: www.independent.co.uk
International Herald Tribune: www.iht.com
New York Times: www.nytimes.com
Reuters: www.reuters.com
UNHCR: www.unhcr.ch/refworld/refbib/refstat/1998/98tab26.htm.
UNHCR Kosovo Crisis Update: www.unhcr.ch/news/media/kosovo.htm
Washington Post: www.washingtonpost.com

CHAPTER TWO

Germany: protection for refugees or protection from refugees?

KHALID KOSER

Introduction

Of all the countries in the European Union (EU), Germany might well have been expected to be best prepared to receive Kosovar Albanian 'refugees' during the Kosovo crisis in 1999. A few years earlier, Germany had received the lion's share of refugees displaced within the EU from Bosnia. Not only had Germany coped with what possibly constituted the largest sudden mass displacement experienced by any EU state since the end of the Second World War, but lessons had also been learned, and Germany had added to its statute books a new 'temporary protection' status specifically for 'refugees' fleeing civil wars. Furthermore, albeit controversially, Germany had succeeded, where all other EU member states failed, in returning the majority of its Bosnian 'refugees' after the Dayton Peace Accords. Finally, even before the Kosovo crisis, there was already a large Kosovar Albanian population resident in Germany, to whom the *Länder* might turn for sponsorship and offers of support to family members fleeing Kosovo.

Yet each of these 'predisposing factors' can easily also be portrayed as disincentives for Germany to receive large numbers of Kosovar Albanian 'refugees'. Already bearing the weight of the repatriation of *Aussiedler*, and the brunt of asylum applications in the EU, Germany thought it grossly unfair that the EU did not properly share the 'burden' of Bosnian 'refugees'. Perhaps the Kosovo crisis would provide the opportunity for the other EU countries to make amends. Meanwhile, although the majority of Bosnian 'refugees' had departed Germany by the beginning of the Kosovar Albanian displacement, Germany was even then still host to more Bosnian 'refugees' than any other EU state had accepted in the first place. Relative to other EU states, Germany still had an overloaded temporary protection system. And finally, just as had been the case with Bosnians, it was inevitable that 'informal' or 'clandestine' migration between Kosovo and Germany would take place on the basis of social networks centred on Kosovars already resident in Germany. Perhaps Germany should focus its energies on managing and regularizing these flows, leaving other member states to publish quotas and deal with formal resettlement.

It is in the context of these contradictions that this chapter describes and analyses the German response to the Kosovar Albanian 'refugee crisis'. The main focus is the reception of 'refugees'. This is because it is too early yet to assess properly how Germany is coping with the return of Kosovar Albanian 'refugees'. (At the time of writing it is also too early to assess how Germany is coping with the new 'refugee' flow from Kosovo of ethnic Serbs.) Although they do not form a focus, the chapter does touch upon the equally contentious issues of German military participation in and funding of the NATO exercise in Kosovo.

This chapter has three main parts. The first outlines the Kosovar Albanian displacement to Germany. It emphasizes that Germany experienced at least three types of migration, distinguishing between asylum seekers, 'quota refugees' and clandestine migrants, and it describes how the country responded to each of these types.

The second part of the chapter turns to analysing the German response to Kosovar Albanian 'refugees', with analysis structured around three main themes. The first theme concerns the extent to which Germany's response was informed by the Bosnian 'refugee' experience a few years earlier. The second places the response in the context of national debates about asylum and immigration in Germany. The third theme is to examine the influence of EU integration – or rather, at least from a German perspective, the lack of EU integration – on the German response, and Germany's attempts to influence an EU-level response. The final part of the chapter turns to considering some of the wider theoretical issues arising from the German case study, particularly focusing on the linkages between security and refugee movements. The conclusion provides a brief update on developments in Germany since the end of the Kosovo crisis.

This chapter draws on two main periods of fieldwork in Germany. The first, in May 1997, focused on the reception and return of Bosnian 'refugees'.[1] The second took place between March and May 1999, coinciding with the NATO military campaign in Kosovo and covering the crucial months of decision-making in Germany over the reception of Kosovar Albanian 'refugees'. During both visits, interviews were conducted with government, refugee organizations and other non-governmental organizations (NGOs). During the 1999 visit, media – particularly newspapers – were closely monitored.

KHALID KOSER

Background to the Kosovar Albanian influx and the German response

It is possible to distinguish three main types of migration flows which Germany experienced as a result of the crisis in Kosovo, although the distinctions between each type were not always clear during the peak of displacement. Each elicited a different set of responses from the German government, and vacillation might fairly be described as a hallmark of each set of responses.

The earliest flow consisted of asylum seekers. In 1998 over 30,000 Kosovars applied for asylum in Germany. Monthly applications rose steadily, from 1400 in February to 5090 in October (Table 2.1). Although these applications have not been disaggregated according to ethnic origin, it seems reasonable to assume that the vast majority were from Kosovar Albanians. The limited data which are available indicate that asylum applications in Germany by Kosovar Albanians continued at a substantial rate during early 1999. Applications from former Yugoslavia numbered 2736 in March, 2099 in April and 2808 in May, of which it is estimated that some 80 per cent were by Kosovar Albanians.[2]

The response to asylum seekers who arrived prior to the commencement of the NATO campaign has since been heavily criticized by NGOs and human rights lawyers in Germany. In February 1999 – just one month before the campaign began – the administrative court of Hessen established that, in principle, Kosovar Albanians returning to Yugoslavia were not subject to state persecution, and that asylum seekers could thus

Table 2.1 Monthly asylum applications by Kosovars in Germany, 1998

Month	Number of applications
January	1,690
February	1,400
March	1,840
April	1,610
May	2,070
June	2,800
July	3,000
August	3,430
September	4,430
October	5,090
November	4,500
Total	31,860

Source: UNHCR Statistical Unit (1999)[3]

26

safely be returned. The court elaborated that there was no basis to support claims of ethnic persecution or 'ethnic cleansing', and that the situation in Kosovo had become 'fairly stable' since autumn 1998. The court proceeded to withdraw this principle in April 1999, recognizing that Kosovar Albanian asylum seekers had a right to political asylum. According to 'Ialana', an association of lawyers, the court's initial decision had been made on the basis of 'antiquated' and 'unrealistic' reports on the situation in Kosovo supplied by the Foreign Ministry. These reports were withdrawn at the end of April.[4]

A second flow of 'refugees' from Kosovo arrived between April and May 1999 under a German quota. On 6 April 1999 the federal and *Länder* Interior Ministers announced the acceptance of an initial quota of 10,000 Kosovar Albanian 'refugees' from camps in Macedonia. This quota was at least double the quotas announced in every other EU member state. On 7 April the first 700 'quota refugees' arrived in Nuremberg. Within one month, according to data from the United Nations High Commissioner for Refugees (UNHCR), 9974 Kosovar Albanian 'refugees' had been received in Germany.

While it cannot be denied that Germany received Kosovar Albanian 'refugees' more generously and more rapidly than the rest of the EU, it needs to be acknowledged at the same time that on the whole the EU's record on receiving 'refugees' from the Kosovo crisis was lamentable and hardly set a meaningful benchmark against which to measure German vacillation. Measured instead against a total refugee population of at least 500,000 people in countries neighbouring Kosovo, a quota of 10,000 seems rather less generous. This is particularly true in the context of the quid pro quo stance adopted by Macedonia at various times during the Kosovo conflict, that it would admit from Kosovo only the same number of refugees as had been evacuated and temporarily resettled from Macedonia.[5]

Furthermore, Germany did vacillate at a later stage. In an interview with the *Süddeutsche Zeitung* on 8 April, the federal Interior Minister, Otto Schily, said that the quota of 10,000 was not necessarily an upper limit, and that its extension would depend on how the refugee crisis in Macedonia developed.[6] On 3 May, Mr Schily announced his intention to double the initial quota, by admitting a further 10,000 Kosovar Albanian 'refugees'. During a telephone conference that day, his proposal was rejected by several *Länder* Interior Ministers – a veto by just one being sufficient to block the proposal. However, just a few days later on 6 May, agreement was reached to double the quota during a reconvened telephone conference. Eventually, about 15,000 Kosovar Albanians were admitted into Germany as 'quota refugees'.[7]

A third flow consisted of 'clandestine' migrants. Their arrivals were probably largely organized through social networks based on the substantial Kosovar Albanian population already present in Germany prior to the conflict. In an interview in the *Süddeutsche Zeitung* at the beginning of April 1999, Michael Ziegler, from the Bavarian Interior Ministry, estimated that the Kosovar population in Germany prior to the conflict already amounted to some 320,000. 'A quarter of Kosovo is already here,' he said[8] – although this estimate probably includes both Kosovar Albanians and Kosovar Serbs. Neither does the number disaggregate Kosovar Albanians who arrived in Germany as labour migrants during the 1960s and 1970s, and have permanent resident rights, from those such as more recent asylum seekers who do not.

By their very nature, 'clandestine' flows are the hardest to quantify, but most people assume that they accounted for the largest number of Kosovar Albanian arrivals in Germany during 1998 and the first months of 1999. During the Bosnian crisis Germany accepted a quota of 13,000 refugees, in addition to which number some 330,000 arrived 'spontaneously', based similarly on social networks with Bosnians resident in Germany. During April and May several government representatives conceded in interview that they expected just as many 'spontaneous' arrivals from Kosovo. The relatively short duration of the conflict almost certainly means that their predictions were grossly overestimated.

Visa policy towards relatives of Kosovar Albanians already resident in Germany changed repeatedly during the period 1998-9. In April 1999 the German embassy in Macedonia started to issue visas once more, having stopped issuing them about a month before. During the telephone conference on 3 May, another proposal floated by Otto Schily, and supported by several *Länder*, was to announce a quota for family reunification for relatives of Kosovar Albanians already resident in Germany, on the condition that the families in Germany assumed full financial responsibility for the new arrivals. As with the proposal to double the 'refugee' quota, this proposal was also vetoed by several *Länder*.

Lessons from the Bosnian 'refugee crisis'

Germany's experience of the Bosnian 'refugee crisis' was quite different from that of all other EU member states for two main reasons. First, Germany received by far the largest number of Bosnian 'refugees'. At the beginning of 1997, of a total of some 584,000 Bosnian 'refugees' in the EU, some 342,000 – or almost 60 per cent – were in Germany alone (see Appendix 2, Table 5), although the size of the Bosnian population as a proportion of the host population as a whole is of course an important consideration.

Second, and largely as a result of the size of the Bosnian influx,

Germany adopted a stance to the return of Bosnians that was quite different from that adopted in most other EU member states. Although Bosnian 'refugees' were granted only 'temporary protection' in most EU member states, by the time of the Dayton Peace Accords, provision had been made in all the states with the exception of Germany for the transferral of the temporary status of a majority of Bosnians to a more permanent one. The outcome was that from all states other than Germany, return to Bosnia has proceeded at a low rate. By the end of 1997, return from Germany accounted for almost 95 per cent of total returns from the EU (Appendix 2, Table 5).

There were two distinctive – and notorious – features about the return of Bosnians from Germany. In some *Länder* – particularly Bavaria and Berlin – a relatively small number of Bosnians have been forced to return. By the end of 1997 there had been a total of 440 forced returns from Germany. The claim was that limited forced return was necessary to provide the threat needed to encourage voluntary return, although analysis of return rates by *Länder* does not support this claim.[9] In addition, Germany was the only member state which did not conform to UNHCR guidelines concerning return to Bosnia.[10] Specifically, the UNHCR stipulated that whereas it was safe for Bosnians to return to areas where people of their ethnic origin comprised a majority, it was unsafe for them to return to so-called 'minority areas'. In contrast, ethnic origin was not one of the criteria used by Germany to prioritize return.[11]

However controversial the return of Bosnians has been, a tempting line of analysis is to suggest that it is the 'success' of achieving the return of Bosnians which gave Germany the confidence to receive Kosovar Albanian 'refugees' relatively generously and rapidly. As a corollary, it might equally be argued that the initial reluctance of so many other EU states to receive Kosovar Albanian 'refugees' stemmed from their inability to return Bosnians. Indeed, several German government representatives in interview expressed the opinion that it would have been harder to persuade the German public to adopt a sympathetic stance towards Kosovar Albanian 'refugees' had it not been possible at the same time to assure them that the sojourn of the 'refugees' was to be only temporary, just like that of the Bosnians.

Nevertheless, what this line of analysis underestimates is how protracted and costly the Bosnian return has been for Germany. Return to Bosnia has proceeded at a far slower rate even from Germany than was initially projected. By 1999 it was estimated that two-thirds of Bosnian 'refugees' had departed Germany – although it is not always clear whether they have returned to Bosnia.[12] Nevertheless, this means that some 100,000 Bosnians still remain. In other words, even after a massive repatriation operation, Germany is still host to more Bosnians than any other EU state was during the peak of the Bosnian displacement.

Indeed the continuing presence of so many Bosnians was probably one reason for certain *Länder* to block Otto Schily's proposal to enlarge the quota for Kosovar Albanians. Certainly, the arrival of quota 'refugees' from Kosovo was used to bring pressure to bear on remaining Bosnians to return. The Bavarian Interior Minister, Hermann Regensburger, insisted that with the influx of new 'refugees' from Kosovo, 1999 must be the 'year of repatriation for Bosnians'.[13] Lydia Jendryschik, from the Interior Ministry of North Rhine-Westphalia, made it clear in an interview with the *Süddeutsche Zeitung* that Bosnian refugees 'must go home, to make space for the next wave of refugees'.[14]

In addition, Bosnian return has proved very costly for Germany. The primary programme for assisted return to Bosnia from Germany has been coordinated by the International Organization for Migration (IOM), and combines the Reintegration and Emigration Programme for Asylum Seekers in Germany (REAG) with the Government Assisted Return Programme (GARP). REAG is funded by the Federal Ministry for Family Welfare. In 1997 the annual payment to the IOM of DM 8 million (4.1 million euros) was increased to DM 20 million (10.2 million euros). GARP is funded by the federal Ministry of the Interior. In 1997 GARP payments were increased to DM 15 million (7.7 million euros). Crucially, for both REAG and GARP, payments by the federal ministries are matched by the *Länder* per returnee from that *Land*.

The implication is that while other EU states may have vacillated in receiving Kosovar Albanians because of their experience of not having been able to return Bosnians, Germany may equally have vacillated precisely because of the experience of having returned Bosnians.

National debates on asylum and immigration

One important reason why comparison with the Bosnian experience is relevant to only a limited extent is that those Kosovar Albanian 'refugees' who arrived under Germany's quota have been granted a status quite different from any status given to Bosnian 'refugees' – whether quota 'refugees' or 'spontaneous refugees'. This status is known as 'paragraph 32a' status, and is named simply after the paragraph in which it is contained in the German Law for Foreigners (*Deutsches Ausländer-recht*).[15]

Paragraph 32a status emerged from the national debate on asylum during 1992 and 1993. After years of pressure from the Christian Democrats (and Christian Socialists) to abolish or at least qualify the constitutional right for asylum, the constitution was finally duly amended on 6 December 1992. According to several commentators, the amendment was largely driven by the increase in racist and xenophobic violence in Germany, which fuelled extreme right-wing parties.[16] It brought Germany much more closely into line with restrictive asylum practices in other EU states. For the first time, so-called 'safe countries of first asylum' were identified by Germany, and Germany began to sign a series of 'readmission agreements'. Also, a so-called 'white list' was drawn up, listing 'safe countries of origin' with no presence of persecution, from which asylum seekers would not be accepted.[17]

From the amendments, the Social Democrats succeeded in wrangling an 'asylum compromise', one of the elements of which was paragraph 32a, which entered the statute books on 30 June 1993. Paragraph 32a applies specifically to 'war and civil war refugees', and was written with Bosnian 'refugees' in mind. It is intended to bypass the asylum procedure, and provide 'temporary protection' on a group – as opposed to individual – basis. Paragraph 32a status is initially granted for a period of three months, but can be extended should the war continue. The expectation is that once it is safe to return, recipients of the status should do so. The status entails a series of restrictions, including restricted movement within Germany, but most importantly the withdrawal of the right for the recipient to apply for refugee status.

It is significant that even though paragraph 32a was written principally for Bosnian 'refugees', it was never invoked during the Bosnian displacement in Germany; instead, a series of far more restrictive statuses where granted.[18] By the time the amendment had entered the statute books, the initial quota of Bosnian 'refugees' had already arrived, and it was decided not to apply the new status to the large numbers of 'spontaneous arrivals'. Many German NGOs criticized that decision, but were also critical that the government waited until April 1999 to invoke paragraph 32a and publish a quota for Kosovar Albanian 'refugees'. And throughout the Kosovo conflict, they pressurized the government to apply the new status more widely, either by increasing the quota or by granting the status to Kosovar Albanian asylum seekers.

A focus on the implications of paragraph 32a status provides some insight into the government's steadfastness in the face of this NGO pressure. First, and perhaps most crucially, recipients of paragraph 32a status have the right to seek family reunification, and their close family the right to receive the same status. In interviews, government representatives repeatedly emphasized that an initial quota of 10,000 should be expected to increase to as many as 30,000 through this process of family reunification.

This 'multiplier effect' of the quota system was of particular concern to the *Länder*, which were required to bear a significant proportion of the costs of housing and providing welfare for the quota 'refugees'. According to the stipulations of the German Law for Foreigners, paragraph 32a 'refugees' are distributed between the *Länder* in direct proportion to the each *Land*'s population. Table 2.2 shows the distribution of the 10,000 Kosovar Albanian paragraph 32a 'refugees' within Germany on this basis. The costs of providing for the 'refugees' varied between *Länder*, from a monthly maximum of about DM 1300 (665 euros) in Bavaria to a monthly minimum of about DM 700 (358 euros) in Hessen. When the original quota of 10,000 was agreed by the federal and *Länder* Interior Ministries, it was on the understanding that the federal government would pay each *Land* DM 500 (257 euros) per 'refugee' for six months, to meet part of the costs of resettling Kosovar Albanian refugees.

Cost became one of the principal issues that led several *Länder* to block Otto Schily's subsequent proposal to increase the quota. First, especially for more expensive *Länder* such as Bavaria which was resettling a fairly significant proportion of the 'refugees', the shortfall between the federal government's subsidy and actual costs per 'refugee' became significant. Second, at the time when the proposal was considered – in early May 1999 – many commentators expected the Kosovar conflict to last far longer than it eventually did, and several *Länder* were concerned that the stipulation that the federal government

Table 2.2 Distribution of Kosovar Albanian 'paragraph 32a refugees' in Germany

Land	Number
Baden-Württemberg	1,220
Bavaria	1,400
Berlin	220
Brandenburg	350
Bremen	100
Hamburg	260
Hesse	740
Lower Saxony	930
Mecklenburg-West Pomerania	270
North Rhine-Westphalia	2,240
Rhineland-Palatinate	470
Saarland	140
Saxony	650
Saxony-Anhalt	400
Schleswig-Holstein	280
Thuringia	330
Total	10,000

Source: Calculated from *Deutsches Ausländerrecht*[19] for 10,000 'refugees'

would pay a subsidy only for the limited period of six months would leave them picking up a far higher bill for an unspecified period of time. Third, the cost of supporting the 'quota' refugees was being compounded by the costs of managing and supporting the far larger numbers of 'spontaneous' arrivals from Kosovo during the same period – as well as the continuing costs of supporting Bosnian 'refugees' who still remained.

In contrast, cost was not the obstacle which persuaded several *Länder* to veto Otto Schily's other proposal on 3 May 1999 to produce a quota for family reunification. Rather, the main obstacle arose from the question of how to choose which 'refugees' to include in the quota. The federal government proposed that this should be the decision of the various receiving *Länder*. Several *Länder* argued that they could not possibly make a decision about which 'refugees' should have the highest priorities as they did not have direct representations in the refugee camps in Macedonia and elsewhere. The decision, they maintained, should be made by local embassies, and was ultimately thus the responsibility of the Foreign Office. It seems that the Foreign Office, having already prevaricated over issuing visas, was unwilling to assume this new responsibility.[20]

Looking beyond the specific implications of implementing paragraph 32a status, it is also worth placing Germany's reaction to receiving Kosovar Albanian 'refugees' in the context of another national debate on citizenship which coincided with the Kosovo crisis. This debate, a long one, finally ended when the *Bundesrat* (Parliament) ratified a citizenship law reform on 31 May 1999. It replaces Germany's famous *jus sanguinis* principle on citizenship, by determining that children born in Germany to foreign parents after 1 January 2000 will acquire German nationality in addition to their parents' nationality via *jus soli*, although they will be required to decide which nationality they wish to retain by the age of 23. Although no direct link was made during interviews between this new citizenship law and the Kosovar Albanian 'refugee' quota, the law does potentially introduce a 'multiplier effect' additional to that already entailed by the right to family reunification.

The impact of EU integration

'Burden sharing' by other EU member states evolved quite clearly as a crucial factor in explaining Germany's reaction to Kosovar Albanian 'refugees'. First, a lack of 'burden sharing' by other EU member states was the other main reason – besides cost and the implications of family reunification – given by the *Länder* on 3 May in objecting to the proposal to double Germany's quota. Second, the decision only three days later to double the quota after all was driven quite directly by commitments in other EU states – and especially the UK – to increase their own quotas.

Given its significance in determining German policy, it is worth considering in closer detail the 'burden-sharing' argument from the German perspective. By 3 May Germany's quota was double the size of the next largest quota ('up to 5000' in Austria) in any other EU member state, with the exception of Italy, which had officially received no Kosovar Albanian 'refugees' by this date (Appendix 2, Table 3). And by 5 May, within one month of announcing its quota, Germany was one of only three EU states which had already filled its published quota. The only other two states which had filled their quotas – The Netherlands and Belgium – had far smaller quotas of 2000 and 1200 respectively.

Particular criticism was launched at the UK, where only 330 Kosovar Albanian 'refugees' had been resettled by this date – the same number as in one of the smaller *Länder* in Germany, Thuringia.[21] During a speech in London on 5 May the former chancellor, Helmut Kohl, described the EU's refugee politics as 'scandalous'.[22] Unlike the other main obstacles to the expansion of the quota, the 'burden-sharing' obstacle was one upon which *Länder* led by both Social Democrats and Christian Democrats agreed.

'The main lesson that Germany has learned from the Bosnian displacement is that other EU states refuse to share the burden.' In order fully to understand the power of the 'burden-sharing argument', it is important to realize that, as implied by this quotation from an interview with a representative of the Interior Ministry of Hesse, Germany entered the Kosovo crisis almost with the expectation that other EU states would avoid assuming responsibility for Kosovo's 'refugees' if they could. The background to this assumption is the fact that during the 1990s, Germany tended to receive the lion's share of asylum applications in the EU.[23] For example, it is indicative to consider that even during the peak of displacement from Kosovo, Kosovars accounted for only about one-third of asylum applications in Germany, which totalled 7333 in February 1999, 7925 in March 1999 and 6491 in April. Other important countries of origin were Turkey, Iraq, Afghanistan and Iran.[24]

The perception that the rest of the EU would be unwilling to share the 'refugee burden' was fuelled by the eventual distribution of Bosnian 'refugees' through the EU countries (Appendix 2, Table 5). When faced with criticism over their use of forced return to facilitate the voluntary return of Bosnian 'refugees', German politicians have consistently replied that they would not have been forced to adapt such drastic measures had the rest of the EU relieved Germany of such high numbers of Bosnians.

Indignation was compounded even further through the realization that Germany not only had announced and filled the largest quota in the EU for 'refugees' from Kosovo, but also was bearing the brunt of asylum applications and 'spontaneous' arrivals in the EU. In May 1999 Germany received 2808 asylum applications from former Yugoslavia, accounting for 24 per cent of the EU total. In June 1999 the number increased to 4811, and accounted for 26.1 per cent of the EU total. These applications in turn respectively comprised only 40 per cent and 49 per cent of total asylum applications in Germany, which in both months received over 25 per cent of total asylum applications in the EU.[25]

Several commentators have accused Germany of placing too much emphasis on this 'burden-sharing argument'. First, a focus on absolute numbers of refugees ignores what is probably a more important measure of 'burden' borne: namely the proportional size of the 'refugee' population in relation to the host population as a whole. Against this measure, the gap implied by absolute numbers between Germany's quota and that in Austria, for example, reduces, as does the gap between the number of 'refugees' received in Germany and those in Belgium or The Netherlands. Second, looking outside the EU, significantly more asylum applications were received from former Yugoslavia during May and June 1999 in Switzerland than in Germany. Third, Germany has not been alone in receiving substantial numbers of 'spontaneous arrivals'. It was estimated in June 1999, for example, that there were some 7600 Kosovar Albanians in Italy who had arrived outside any quota.

Another argument views the reception of refugees as just one element of an integrated 'package' of EU commitments to the Kosovo crisis. On 8 May 1999, Digby Waller of the International Institute for Strategic Studies in London commented that 'There's an attempt to free-ride on the military spending by opting for soft burdens such as aiding refugees. Germany is doing that'.[26] The article points out that Germany committed significantly fewer troops to Kosovo than the UK, only one frigate to the UK's eight and France's five and fewer combat aircraft than the UK, France, Italy and The Netherlands. Similarly, by April 1999 Germany had pledged US$1.8 million (1.7 million euros) to relief operations for refugees from Kosovo, significantly less than pledges from The Netherlands and Italy (although larger than the paltry pledges from the UK and France).

Wider theoretical issues

This final section turns to considering some of the wider theoretical issues arising from the preceding analysis of Germany's response to Kosovar Albanian 'refugees'.[27] It focuses specifically on the contemporary debate on the linkages between security and refugee movements. It is possible to discern two contradictory prevailing analyses of these linkages, which can, in the simplest terms, be summarized as follows. According to one analysis, refugees (as well as other immigrants) can comprise a threat to the security of societies and national identities, and it is the responsibility of states to nullify the threat through controlling entry. Alternatively, it is refugees who have been threatened in their home countries, and it is the responsibility of more stable societies to develop a system for protecting them for the duration of the threat.

Protection from refugees?

The first of these analyses arises from literature emanating from the so-called Copenhagen School, focusing on the 'new security framework' in the EU.[28] For the purposes of this analysis, there are three key elements of the 'new security framework'. First, in the post-Cold War era, security concerns in the EU have been refocused from the state to society. Second, replacing the primarily military threat to states, there are a range of new threats to 'societal security', one of which is the threat that immigration poses to identity. One of the causes of increased immigration is posited to be the process of EU integration, and a third element is the potential for a backlash against integration where national identities are threatened by its consequences.

It would be reasonable to suppose that this framework applies to Germany perhaps more than any other EU member state. First, Germany has probably been the greatest advocate for rolling back state boundaries through EU integration in favour of a 'European' society. Second, Germany has come to be particularly associated with incidents of racist and xenophobic violence against immigrants and asylum seekers, at least in media and popular perceptions. Third, one of the implications of opening borders within the EU has been to place disproportionate pressure on geographically peripheral countries such as Germany as migration 'buffer zones'.

Indeed, there are clear indications from the preceding analysis that 'societal security' has been a significant factor in determining Germany's response to Kosovar Albanian 'refugees'. It is clear, for example, that a concern to avoid the racist and xenophobic violence which preceded the 1992 amendment to the constitution has been a continual underlying motivation for trying to control immigration to Germany since 1993. This underlying concern was one of the main factors accounting for Germany's decision to return Bosnian refugees, even at the cost of attracting international criticism. It has also been shown in this chapter how a direct link was made between the number of Bosnians still present in Germany and the number of Kosovar Albanian 'refugees' who should be admitted, again in a concern not to provoke negative public and media reactions by being 'overburdened' by 'refugees'. Similarly, one of the ways in which the German government 'sold' its quota for Kosovar Albanians to the German public was by offering assurances that the 'refugees' would not stay permanently.

Nevertheless, analysis of Germany's response to Kosovar Albanian 'refugees' can quite easily also be directed to reinforce criticisms of elements of the 'new security framework'.[29] One criticism is that the notion that 'societal security' can be threatened by immigration ignores the reality of long-standing multicultural societies in most EU countries. In Germany, Kosovar Albanians already constituted an integral part of society and arguably national identity even before the Kosovo crisis. Notwithstanding tensions which are often found in host countries between older and newer immigrant arrivals from the same country of origin, this observation renders rather problematic the assertion that the German society and identity might have been threatened by Kosovar Albanian 'refugees'. The assertion also depends on a static view of society. The new citizenship law reform in Germany, referred to above, provides an excellent example of the dynamism of societies.

A second criticism has been that there are very few examples of refugees or immigrants actually posing a 'threat' to, or endangering, host societies. The same observation stands for Kosovar Albanian 'refugees' in Germany. It may be argued that such a 'threat' might only become apparent after a period of time, but then it is significant to observe that even though many Bosnian 'refugees' have been in Germany for almost ten years, they have not been associated with a discernible 'threat' to society. Indeed, one of the reasons why the other EU states eventually provided permanent residence rights for most Bosnian 'refugees' was their apparent success in becoming economically and socially integrated.[30] Had Bosnians not been denied the opportunity to integrate in Germany, perhaps they would have succeeded there too. The reality is that it is usually racists and xenophobes within host societies who are guilty of threatening immigrants, and not immigrants who threaten society.

Protection for refugees?

According to an alternative analysis of the linkages between security and refugee movements, it is the security of refugees that has been threatened and host states which should be criticized for not adequately providing for their protection for the duration of the threat. The criticisms which recur most regularly concern the strict adherence to the 1951 Geneva Convention definition of a refugee, which automatically excludes from consideration many contemporary 'refugees', and the increasing range of restrictions which are imposed upon all asylum seekers.[31] For many commentators, the Bosnian displacement provided the impetus for the development of a new European refugee regime with the potential to incorporate such criticisms. German (as well as other EU) responses to the Kosovar displacement provide the opportunity to assess what progress has been made.

One of the main implications of the Bosnian experience was a growing consensus within the EU that the concept of 'temporary protection' should form a central pillar of a new regime. Indeed, the introduction into the German statute books of paragraph 32a for 'civil war refugees' was a direct response to that consensus. The most recent report on the state of the world's refugees published by the Office of the UN High Commissioner cites three main benefits of a system of 'temporary protection'. The first is that it has signalled acknowledgement on the part of states in the EU of a humanitarian obligation to provide a place of safety for people who have fled from a war-torn state; the second is that it has helped to reassert the principle of international responsibility – or burden sharing; while the third is that it is a solution-oriented approach, explicitly focused on voluntary repatriation.[32]

These three proposed benefits provide a convenient framework within which to analyse the German response to 'refugees' from Kosovo. First, to what extent has the German response signalled a wider humanitarian obligation? As alluded to in the preceding analysis, even though paragraph 32a status was on the statute books by the time the majority of Bosnian 'refugees' arrived in Germany, it was never used for their reception. In this context a new willingness to use the more liberal status to receive Kosovar Albanian 'refugees' might be taken as a fulfilment by the German authorities of a wider humanitarian obligation towards people who do not necessarily satisfy strict criteria of refugee definition.

On the other hand, German non-governmental organizations were very critical of the way in which paragraph 32a status was used. They argue that it was introduced on political and not humanitarian motivations, and only after the NATO campaign began, instead of in response to growing numbers of asylum seekers from Kosovo. Furthermore, its use was strictly limited: the initial quota of 10,000 was not substantially increased, and the status was not granted to asylum seekers or 'spontaneous' arrivals who had fled at the same time and presumably from the same threats. The implication is that a broader humanitarian obligation was acknowledged only towards a minority of 'refugees' from Kosovo.

Even if the response to Kosovar Albanian 'refugees' is accepted as indicative of a broader humanitarian obligation on the part of Germany, another question which needs to be asked is to what extent this obligation extends beyond them. Will it be extended to ethnic Serbs currently fleeing retaliation in Kosovo? Will it be extended to 'refugees' fleeing civil wars which take place outside Europe? It is salutary to observe that recognition rates for all asylum seekers in Germany stood at about 2 per cent between January and June 1999.[33]

Second, to what extent has the EU response to Kosovar Albanian refugees reasserted the principle of international responsibility? As described in the last section, German politicians were unusually united in their condemnation of other EU member states in their failure to share the 'refugee burden'. More critical analysis, however, suggested that these criticisms result only from a rather narrow interpretation of the concept of burden sharing. There seem to be reasonable grounds to suggest that in fact the EU succeeded in achieving a fairly equitable 'comprehensive approach' to the Kosovo crisis. Joanne van Selm-Thorburn conceives of three stages of a comprehensive approach to a conflict-provoked flight situation: prevention; protection (both locally and internationally); and durable solutions.[34] As suggested in the previous section, while Germany may have taken more responsibility than most other EU states for international protection of refugees, this was arguably compensated by its lighter role in prevention and military intervention, and in funding the local protection of refugees.

The third proposed benefit of a 'temporary protection' approach is that it is 'solution oriented', and oriented specifically towards voluntary repatriation. An orientation towards repatriation was stated as one of the guiding principles for the overall EU approach to the Kosovo crisis, which arguably explains why the emphasis was on trying to protect Kosovar Albanian 'refugees' locally rather than outside the Balkans area. While return particularly from the immediate region has proceeded at a substantial rate since the end of the crisis, this approach has been fiercely criticized for abandoning the 'refugees' in countries ill equipped either to provide for them adequately or to protect them.

Meanwhile, it is still too early to assess the progress and process of return for those relatively few 'refugees' who were protected in Germany (and other EU states). However, one implication of the use of paragraph 32a status is that in the long term it may complicate the return process. This is because it has contributed towards the creation of different categories of Kosovar Albanian 'refugees' in Germany – 'quota refugees', asylum seekers and 'spontaneous' migrants – who will probably require different return approaches.

Conclusion

In trying to describe and analyse Germany's response to Kosovar Albanian 'refugees', this chapter has focused on the period up to mid-May 1999, when the crucial decisions on the reception of the 'refugees' were taken. At the time of writing, the Kosovo crisis has been concluded – although there may be another one in the making, centred this time on Serbs – and the purpose of this conclusion is simply to provide a brief update on the situation of Kosovar Albanian 'refugees' in Germany.

At the beginning of August 1999 it was estimated that about 1500 of the

15,000 'quota refugees' finally accepted in Germany had already returned to Kosovo. Their returns have been completely voluntary, and assisted by both the *Länder* and the federal government. There is some debate about the timing of the return of the remaining 'quota refugees'. The *Länder* of Bavaria and Berlin were pressing for the return to be completed by the end of 1999. However, the federal Defence Ministry has declared that they should be returned only after 'refugees' in the countries neighbouring Kosovo have returned, while the federal Interior Minister, Otto Schily, has stated that the repatriation will probably begin in spring 2000. There has not yet been a formal statement from either the federal government or the *Länder* about whether compulsory repatriation will take place if deemed necessary.[35]

It has been decided to include in the repatriation plans up to 180,000 Kosovar Albanians who are currently in Germany without permanent residence rights. This number mainly comprises asylum seekers who have arrived since the beginning of 1998, as well as 'spontaneous' migrants who have declared themselves. Of course, it is unclear how many 'spontaneous' arrivals have not declared themselves. In addition, since the end of the Kosovo crisis a number of administrative courts have postponed decisions on asylum applications by Kosovar Albanians to see how the peace process develops, so it is also unclear as yet how many of the asylum seekers might be granted refugee status. Finally, it has also recently been reported that Serbs from Kosovo may now be entering Germany 'spontaneously', while Kosovar Albanians are reported to be entering Germany informally from Italy.[36]

Notes

1. R. Black, K. Koser, and M. Walsh, *Conditions for the Return of Displaced Persons from the European Union.* Final Report. Luxembourg: Office for Official Publications of the European Communities (1997).
2. *Migration und Bevölkerung* issue 6 (August 1999).
3. UNHCR Statistical Unit, Kosovo Crisis Update (1999): www.unhcr.ch/news/media/kosovo.htm.
4. European Forum for Migration Studies (EFMS), *Migration Report* (19) (May 1999), Bamberg.
5. United States Committee for Refugees (USCR), *Refugee Reports* 20 (4) (March/April 1999).
6. *Süddeutsche Zeitung*, 7 April 1999.
7. European Forum for Migration Studies (EFMS), *Migration Report* (20) (August 1999), Bamberg.
8. *Süddeutsche Zeitung*, 31 March 1999.
9. Black *et al.*, *Conditions for the Return of Displaced Persons.*
10. *Migration News Sheet* (1997), various issues.

11. K. Koser, M. Walsh, and R. Black, 'Temporary protection and assisted return of refugees from the European Union', *International Journal of Refugee Law* 10 (3) (1998) 444-61.
12. See J. Selm, Chapter 3 of this volume.
13. *Frankfurter Rundschau*, 6 May 1999.
14. *Süddeutsche Zeitung*, 31 March 1999.
15. *Deutsches Ausländerrecht* (1997), Munich: Beck.
16. D. Thränhardt (ed.), *Europe – A New Immigration Continent: Policies and Politics in Comparative Perspective* (Münster: Lit Verlag, 1996).
17. *Ibid.*
18. *Hamburger Abendblatt*, 8 April 1999.
19. *Deutsches Ausländerrecht* (1997).
20. *Der Spiegel*, 3 May 1999.
21. *Berlin Tageszeitung*, 14 April 1999.
22. *15hr Aktuell Berlin*, 5 May 1999.
23. K. Koser, 'Recent asylum migration in Europe: patterns and processes of change', *New Community* 22 (1) (1996), 151-8.
24. EFMS, *Migration Report* (19).
25. UNHCR Statistical Unit, Kosovo Crisis Update.
26. *The Economist*, 8 May 1999.
27. This section draws substantially and gratefully on the work of Joanne van Selm-Thorburn: *Refugee Protection in Europe: Lessons of the Yugoslav Crisis* (The Hague: Martinus Nijhoff, 1998) and 'Kosovo's refugees and the EU: wherein lies the threat?', *Refuge: Canada's Periodical on Refugees* 18 (3) (1999), 47-50.
28. O. Waever, B. Buzan, M. Kelstrup and P. Lemaitre, *Identity, Migration and the New Security Agenda in Europe* (London: Pinter, 1993). Referred to also in the Introduction to this volume.
29. Van Selm, 'Kosovo's refugees and the EU'.
30. Koser *et al.*, 'Temporary protection'.
31. J.C. Hathaway, *Reconceiving International Refugee Law* (The Hague: Martinus Nijhoff, 1997).
32. UNHCR, *The State of the World's Refugees* (Geneva: UNHCR, 1999).
33. UNHCR Statistical Unit, Kosovo Crisis Update.
34. Van Selm-Thorburn, *Refugee Protection in Europe*.
35. EFMS, *Migration Report* (20); Migration und Bevölkerung issue 6.
36. EFMS, *Migration Report* (20).

Bibliography

Books and journal articles

Hathaway, J.C., *Reconceiving International Refugee Law* (The Hague: Martinus Nijhoff, 1997).
Koser, K., 'Recent asylum migration in Europe: patterns and processes of change', *New Community*, 22 (1) (1996), 151-8.

Koser, K., Walsh, M. and Black, R., 'Temporary protection and assisted return of refugees from the European Union', *International Journal of Refugee Law* 10 (3) (1998), 444-61.

Selm-Thorburn, J. van, *Refugee Protection in Europe: Lessons of the Yugoslav Crisis* (The Hague: Martinus Nijhoff, 1998).

Selm, J. van, 'Kosovo's refugees and the EU: wherein lies the threat?', *Refuge: Canada's Periodical on Refugees* 18 (3) (1999), 47–50.

Thränhardt, D. (ed.), *Europe – A New Immigration Continent: Policies and Politics in Comparative Perspective* (Münster: Lit Verlag, 1996).

United Nations High Commissioner for Refugees (UNHCR), *The State of the World's Refugees* (Geneva: UNHCR, 1999).

Waever, O., Buzan, B., Kelstrup, M. and Lemaitre, P., *Identity, Migration and the New Security Agenda in Europe* (London: Pinter, 1993).

Reports and other documents

Black, R., Koser, K. and Walsh, M., *Conditions for the Return of Displaced Persons from the European Union*. Final Report (Luxembourg: Office for Official Publications of the European Communities 1997).

Deutsches Ausländerrecht (Munich: Beck, 1997).

European Forum for Migration Studies (EFMS), *Migration Report* (19) (May 1999), Bamberg.

European Forum for Migration Studies (EFMS), *Migration Report* (20) (August 1999), Bamberg.

International Organization for Migration (IOM), Fact Sheet (September 1997), Sarajevo.

Migration News Sheet (1997), various issues.

Migration und Bevölkerung issue 6, August 1999.

United States Committee for Refugees (USCR), *Refugee Reports* 20 (4), (March/ April 1999).

United Nations High Commissioner for Refugees (UNHCR), *Bosnia and Herzegovina Repatriation and Return Operation*, (October 1997), Geneva.

Web sites

UNHCR Kosovo Crisis Update: www.unhcr.ch/news/media/kosovo.htm

CHAPTER THREE

The Netherlands: the few who made it 'won't be staying'

JOANNE VAN SELM

Introduction

The active response in The Netherlands to receiving Bosnians and the creation of specific legal instruments as early as 1994 to deal with the temporary protection of displaced persons may have inspired a hope that the Dutch would once more protect large groups in need if a situation requiring such protection would arise again. However, the response to the massive exodus of ethnic Albanians from Kosovo was much more hesitant and limited in scope. In large part this was due to the altered political context with regard to asylum and immigration issues, both domestically and at European Union (EU) level. The displacements from Kosovo and discussion of evacuations from the neighbouring states came at a moment at which The Netherlands was already deep in a political discussion about asylum seekers and refugee reception and admission. This discussion was largely inspired by the rising numbers of applicants year on year, both in actual numbers and as a relative percentage of total applicants in EU states.[1] Given that the debate of the previous months had most frequently given rise to the mantra of a solution to be found only at EU level, it is perhaps not surprising that The Netherlands' response to the massive displacements once the NATO bombing campaign began was to look to its EU partners to create a collective approach, if not solution, to the refugee crisis.

This chapter will suggest that the expression of the Dutch search for an EU-level common approach to asylum issues is leading The Netherlands down a path of restriction and 'back-seat' passiveness, as evidenced by its political approach to Kosovo's refugees. This is not in keeping with its history on this issue, both recent and more distant, and its position of apparent attraction to asylum seekers. This history indicates rather that The Netherlands could take the political lead and encourage its partners to be both more pragmatic and more liberal in their asylum policies. In not taking such a lead, the Dutch government leaves itself open to critical analysis of the way in which it listens and responds to both its EU partners and its domestic parties and voters, analysis sharpened by the contrast with its explicit policy goal of seeking an EU-level approach. Therefore, the question becomes: is The Netherlands powerless in the face of immigration and is that the reason for the shift of attention to EU level, or is it simply seeking pragmatic reinforcement?

Picking up the four key themes of this book,

1   the lessons of the reception and statuses accorded to Bosnians drawn on in dealing with the displacements of Kosovars;
2   the national debates on asylum and immigration within which this crisis took place and which influence policy making;
3   the wider theoretical issues;
4   the way EU integration (or not) on the subject is impacting policy-making in the different states,

this chapter will demonstrate how this passive stance is a departure from the Dutch approach in the recent past, and suggest potential motives behind this change.

The first five sections of the chapter involve a description and analysis of the Dutch position on protection for persons from the Balkans in the context of domestic expressions of political and public interest. These sections develop the context for the sixth section, which addresses the thesis of this chapter concerning the Dutch position on how asylum and immigration can be addressed in the EU, and the means employed in seeking the goal of a common approach in the specific situation of displacements from Kosovo. The first three sections describe the Dutch political context on asylum matters when the Kosovo displacements took place; set out a history of the protection of Bosnians displaced by the Balkan conflict of 1992–5 with a focus on the legal and political measures introduced and the lessons which might have been learned; and describe the specific Dutch approach to the notion of protecting the ethnic Albanians driven into Macedonia and Albania, in particular from March to June 1999, and the possibility that some of those displaced could be protected in The Netherlands. The fourth section provides an analysis of some lessons which could have been learned from the experience of Bosnian displacements, in terms both of protection in The Netherlands and protection closer to home. The fifth section turns to analysis from the perspective of so-called 'societal security', focusing on the duplicitous reactions to xenophobia demonstrated. The perspective of 'societal security' as a way of explaining the Dutch response will be linked to and contrasted with the analysis of the Dutch position within the EU on this issue, which will be shown to be a statist attempt to influence the integration process towards the national ideal of a common EU approach to asylum policy.

The focus of this chapter, as of others in this volume, will rest on Kosovo's Albanians. Few Serbs from Kosovo appear to have applied for asylum in The Netherlands.

The context of the Dutch approach to Kosovo's refugees

As background to any discussion of the approach taken by the Dutch government to the displacements in Kosovo and the question of receiving Kosovars in The Netherlands, it is necessary to sketch the context with regard to asylum and immigration politics. The asylum issue is never very far from the centre of Dutch political debate, and it has become a key issue in the latter half of the 1990s. Asylum policy and practice in The Netherlands in the past decade can be characterized as increasingly restrictive, but also as paradoxical and introspective. The Netherlands has seen its ranking in statistical tables rise, as regards both the number and the proportion of asylum applicants in the EU. Meanwhile, the Dutch are also popularly aware of their ranking in terms of population density: a 'small country' ($37,330$ km^2) with a population of 15.8 million. The presentation of this chart-topping can certainly lead to many less than welcoming reactions towards asylum seekers. However, many of the open anti-immigrant reactions which could be expected, and which some extreme-right political figures would instinctively display, are repressed, as the key anti-immigrant party has been suppressed in the Dutch political system.[2]

Asylum law in The Netherlands is based on the 1965 Aliens Law, which was little changed until the late 1980s, and on other administrative instructions. The most recent changes to the major law took place in 1994, and more are proposed for 2000.[3] The 1994 changes included the addition of a legally based category of temporary protection for displaced and tolerated persons, created specifically in reaction to the influx of Bosnians. The changes proposed for 2000 focus on restricting refugee categorizations to one status only: a temporary status for three years, beyond which a permanent status will be granted to those deemed unable to return. While the legal changes as such may have been relatively limited in number if not scope, political debate and the practice of granting and enacting protection have undergone many more subtle and continuous changes since the numbers of spontaneous asylum applicants started to rise in the mid-1980s.

In the 1994 elections the right-leaning liberal VVD party (Volkspartij voor Vrijheid en Democratie: People's Party for Freedom and Democracy) under the leadership of Frits Bolkestein (who became a European Commissioner in 1999) broke the tacit taboo on raising the immigration issue in electioneering. By the time of the 1998 elections the issue was a subject of open election debate.[4] October 1998 saw a major crisis for the Dutch way of receiving refugees when the number of applicants soared to new levels, and reception facilities – asylum seeker centres – were so crowded that no new applicants could be housed. Reception forms a cherished heart of the Dutch approach to asylum seekers, distinguishing it from many fellow EU states which take a more *'laissez-faire'* or less welfare-oriented approach to the housing and placement of both asylum seekers and refugees. From 12 October 1998 waiting lists were established for people already in the country who wished to file an asylum application, and those waiting were sheltered in tents. By 1 January 1999, 758 people were on the waiting list, of whom 359 were housed in tents.[5] Those same tents would later be used to house Kosovars evacuated from Macedonia.[6]

The establishment of the waiting lists and the overcrowding coincided, in the public presentation of the issues at least, with major question marks being raised over how the Dublin Convention was being put into effect, and with the arrival in The Netherlands of dozens of Bosnians who had been forced or encouraged to leave Germany. The impact of the Dublin Convention, determining Germany to be the state which should assess the claims of Bosnians who had first applied for asylum there, meant that since the Bosnians could not officially apply for asylum in The Netherlands, they could not go on a waiting list and could not be sheltered, even in tents, by the organizations mandated to deal with reception of asylum seekers. The fact that the limited number of Bosnians then arriving in The Netherlands were often people who had spent years in Germany, and that Germany was 'returning' or 'resettling' significant numbers of Bosnians who had sought protection there, and had been tolerated until the end of the conflict in Bosnia, caused some Dutch political parties, including two of the coalition partners, to raise the spectre of return for Bosnians from The Netherlands too. That could, according to the political statements made at the time, mean enacting the notion of cessation of the refugee status, and returning not only those who had initially received temporary protection and later a humanitarian status, but also those who had been accorded Convention status.[7]

The protection of Bosnians in The Netherlands[8]

The Netherlands was one of only a few EU states to enact legislation on temporary protection during the influx of Bosnians. Under the 1994 Act a temporary protection scheme was created which not only could be used in response to the Bosnian displacements (the reason for its creation), but would also, very specifically, be in place for any future mass displacement crises. The Act introduced the 'F' document to the array of Dutch 'refugee' statuses under the VVTV regulations (*Voorwaardelijk Vergunning tot Verblijf*: Conditional Permission to Remain). This legally based temporary protection scheme followed from a dual-track *ad hoc* system.

A rise in the influx of spontaneous Bosnian arrivals in 1992 prompted the initial political decision in The Netherlands to create an *ad hoc* regulation allowing for the admission and reception of persons from former Yugoslavia who would be permitted to remain on a temporary basis, in line with the existing regulations in the old Asylum Act. In addition to the creation of an *ad hoc* regulation, The Netherlands' government sent a mission to Croatia in August 1992 to organize the transportation of groups invited to go to The Netherlands, including ex-detainees, women, children and the sick and injured.

At that time it was thought that planning for a period of three to six months would be sufficient. Largely with the aim of keeping down the number of people entering the slow individualized procedures, a combined scheme with a limited and provisional legal basis was set in motion. There were two short-term programmes, both known as TROO (*Tijdelijke Regeling Opvang Ontheemden* – Temporary Arrangement for the Reception of Displaced Persons). One of the TROO programmes dealt with admission arrangements and was the responsibility of the Justice Ministry; the other dealt with reception arrangements and fell under the Welfare Ministry. This division of responsibilities led to significant confusion, not least where financing was concerned. The TROO schemes gave recipients a place in a reception centre, or funding for their hosts if they were accommodated with family members or friends. Additional centres specifically for Bosnians were established, at which costs were to be kept below the level of those for regular asylum seekers.[9] The deadline for the closure of the TROO scheme was originally 1 January 1994, although this was extended to 1 January 1995 when passage of the New Aliens Act, including VVTV status, was delayed.

The initial schemes were a response to appeals in August 1992 by the United Nations High Commissioner for Refugees (UNHCR) for temporary protection of persons displaced by the conflict in former Yugoslavia, and were, until 14 April 1993, open to people from all republics, provided that they could not be returned to a safe third country and that they did not pose a serious threat to public order, peace and national security in The Netherlands.

As the conflict in Bosnia and Herzegovina continued into 1993, it was appreciated that this short-term, non-regulated policy was not satisfactory, either for the displaced persons or for the Dutch government and people. Two decisions were therefore taken: the first was to establish in law a scheme for provisional protection and the second to accord Geneva Convention or humanitarian status[10] to all those who had entered The Netherlands during 1992 and before 14 April 1993, and had applied for asylum. For those who arrived after that date, people from Bosnia and Herzegovina would still be covered by the TROO scheme. Other people from former Yugoslavia had to enter the regular procedures. The granting of 'A' status to the earlier groups was forced both by the provisions of the old Aliens Act and by a speech by the Justice Minister in Parliament announcing that the accordance of Convention Status to persons from Bosnia and Herzegovina already in The Netherlands would be the most likely course. It should be noted, however, that many of those who were in The Netherlands had not filed an application specifically because they hoped their stay would be brief, and were treating it as a brief visit to family or friends already in The Netherlands.

Later a parliamentary decision established an invitation for 1500 people to go to The Netherlands from Bosnia and Herzegovina, with transport arranged, in partial cooperation with the UNHCR.

Temporary protection under the 1994 Act and in practice

The 'New Dutch Aliens Act' of February 1994 introduced VVTV. This status can be granted to two categories of recipients: displaced persons and tolerated persons. The former are defined by the size of the influx, the latter by the flight motive. Essentially the 'tolerated' category indicates that the only barrier to return is a 'technical' one. This is a status which is open to both groups and individuals. The permit or 'F' document is renewable annually for up to three years, with an accumulation of rights and entitlements gradually, year on year. If the reason for flight is removed during the first three years, then the status can be withdrawn. If there is no change in the situation, then the status is automatically converted to an unlimited residence status on humanitarian grounds after three years. Any asylum request which is suspended on receipt of this temporary status would be reactivated if the status were withdrawn.

Initially the government appeared to be applying the new status only to very limited categories of people, largely to limit the attractiveness of The Netherlands as a haven. This restrictiveness in implementation did not necessarily mean a restrictive approach to protection generally at first. On the contrary, in 1994 one-third of applicants from Bosnia and

48

Herzegovina received VVTV, while almost half received Convention status. However, since 1995 the status has increasingly been applied to persons falling into the 'tolerated' category, and it seems that the tolerated category is gradually expanding to cover many people who might previously have been granted either a humanitarian ('C') status or Convention ('A') status. In other words, the 'F' status has become the means of restricting application of the 'A' and 'C' statuses. It is not possible to apply specifically for VVTV; rather, it is one of the options for the decision-maker which can result from the dual-track application for asylum and residence. In the case of the ethnic Albanian Kosovars evacuated from Macedonia to The Netherlands, however, the status was granted to them a priori, without their having to file applications for asylum and residence. This point will be returned to below.

The lessons learned from the experience with the Bosnian displaced

At first sight, the major lesson which one would assume the Dutch political leaders had learned from the experience of Bosnian displacements from 1992 to 1995 was how to use efficiently a protection mechanism based in law, allowing for management of a significant influx. However, both the proposals for a new 'Aliens Law' and the approach to the Kosovo displacements indicate that that was not a lesson learned. The Kosovars evacuated from Macedonia and those who arrived spontaneously before and during the NATO campaign were in general accorded the VVTV status. Many non-governmental organizations and academic experts on immigration and asylum law felt that the Kosovars should have been accorded Convention status. The numbers involved hardly constituted a 'mass influx' – the ill-defined criterion for the 'displaced persons' category under VVTV – and while NATO bombing, with Dutch participation, was taking place with the motive of protecting 'the refugees' from the implementation of 'ethnic cleansing and killing' policies, it could hardly be suggested that the only barrier to return was technical, and that the Kosovars in The Netherlands were therefore only 'tolerated persons'.

Given the traumatic experiences in Srebrenica, where the 'safe area' under Dutchbat authority fell to the Serbs in 1995, leading to the mass execution of thousands of Muslims whose graves are still being discovered, and all the recriminations and inquiries which have taken place in the intervening years, one might also imagine that the Dutch government would be opposed to the notion of trying to keep the displaced persons, in need of international protection, close to their homes.[11] However, the notion that reception in the neighbouring states would be best for all concerned had much credence in Dutch political circles.

In fact, the major lesson which the Dutch authorities seemed to have picked up from both the protection of Bosnians and asylum practice generally was that The Netherlands often took on 'more than its fair share' of the responsibility for refugees in Europe. This is a similar lesson to the one Germany is suggested by Koser to have learned.[12] Not only have the numbers of asylum seekers in The Netherlands been rising during the 1990s, the proportions compared to EU partner states have also been shifting, indicating a heavier 'burden' for The Netherlands than would be the norm if population, and particularly population density, indicators were to be taken into account in some idealized system of solidarity between EU states in receiving, protecting and accepting asylum seekers. Furthermore, a majority of the Bosnians who had received protection in The Netherlands were still in the country four years after the Dayton Agreements, and this in spite of the practice of allowing 'go and see' visits with the guaranteed possibility of return to The Netherlands if a new life in Bosnia did not work out. While Germany seemed to be successfully, if not uncontroversially, 'returning' many of the Bosnians who had received a *Duldung* or 'tolerated' status, those who had been protected in The Netherlands seemed to be proving the point of those critics who suggested that 'there is nothing more permanent than temporary protection'.[13]

The Dutch approach to Kosovo's refugees

The initial Dutch approach to the mass exodus from Kosovo into the neighbouring countries was twofold. On the one hand the government sought to support protection of the displaced in the neighbouring countries, under the title of 'reception in the region'. On the other hand it sought an EU-level approach: that is, the Dutch response was to take no unilateral position but to seek a European approach.

In support of the neighbouring states, The Netherlands donated some 3.5 million euros in the first week of the NATO bombing campaign. The money was divided between the UNHCR (1.5 million euros), the World Food Programme (WFP) (750,000 euros), the Red Cross (ICRC) (1 million euros) and UNICEF (300,000 euros).[14] It also considered using employees of the COA (Centraal Orgaan Opvang Asielzoekers – Central Body for the Reception of Asylum Seekers) to organize 'reception in the region'. Employees of the organization were in any case part of two missions sent to Macedonia to select those people to be evacuated to The Netherlands under the programme agreed.

As part of the promotion of an EU rather than national approach to the protection of the displaced, The Netherlands called for discussion of the subject to be placed on the agenda of the K4 committee meeting under the German presidency.[15] The Dutch government called for this EU approach because of 'the humanitarian concerns at stake and of the proximity of the conflict'.[16] The Dutch government's position in that meeting would be that reception in the region should be the main theme of the EU's approach, the 'region' being understood as Serbia's neighbouring states, as the acceptance of Kosovo's displaced in the wider European region would be a sign that ethnic cleansing was being accepted.

While seeking this two-pronged approach, amounting to a desire to see the vast majority of the displaced remain outside the EU, the Secretary of State for Justice, Job Cohen (PvdA: Partij van de Arbeid – the Dutch Labour Party), assured Parliament in his letter of 31 March 1999 that The Netherlands would not shirk its responsibility towards those Kosovar Albanians who arrived spontaneously in The Netherlands. He did not elaborate on the form that responsibility would take. In other words, he made no statements with regard to the status those asylum seekers might be granted, or the likelihood of the a priori acceptability of their cases for admission under any status at all.

By 20 April the government had decided to create a quota for Kosovar Albanians to be evacuated from Macedonia under the supervision of the UNHCR. In a letter to the upper chamber of Parliament, the Secretary of State explained that The Netherlands would initially accept 1000 people. This total could be increased to 2000 at a later stage. The emphasis would be on those who volunteered to be evacuated to The Netherlands, on family unity and on reunification and medical cases. Those brought to The Netherlands would receive temporary protection, be housed in temporary emergency shelters in the rural towns of Ermelo and Ter Apel, and be given the opportunity to make an application for admission and asylum.[17] The first arrivals were in Ermelo on 24 April.

Status

As mentioned above, the Kosovar Albanians who arrived on the evacuation programme were given, a priori, the VVTV status, which granted temporary protection for one year, renewable (with increasing social entitlements) for up to three years. The reason for granting this status, rather than a Convention status, is questionable: the group of some 4000 arriving over a six-week period could not reasonably be called a 'mass influx' in a country which regularly receives some 4000 asylum applications per month. If the sole reason was to limit the potential length of protection, then this strongly indicates a lack of political will to employ the cessation clause of the Convention (article 1C, which refers to the change of circumstances in the country of origin). At the same time, granting the status, unusually, a priori meant the individuals who made up that evacuated group had no suspended asylum claim on which they could call to maintain a status if the VVTV status were to be either withdrawn or not renewed.

It is also interesting to consider the situation of some Kosovar Albanians who had arrived in previous years, and were granted nothing more than a stay of deportation on the basis that technical reasons prevented their return. Once the situation in Serbia for ethnic Albanians was considered to have deteriorated to the extent that statuses were more often being granted (March 1999), and some rejected applicants who nonetheless were not required to return had been in the Netherlands with exceptional leave (*uitstel van vertrek*) for almost three years (the time period after which they would automatically be granted a long-term status), VVTVs started to be granted. Those who had lived for almost three years in uncertainty were thereby granted another period of uncertainty in temporary protection, the two periods not being cumulative with regard to the granting of permanent residence status.[18] Once the VVTV statuses were withdrawn, those who had not yet made an asylum application but wished to do so could. Those whose previous application had been rejected, but who had been granted an exceptional leave prior to departure, returned to the vague status of exceptional leave. Once they have spent three years with exceptional leave, for which the period of VVTV will not count, they will be granted a humanitarian permit to remain. Although the government has withdrawn the VVTV statuses on the basis that the situation has changed and return has become possible, there is as yet (October 1999) no official circular (*ambtsbericht*) indicating that there was no reason for delaying departure. Indeed, the *ambtsbericht* of 19 August 1999 provided a broad overview of the situation, but no conclusions which would suggest safety in Kosovo. In fact, it pointed out that K-FOR could not be expected, as yet, to provide security in the whole province.[19]

Numbers and the EU context

Political discussion in The Netherlands focused, perhaps unsurprisingly given the debate of the previous year, on numbers. Many of the political parties in Parliament, including those making up the coalition cabinet, found the figures of 1000 increasing to 2000 too little and too late.[20] Waiting for the European approach for which it hoped, the Dutch government formulated no specific offer to the UNHCR, while its EU partners and other states did. Clearly it must have felt that its best bargaining strategy was not to show its hand too soon. Newspaper reports of Iceland and Finland opening quotas and accepting refugees while the Dutch waited seemed at least to be part of the process of almost shaming the Dutch government into actual action in protecting the refugees rather than discussion of how the EU could do that together. One of the coalition partners, D66, noted that it was painful to see The Netherlands, at a late stage, limping along behind fellow European states who were announcing quotas of a far higher order. Those cited included Finland (10,000), Norway (6000) and Sweden (5000). The search for an EU approach was not dealt with by 'leading by example'. The Netherlands was not alone in wanting to stimulate solidarity. However, the German government's decision to close Germany's quota at 10,000 and reopen it only once other EU states had taken action was perhaps a more active effort at stimulating solidarity and thereby a semblance of EU collective action.[21] The Netherlands was one of the few other EU states to have filled its quota when Germany restarted its evacuation programme. However, as the quota was so relatively low, this fulfilment only raises further questions about the purpose of such quotas, both in respect to the displaced persons concerned and in the internal relations between EU states and their visions of the collective or independent action the quotas could be taken to represent.[22]

Another coalition partner, the VVD, sought clarity from the UNHCR on the exact numbers of people it could manage to protect within Macedonia and Albania, and figures from the UNHCR indicating how many people it expected EU states to take, rather than vice versa. That party sought a common EU approach to the reception of the Kosovars: giving shelter, but no legal status, and guaranteeing return as soon as possible. All other political parties, both in the governing coalition and in the opposition, appeared to agree on the granting of the temporary status ('F') in the short term, with eventual extension of the 'A' status if the reason for flight persisted.

Political and public debate

On the one hand, therefore, one saw the majority of political parties supporting the welcoming and protection of significant numbers of ethnic Albanians from Kosovo, under EU cooperation. On the other hand, the political party which was perceived as having substantially improved its electoral record partly on the basis of its opposition to further immigration (while integrating those immigrants already in The Netherlands) supported EU cooperation, but opposed the entry into The Netherlands of significant numbers of Kosovars and the accordance of a legal status to those who did arrive.[23]

The media highlighted individual tales of those ethnic Albanians who were eventually evacuated to The Netherlands. The *Volkskrant* reported at various stages on one family whose initial reaction to the move to The

Netherlands was portrayed under the headline 'I'll gladly go to The Netherlands, but sorry, I won't be staying'.[24] The message was clear: these refugees wanted to be safe, were grateful for the protection they received, but would rather be back home with their entire family in a peaceful Kosovo. After the bombing, and once K-FOR was in place, the same family was reported to be returning, travelling in a second-hand car they had bought using benefits from the Dutch social services.[25] The newspaper talked of 7000 Kosovars in The Netherlands, most of whom could not afford to make such a journey and must thus wait for the International Organization for Migration (IOM) to get organized. Many wanted to return, to see their homes and because they did not like living in Dutch tent cities. Others, however, were reported as wanting to stay a while longer to be sure Kosovo would be safe for them, or because their treatment (e.g. for medical conditions) was better in The Netherlands. Yet others said they could not take the psychological pain of more personal bad news: they had found peace in The Netherlands.

Both TV and newspaper portrayal of specific 'real' families was surely a component of the generally expressed sentiment of compassion. A cynic (or pragmatist) could suggest that the Dutch government had also decided to include a large proportion of people with medical needs as a public relations exercise, trying to make up for not having acted in line with public sentiment in the initial days of the NATO campaign and massive exodus. Indeed, many media items, and particularly interviews with political leaders, highlighted the Dutch focus on those in need of medical treatment as something which distinguished The Netherland's approach from that of other host states. However, public relations strategy or not, such an approach could, in the rock-hard terms of 'return as success', be said to guarantee failure: acceptance of the most vulnerable must be morally worthwhile, but will not stimulate high return figures if that is also a policy goal.

By the end of the NATO bombing and the period of major evacuations, The Netherlands had accepted a total of 4060 evacuees.[26] This was 7.7 per cent of those ethnic Albanians evacuated from Macedonia to EU states. By mid-August 1999 approximately 2000 of those people had left The Netherlands, approximately half of them on an IOM programme (see below). Almost none of those evacuated with a temporary status had in fact formally claimed asylum in The Netherlands. Some 2100 Kosovars, spontaneous arrivals in The Netherlands, had requested asylum between January and August 1999.[27] For those people the only way legally to remain in The Netherlands is to file such a claim. UNHCR statistics show that 2168 people from the Federal Republic of Yugoslavia had filed asylum applications in The Netherlands between January and June 1999. Given that these are all provisional statistics and that rounding takes place in some sources and not others, it seems reasonable to suggest that there were almost no asylum requests from Serbs in The Netherlands in the first six months of 1999.

Return

A return programme was established under the Netherlands office of the IOM. By 28 July IOM-Nederland had received 735 applications, and the first returns had taken place on 20 July, via Skopje. By 27 August the return numbers on the IOM programme had risen to 1319.[28] Each person or family returning on the programme was promised a monetary reward: 570 euros (Dfl 1250) per person for individuals or 800 euros (Dfl 1750) per family. From 29 July onwards those who had arrived in The Netherlands before 16 July could also be awarded a reintegration premium of DM 1000 (510 euros) per adult and DM 500 (255 euros) per child by the Department for Development. The maximum per family which this latter award could reach was 4,000 DM (2040 euros). Those people who still did not have identity papers could travel (a great irony when one considers that entering The Netherlands without ID documentation is enough to invalidate a claim to asylum). Those returning on the specially arranged flights from Rotterdam to Skopje could take 30 kg of luggage.[29]

'Societal security' and The Netherlands: racism – beat it?[30]

Visiting the Second World War concentration camp Majdanek, in Poland, on 13 May 1999, the Dutch Prime Minister, Wim Kok, compared the ethnic cleansing taking place in Kosovo with the actions of the regime in Nazi Germany. 'During the war people were judged on the basis of their origins,' he said. 'After that we said: this must never happen again. But, alas, it is now, once more, a topical subject.'[31] He could have added that before the Second World War, in 1938, leaders of several Western states meeting in Evian made a political decision not to accept Jewish refugees. Loescher describes how delegates to that conference

> noted that the movement of Jewish refugees was 'disturbing to the general economy,' since those in flight were seeking refuge at a time of serious unemployment. Jewish refugees posed a 'severe strain on the administrative facilities and absorptive capacities of the receiving nations,' racial and religious problems were rendered more acute, international unrest increased, and 'the process of appeasement in international relations' might be hindered.[32]

Part of the 'never again' approach to post-Second World War politics on humanitarian issues involved, in the immediate aftermath of the war, the decision that refugees should be accorded an internationally agreed and recognized status, set out in the 1951 Convention. However, current EU leaders appear very able to maintain the topicality of the non-protection of those seeking asylum, whatever the cause of their displacement and search for protection.

In The Netherlands, as in many other EU states, the overwhelming picture portrayed of public attitudes towards ethnic Albanians from Kosovo during the height of the displacements was one of strong sympathy and willingness to help, including offering shelter if necessary. Of course political leaders have to take much more into account than appearances of public sentiment. However, the impression given in some EU states, including The Netherlands, was that the political leadership was more willing to accept the image and accounts of a xenophobic electorate uncomfortable with the arrival of immigrants and asylum seekers than that version of public opinion which demonstrated compassion and a humble and perhaps naive desire to protect the displaced and assist the neighbouring states. In the Dutch case in particular, it may (paradoxically) be the case that political awareness of the extent of xenophobia or its inverse has been distorted by the suppression of the anti-immigrant party.[33] Anti-immigrant sentiment may have been overestimated, particularly as it is in part presumed to be indicated by the electoral support for the VVD, whose supporters in fact may well vote for it for many reasons other than its relatively anti-immigration stance.

That former, xenophobic image is at the root of thinking on the so-called new security issues on the post-Cold War security agenda. As described in the Introduction to this volume, a vision of 'societal security' has been set out by some writers in the field of international relations, portraying identity as one of the cherished and threatened values at stake in the post-Cold War world. The threat to identity is not necessarily to be found in the intentions of other states, although one aspect of the threat to a national identity in the European context is the gradual process of integration within the EU.[34] The purported threat comes rather from individuals and population groups with other cultural, linguistic and identifying characteristics. That the threat to identity could come rather from a nation's own xenophobes is a line of thought which deserves further consideration and which would critically challenge this vision of 'societal security' in which the state, understood as society, finds its identity challenged only from the outside.

To take the Dutch case: The Netherlands is popularly characterized as a liberal and humanitarian state and society. While that liberal identity is chiefly, and stereotypically, seen as apparent in the approach to other public policy areas such as soft drug use and euthanasia, the humanitarian identity has also, through the decades, been based on the Dutch acceptance of foreigners, either as immigrants in the widest sense or those seeking a refuge.[35] The country has its own less than humanitarian record in colonization, although some writers find the Dutch record less oppressive than those of other empire-building European nations. It is also seen as a multicultural society by many Dutch thinkers, although while there has been political acceptance of the notion of multi-culturalism, the label 'immigration country' has been less politically attractive.

One possible analysis of the stance taken with regard to Kosovo's refugees would be that fearing a xenophobic and exclusionary reaction from segments of the population (not unlikely, given the context of the asylum debate in the months prior to the Kosovar exodus), the government raised a challenge from within to the identity of a humanitarian, liberal, multicultural and prosperous state. In trying to defuse the more vocal and violent problems posed by xenophobes and racists, the government's decision to allow only a minimal number of ethnic Albanians into the country on organized evacuation programmes, and to accord in general only limited protection to the relatively small numbers of spontaneous arrivals, denied the expression of identity of the suddenly vocal element of the population which sought a compassionate and welcoming approach. This analysis, suggesting submission to domestic xenophobes, raises questions of continuity when the argumen-tation used is that submitting to Milošević's ethnic cleansing would be a 'bad thing'.

Demonstrations of the compassion for Kosovo's ethnic Albanian displaced were manifold. Town councils and various action groups prepared shelter for thousands of Kosovo's refugees who either never came or were never 'invited'. During the three months of intense media attention linked to the NATO bombing, decisions which had been taken on the subject of asylum seekers generally during the previous months were seen in a new light, and thus reviewed. One example would be the town of Vught, where wealthy residents had bought a residential complex with the aim of keeping it out of the hands of the COA, which planned to house asylum seekers in it. During the NATO bombing those same wealthy residents decided to offer the residential centre for use as shelter for Kosovars only. At the same time, decisions taken during the bombing campaign to open and reuse old army barracks as shelter were overturned once the 'crisis' was over and it became clear that Kosovars would not be the only or even the majority of asylum seekers to be housed there.[36] Such action and sentiment on behalf of Kosovo's fleeing Serb population has been less evident.

In essence the use of 'societal security' or 'new security' thinking to explain decisions to reject immigrants, even when they are in genuine search of safety and protection, does seem, as Shaw suggests, to come down to straightforward realist politics.[37] Judgements are made on the basis of xenophobic positions perceived (perhaps incorrectly) through voting patterns and other manifestations suggesting that exclusion of 'others' is in society's and therefore the nation's interest. However, in making such realist judgements politicians run the serious risk of not fulfilling their international obligations and of alienating those perhaps normally less vocal segments of the population who do not wish to see people in need being excluded on the implicit basis of the changes they may bring to the cultural make-up of a country. That a self-reputed 'multicultural' state should turn to exclusion seems particularly paradoxical. However, the depth of paradox would depend on the understanding of 'multiculturalism' (presumably based on a form of 'contract nationalism') and how far the multicultural state is prepared to further embrace newcomers and expand on the mix of cultures presumed to inform its identity and self-image.[38]

The Dutch decision to implement a relatively small quota could, however, be a symptom of concern other than the (potential) xenophobia of Dutch citizens. It could, for example, indicate a willingness to stand up to EU partners on the issue of solidarity at the expense of domestic support, international commitment and the protection of both the lives of the refugees and the stability of neighbouring states. Alternatively, it could be simple pragmatism: a desire to set a quota which could realistically be filled and thus 'achieved' rather than an inflated quota which would be unlikely to be filled.

Expectations in and of the EU

As clearly demonstrated in the Secretary of State's letter to Parliament cited above, The Netherlands was seeking a common EU approach to the displacements from Kosovo. During the political discussions of the previous months the need for an EU solution had been stressed consistently by all political actors, and this was re-emphasized in the early days of the NATO campaign. On the one hand this can seem logical: the EU is working on further cooperation on immigration and asylum, as manifest by the major institutional and practical changes set out in Title IV of the Amsterdam Treaty, negotiated under a Dutch EU presidency. However, taking such a position can also seem like abrogating responsibility: saying to the voting public that because immigration is increasingly a matter affecting all EU states, and because of earlier arrangements and anticipated future progress, the national government is not going to take on what is still, in fact, a matter of national policy.

One of the particular features of the EU approach to asylum and immigration which is impacting on The Netherlands, and which is part of the issue of solidarity, is the implementation of the Dublin Convention determining the state responsible for assessing an asylum application.[39] In 1998 The Netherlands received 892 claims from fellow member states who viewed the Dutch state as responsible, according to the Dublin criteria, for considering the applications for asylum they had received. The Netherlands made 6142 claims on other EU states: most of these (72 per cent) were made to Germany.[40] According to the Dublin criteria, of course, The Netherlands should in general be responsible for very few asylum claims: of new arrivals in the EU without family members already present in, or with a visa for, The Netherlands, only those arriving from beyond the EU's borders by air or sea should be the responsibility of The Netherlands. Therefore, under Dublin as it stands, The Netherlands should have a very small role to play in EU 'solidarity' or responsibility sharing.[41] A minor role in the assessment of spontaneous arrivals should not necessarily, however, indicate that a minor role should also be played in quota arrivals.

A further indication of the Dutch government's desire to see greater EU-level coordination on asylum matters came in mid-May when the Prime Minister, Wim Kok, called for the creation of a post of European commissioner to deal soley with asylum issues.[42] This call came during the vacuum caused by the resignation of the entire European Commission, and as the Commission President-to-be, Romano Prodi, was assembling his new Commission. Kok suggested that such a commissioner could act within the present structure. Many commentators, including former MEP Hedy d'Ancona (chair of the European Parliament's Civil Liberties Committee from 1995 to 1999), pointed out that such a commissioner already existed: Anita Gradin had had the entire Justice and Home Affairs (JHA) area in her portfolio under the Santer Commission, as had Padraig Flynn in the previous Delors Commission. Discussion never went so far as to indicate whether the call was in fact for not only the separation of asylum and immigration matters from other JHA affairs but also the addition of elements of humanitarian affairs (dealing with the favoured plan of aid and 'protection' within the region) and even foreign policy matters. No such position was created, although the new JHA commissioner, Mr António Vitorino, does not have matters of fraud in his portfolio, as Ms Gradin did.[43]

It is apparent from this description of the Dutch position, portrayed domestically and as taken during various meetings of Justice and Home Affairs Departments and asylum and immigration groups, that there is a strong belief in, and wholehearted desire for, an EU-level approach to asylum and immigration matters. The approach as seen here is one of first seeking EU-level agreement, and only later acting and imposing limitations on that action in comparison to fellow EU member states and the traditional reactions of the state itself to similar crises. The question is whether such an approach is understandable, and appropriate, from the point of view of domestic politics and international relations.

From the point of view of the Dutch government, wishing not to be seen in the eyes of the national voters as being taken advantage of, either by EU partners or by potential immigrants, it was perhaps logical that a position of restriction and limitation would be taken. However, that position did not achieve the goal of seeing a common approach to the protection of the displaced, nor did it achieve the proclaimed goal of the NATO campaign itself: the protection of the refugees.

Internationally, the Dutch approach could be said to have been one of seeking the national interest, both with regard to maintaining control over admission to the national territory and with regard to making explicit the national perspective on immigration: namely that after fifteen years of gradual harmonization on this subject and almost fifty years of gradual integration in other policy areas which impact on the ability of people to move between and into the member states, it is time to adopt an EU approach. This analysis would suggest that seeing a crisis developing, potentially of enormous proportions in terms of the influx to the EU states if the magnitude of the exodus from Kosovo itself was anything to go by, and if the cause of displacement were not to be resolved in such a way that Kosovars would believe a rapid return to be possible, the Dutch government saw its opportunity to create the EU approach it desired. As the influx to the EU states turned out to be manageable and minimal in the three main crisis months, and returns became possible, making temporary protection (whether in neighbouring first states of asylum or further afield in the EU) truly short term, the moment for developing that precedent for common approach was lost.

Conclusion

The analysis of this chapter has been twofold: using both questions of 'societal security' or concerns about xenophobia, and matters of European integration, specifically in the area of asylum and immigration policies, to explain and illuminate what has here been characterized as a hesitant and passive approach on the part of the Dutch government towards the reception of refugees from Kosovo.

From the societal security perspective it has been shown that concerns about xenophobia in The Netherlands may be one way of explaining why other means for protection of the rights of displaced persons were emphasized in this case – in particular, 'reception in the region'. However, it has also been suggested that this belief in the potential challenge to the *status quo* of Dutch identity could in itself be a threat to characteristics understood as inherent in that same identity. In particular, it has been suggested that the humanitarian nature of what is portrayed as 'being Dutch' may have been challenged by the government's apparent willingness to believe in the story of anti-immigrant public opinion, and its decision to respond only to that vision of public opinion which was pro-protection to the extent of trying to promote protective measures beyond Dutch borders. Such protection raises many further questions about the nature of sovereignty and intervention. Perhaps there is an element of 'luck' at work here: the NATO bombing can be portrayed as having been successful enough to permit rapid return, and to have allowed for assistance in neighbouring states for the overwhelming majority of Kosovars without the situation having got so out of hand that conflict spread, caused by the enormous presence of the refugees.

In terms of the process of European integration in asylum and immigration policies, the Dutch government appears to have been chasing an ideal of solidarity through evacuation quotas. Perhaps expecting German support (Germany having been the state which has pushed hardest for 'responsibility sharing' since 1994), the Dutch government seems to have played from what it thought would be a position of strength. The publicly stated goal was a quota definition before reception got under way. However, the stronger of the two partners seeking burden sharing took a more active stance by first taking 10,000 Kosovars on its quota – leaving the Dutch to rapidly establish and fill a smaller programme. In terms of stimulating fellow member states to accept refugees, and take some of their share (however defined), the active German method appears to have been more successful than the passive Dutch one.

Another characteristic of Dutch identity is often said to be the search for compromise, most prominently displayed in the much-talked-of 'polder model' in which government, employers and unions come together to agree the way ahead for economic growth. While the humanitarian and multicultural nature of the stereotypical Dutch identity might have taken a knock, as suggested here, one could (mischievously perhaps) suggest that the search for compromise remained paramount; it was merely that The Netherlands' partners were not playing the same game, or at least not by the same rules. The search for those rules goes on, the dilemmas persist, states muddle through, and the Dutch state, like other EU states, continues to raise restrictions from a human rights perspective, and, from a statist perspective, to defend the national interest (be that economic or cultural) and 'national identity'.

Notes

1. See statistics in Appendix 2, Table 7.
2. See M. Fennema, 'Extreem-rechts en de democratie', *Socialisme en Democratie* 54 (2) (1997), 51–62.
3. The proposed changes were submitted to Parliament in September 1999. *Vreemdelingen Wet 2000*: www.minjust.nl/c_actual/persber/pb0487.htm.
4. For a description of asylum policies in The Netherlands and political changes from 1994 to 1999, see J. van Selm, 'Asylum in the Netherlands: a hazy shade of purple', *Journal of Refugee Studies* (forthcoming, 2000).
5. Ministry of Justice (Immigration and Naturalization Service), *Keten in kaart, 1998: trends en ontwikkelingen in de vreemdelingenketen in 1998* (Charting the chain 1998: trends and developments in the migration chain in 1998) (The Hague: Ministry of Justice, August 1999), pp. 22–3.
6. The closure of the tent camp was in fact announced on 12 January 1999, three months earlier than had been originally agreed.
7. D66 (the centrist Democratic party, established in 1966) adopted a position suggesting that discussion of the return of both Convention refugees and those with limited statuses (VVTV) should not be taboo. It also insisted that the fact that thousands of Bosnians had been able automatically to receive an 'A' status (in fact, more likely was a 'C' status with a permanent residence permit) showed that many people had received what should be an individualized status *en masse*. The greatest sticking point to return, according to D66, was whether or not the Immigration and Naturalization Service could cope with it. ('Toelichting D66-standpunt bosnische asielzoekers' [Explanation of D66's position on Bosnian asylum seekers] – www.d66.nl/nieuws/toevluch.html). The VVD also took, at various points in the debate, a strong stance on the potential for returning or deporting Bosnians. The VVD and D66 have been partners with the Labour/Social Democratic Party (PvdA, Partij van de Arbeid) in the 'Purple Coalition' since 1994.
8. Parts of this section draw on J. van Selm-Thorburn, *Refugee Protection in Europe: Lessons of the Yugoslav Crisis* (Dordrecht: Martinus Nijhoff, 1998), Chapter 10.
9. This division of centres was one aspect of overall policy which disappeared when the scheme was abolished.
10. The attraction of Convention refugee status for the displaced persons would be the accompanying travel documents. For people who might wish to remain indefinitely, however, the humanitarian status would ultimately be more attractive, as it does not appear to include a cessation clause. There was a rejection rate of only 10 per cent for asylum seekers who had been covered by TROO.
11. On the Dutch, and wider, experiences in Srebrenica, see, for example, J.W. Honig and N. Both, *Srebrenica: Record of a War Crime* (London: Penguin, 1996). Dutchbat was the abbreviation for the Dutch battalion.
12. See Chapter 2 in this volume.
13. M. Krikorian, 'Here to stay: there's nothing as permanent as a temporary

refugee', Center for Immigration Studies, Backgrounder (August 1999): www.cis.org/back899.pdf.

14. Letter to the lower chamber of Parliament about the situation of refugees from Kosovo, 31 March 1999, Reference 748763/99/DVB.

15. The K4 Committee which met during the period in which asylum and immigration fell clearly under the third pillar according to the Maastricht Treaty on European Union was named after the article (K4) of that treaty which dealt with work to be undertaken on those matters and its institutional setting.

16. Letter to Parliament, 31 March 1999. Author's translation.

17. Letter to the upper chamber of Parliament, 20 April 1999, reference 753494/99/DVB.

18. See Rechtseenheidskamer, Rechtbank 's-Gravenhage (Court, The Hague), 17 November 1998 (published by Sdu Uitgevers Cd Vreemdelingen- en Asielrecht) – judgement on the handling of the case of A., an asylum applicant of ethnic Albanian origin from Yugoslavia whose application of 7 October 1994 had been judged inadmissible, although he was exempted from deportation for 'technical reasons'. Although there was reason enough, in the court's opinion, to grant a VVTV status, the minister had not done so. The court requested clarification from the Minister about the relative weight accorded to the criteria deemed necessary in the granting of temporary protection. It appeared rather that the political approach was to limit 'permanent' status by granting the temporary status of three years only at the latest possible date. I am grateful to Thomas Spijkerboer for this point.

19. Ministry of Foreign Affairs, Ambtsbericht: 'Situatie (van etnisch Albanezen) in Kosovo' ('The situation (of ethnic Albanians) in Kosovo'), The Hague, 19 August 1999, p. 46.

20. 'Standpunt D66 m.b.t. de opvang etnische Albanezen uit Kosovo' (Position of D66 on the reception of ethnic Albanians from Kosovo): www.d66.nl/tweedekamer/opvang.html. The author, MP Boris Diettrich, cites quotas from other countries. 'Het is pijnlijk om te zien hoe Nederland hier een beetje achteraal hobbelt' (It is painful to see how The Netherlands is limping on behind).

21. UNHCR Daily News (22 April 1999): www.unhcr.ch/news/media/daily.htm. Report from Reuters, citing Interior Minister Otto Schily as saying that 'Germany would not give asylum to any more Kosovo Albanians after already taking in its agreed quota of 10,000 refugees.' He said, 'We have taken in the most refugees. It doesn't make any sense to talk about how many more refugees will come to Germany.' He bemoaned the lack of action by fellow EU member states. Peter Struck, parliamentary leader of the Social Democrats, reiterated these comments: reported by Reuters on 30 April (also UNHCR Daily News). See also Koser in this volume (Chapter 2).

22. The matter of how quotas are created and thinking around them is dealt with in the Conclusion of this volume.

23. PvdA, 'PVDA en VVD oneens over inburgering Kosovaarse Vluchtelingen' (PvdA and VVD disagree over the integration of Kosovar refugees), *Vlugschrift* (Amsterdam, 1 May 1999, no. 151).

24. *Volkskrant*, '"Ik ga graag naar Nederland maar ik blijf niet, sorry"' ('I'll gladly go to the Netherlands, but sorry, I won't be staying'], 26 April 1999, p. 5.

25. *Volkskrant*, 23 June 1999, p. 3.

26. UNHCR figure as of 1 July 1999.

27. *Volkskrant*, '2100 Kosovaren willen asiel in Nederland' (2100 Kosovars apply for asylum in the Netherlands), 26 August 1999, p. 5.

28. IOM Assisted Return to Kosovo – Statistical Update no. 43, 27 August 1999.

29. IOM web site: 209.198.242.125/nonneighbouring/holand/holand.htm.

30. In August 1999 many news reports featured stories of how racism in The Netherlands was declining – a positive account on this subject seeming to make the news for once. In fact the surveys which had been conducted were among young people attending a music festival on 15 August, Racism: Beat It – held every year, but with increasing attendance. The theme of the 1999 festival was 'Respect'.

31. *Volkskrant*, 'Kok: zuivering Kosovo doet denken aan nazi-Duitsland' (Kok: cleansing in Kosovo is a reminder of Nazi Germany), 14 May 1999, p. 3. Author's translation of citation: 'Mensen werden in de oorlog beoordeeld op hun afkomst. Daarna zeiden we: dit nooit weer, maar helaas is het nu weer volop actueel'.

32. G. Loescher, *Beyond Charity: International Cooperation and the Global Refugee Crisis* (Oxford: Oxford University Press, 1993) pp. 44–5. Loescher cites G.S. Goodwin-Gill, 'Different types of forced migration movements and international and national problems', in G. Rystad (ed.) *The Uprooted: Forced Migration as an International Problem in the Post-war Era* (Lund: Lund University Press, 1990), pp. 18–19.

33. I am grateful to Meindert Fennema for this point.

34. This creates spaces for new identity formations which could also challenge and threaten (by altering the status quo) the traditional and 'given' national identities. See O. Waever, B. Buzan, M. Kelstrup and P. Lemaitre, *Identity, Migration and the New Security Agenda in Europe* (London: Pinter, 1993).

35. See J. Lucassen, and R. Peninx, *Newcomers: Immigrants and Their Descendants in The Netherlands 1550–1995* (Amsterdam: Het Spinhuis 1994).

36. *Volkskrant*, 'Kosovaren ondergebracht in Oostzaan en Arnhem' (Kosovars housed in Oostzaan and Arnhem), 11 May 1999, p. 3. The decision to reopen the barracks in Oostzaan was overruled by the council decision late in June.

37. Shaw, Martin, *Global Society and International Relations* (Cambridge: Polity Press, 1994), p. 101.

38. See M. Fennema, and J. Tillie, 'Afstamming of contract: over de aard van het nationalisme' (Descent or contract: on the nature of Dutch nationalism), in K. Koch, and P. Scheffer (eds), *Het nut van Nederland* (The Utility of the Netherlands) (Amsterdam: Bert Bakker, 1996).

39. The Dublin Convention: *Convention Determining the State Responsible for Examining Applications Lodged in One of the Member States of the European Community*, CONV/SILE, (1989). The Dublin Convention came into effect in September 1997.

40. See Ministry of Justice, *Keten in kaart*, pp. 28–30.

41. That the Dublin Convention as it stands in 1999 is not working is a generally

accepted fact in most member states. One suggestion for reform is put forward by the Academic Group [Im]migration – Tampere (AGIT), targeting the European Council special meeting on Justice and Home Affairs in Tampere, Finland, on 15–16 October 1999. The suggestion of that group is that indeed only one state should be responsible for assessing the claim; but that state should be the state of arrival. This would avoid lengthy and costly procedures associated with transfers and the long period of time in which an asylum application is not handled because it is not clear who should assess it. AGIT do suggest financial arrangements for supporting those states who thus receive a significant proportion of claims. See AGIT, 'Efficient, effective and encompassing approaches to a European immigration and asylum policy', *International Journal of Refugee Law* (vol. 11, no. 2, pp. 338–74, 1999); also at www.jur.kun.nl/rit/cmr/articles.

42. *Volkskrant*, 'Kok: EU behoort commissaris voor asielbeleid' (Kok: the EU should have a commissioner for asylum policy), 12 May 1999, p. 3.

43. Prime Minister Kok would have found it difficult to propose the new Dutch commissioner to fill that role, as Frits Bolkestein, when leader of the VVD, had introduced (as described above) immigration as an issue in election campaigning.

Bibliography

Books and journal articles

Fennema, M., 'Extreem-rechts en de democratie', *Socialisme en Democratie* 54 (2) (1997), 51–62.

Fennema, M. and Tillie, J., 'Afstamming of contract: over de aard van het nationalisme', in K. Koch and P. Scheffer (eds) *Het nut van Nederland* (Amsterdam: Bert Bakker, 1996).

Honig, J.W. and Both, N., *Srebrenica: Record of a War Crime* (London: Penguin, 1996).

Loescher, Gil, *Beyond Charity: International Cooperation and the Global Refugee Crisis* (Oxford: Oxford University Press, 1993).

Lucassen, J. and Peninx, R., *Newcomers: Immigrants and Their Descendants in the Netherlands 1550–1995* (Amsterdam: Het Spinhuis 1994).

Selm-Thorburn, J. van, *Refugee Protection in Europe: Lessons of the Yugoslav Crisis* (Dordrecht: Martinus Nijhoff, 1998).

Selm, J. van, 'Asylum in the Netherlands: a hazy shade of purple', *Journal of Refugee Studies* (forthcoming, 2000).

Shaw, M. *Global Society and International Relations* (Cambridge: Polity Press, 1994).

Waever, O., Buzan, B., Kelstrup, M. and Lemaitre, P., *Identity, Migration and the New Security Agenda in Europe* (London: Pinter, 1993).

Reports

AGIT (Academic Group (Im]migration – Tampere), 'Efficient, effective and encompassing approaches to a European immigration and asylum policy', *International Journal of Refugee Law* (forthcoming 1999); also at www.jur.kun.nl/rit/cmr/articles.

D66, 'Toelichting D66-standpunt Bosnische asielzoekers' (Explanation of D66's position on Bosnian asylum seekers): www.d66.nl/nieuws/toevluch.html.

D66, 'Standpunt D66 m.b.t. de opvang etnische Albanezen uit Kosovo' (Position of D66 on the reception of ethnic Albanians from Kosovo): www.d66.nl/ tweedekamer/opvang.html.

Krikorian, M., 'Here to stay: there's nothing as permanent as a temporary refugee', Center for Immigration Studies, Backgrounder (August 1999): www.cis.org/ back899.pdf.

Ministry of Justice (Immigration and Naturalization Service), *Keten in kaart, 1998: trends en ontwikkelingen in de vreemdelingenketen in 1998* (Charting the chain 1998: trends and developments in the migration chain in 1998) (The Hague: Ministry of Justice, August 1999).

PvdA, 'PvdA en VVD oneens over inburgering Kosovaarse Vluchtelingen' (PvdA and VVD disagree over the integration of Kosovar refugees), *Vlugschrift* (Amsterdam, 1 May 1999, no. 151).

Primary sources

Convention Determining the State Responsible for Examining Applications Lodged in One of the Member States of the European Community, CONV/SILE (1989).

Letter to the lower chamber of Parliament about the situation of refugees from Kosovo, 31 March 1999, reference 748763/99/DVB.

Letter to the upper chamber of Parliament, 20 April 1999, reference 753494/99/ DVB.

Rechtseenheidskamer, Rechtbank 's-Gravenhage (Court, The Hague), 17 November 1998 (published by Sdu Uitgevers Cd Vreemdelingen- en Asielrecht).

Ministry of Foreign Affairs, Ambtsbericht: 'Situatie (van etnisch Albanezen) in Kosovo' ('The Situation (of ethnic Albanians) in Kosovo'), The Hague, 19 August 1999.

Web sites

IOM: Assisted Return to Kosovo – Statistical Update no. 43, 27 August 1999: www.iom.ch/kosovo/default.htm

IOM: 209.198.242.125/nonneighbouring/holand/holand.htm

Ministry of Justice: www.minjust.nl

UNHCR Daily News: www.unhcr.ch/news/media/daily.htm

CHAPTER FOUR

The United Kingdom: Kosovar Albanian refugees

ELSPETH GUILD

Introduction

Do countries and their administrations adapt their responses in the light of past experience in the area of forced migration? The example of the Bosnian crisis followed by the Kosovo crisis provides a rare opportunity to test this question within the European context. Throughout the Bosnia crisis the UK was criticized by some other European countries for its failure to take more refugees and displaced persons. How does this compare with the situation during the Kosovo crisis? How did the government and administration respond to the humanitarian crisis in Kosovo and what echoes from the Bosnian crisis can be discerned?

I will approach this question from three perspectives:

1   First, what was the UK's response to the crisis in Kosovo as regards numbers and access to the territory for refugees? This will be contrasted to the treatment of Bosnian refugees during the earlier war.
2   Second, I will look at the treatment of refugees from the region after arrival in the UK. How were refugees from the region treated when they got to the UK and was there consistency in their treatment?
3   Finally, I will consider the national debate on immigration and asylum at the time of the policy-making on Kosovo and seek to determine the extent to which there was any interface between the reception of Kosovo refugees and the wider question of asylum in the UK with reference to the European Union (EU).

This chapter will place substantial emphasis on the legal issues which surround the treatment of Kosovo refugees as in the UK this framework was fundamental to understanding the administrative responses. The

Kosovo crisis came at a time of substantial and increased judicial concern about the treatment of refugees in general which was reflected in the UK court judgements as regards the scope of administrative discretion within which the UK government's margin of action was constrained. The policy response by the government was therefore ring-fenced in a way which had not occurred during the Bosnian humanitarian crisis.

The reception of Kosovo refugees

The bombing of the Federal Republic of Yugoslavia (FRY) by NATO began at the end of March and finished on 10 June 1999. Over the period the UK admitted under its resettlement plan 4346 Kosovo refugees, who were given a specific immigration status which I will discuss in the next section. Over the same period the number of spontaneous arrivals of asylum seekers from former Yugoslavia numbered 3230 (Table 4.1).

The war in Bosnia started in autumn 1992 and the Dayton Peace Accord was signed on 14 December 1995. Over that period 2660 Bosnians[1] were admitted under the programme for Bosnia. The numbers of asylum seekers who arrived spontaneously over that period and their treatment are to be found in Table 4.2. In both cases, before the crises began there were substantial numbers of persons from the area already seeking asylum in the UK.[2] The features of their treatment ran parallel: from a discourse, not long before the wars, of doubt about the genuineness of the applications for asylum, there was an administrative trend towards giving full refugee status, albeit somewhat slowly to asylum

Table 4.1 Spontaneous asylum seekers from former Yugoslavia in the UK, March–June 1999

Month	Number of asylum requests	Decisions taken		
		Refugee status	ELR	Refused any status
March	755	10	—	50
April	690	805	—	20
May	755	2075	—	10
June	1030	N/A	—	N/A

Source: Home Office Immigration Research and Statistics Service, RSD 31/08/99; annex to letter from the service to Kingsley Napley, 7 September 1999

Note: ELR = exceptional leave to remain, a national status less than that of refugee recognized under the Geneva Convention

Table 4.2 Treatment of asylum seekers from former Yugoslavia in the UK, 1992–8

Year	Number of applications for asylum	Recognized as a refugee	Granted exceptional leave to remain	Refused any status
1992	5635	1–2	1–2	125
1993	1830	0	55	125
1994	1385	25	1265	475
1995	1565	285	740	835
1996	1030	1155	335	660
1997	2260	1760	355	550
1998	7980	1010	120	705

applicants whose applications were in the queues. This process accelerated or slowed depending on the general administrative capacity of the authorities at the time.

The Kosovo crisis arrived just as the UK's Immigration and Nationality Directorate (IND) had hit a new low in its functional capacity. Massive inefficiency, the result of implementing a major reorganization and a disastrous computerization programme which when finally on stream proved unable to deal with the requirements of the Directorate, had weakened hugely the administration's ability to deal with any type of application.[3] Further, the physical building of the IND had been closed for renovation and the offices moved around and about in the area of Croydon, south London, for the duration (which is anticipated to last several years). It was in this context of backlogs increasing at a phenomenal rate, public disquiet over the delays and generally low morale that the crisis of Kosovo arrived. On the one hand it permitted some administrative successes and may have increased the morale of the administration as a category of files which could be dealt with quickly was identified: all Kosovar asylum applicants could be processed[4] without provoking too many questions about whether the administration was being sufficiently rigorous in the consideration of the applications in pursuit of the government's stated policy in the field: a fairer, faster and firmer system.[5] This process was also eased by the decision of the Immigration Appeal Tribunal, the second-tier court of the UK immigration system, on 22 July 1996 that Kosovars of Albanian ethnic origin are refugees on account of their race and the history of persecution alone.[6] While the process of recognizing Kosovars as refugees had already begun in the UK after that decision, it was accelerated once the NATO bombing started. I will return to this decision later when looking at the question of treatment of refugees once within the territory.

Indeed, processing these applications quickly was also fulfilling another policy objective: the appearance of responding to the crisis by recognizing Kosovars as refugees without actually admitting many persons from outside the UK into the country. This approach had also been followed during the Bosnia crisis but the territory was less clearly marked out. After a number of initial temporary statuses which were granted to Bosnians seeking asylum in the UK there was a rush of refugee recognitions in 1996, after the Dayton Peace Accord was signed. From 25 persons recognized as refugees in 1994 the number rose to 1155 in 1996.[7] After the signature of the Dayton Peace Accord, this process stopped, and Bosnians whose applications were still pending began to be refused any status in the UK. However, for UK policy the distinctive question was how the refugees arrived on the territory.

Getting to the territory

The UK introduced mandatory visa requirements on nationals of former Yugoslavia on 6 November 1992. This meant that as soon as the Bosnian war began, all nationals caught up in that conflict were no longer able to come to the UK without visas. As there is a general rule that visas will be issued to nationals only in their country of nationality, and as that country was ostensibly Yugoslavia, all applications for visas had to be made at the UK consulate in Belgrade.[8]

The result both for the purposes of the Bosnia conflict and the Kosovo conflict was that not many people arrived after that date in possession of visas issued in Belgrade. They arrived in a variety of different manners, not least – and most pronouncedly for the Kosovars – irregularly (see below). The introduction of mandatory visas for nationals of countries in conflict is a tool increasingly used in UK immigration law.[9] The purpose of visa requirements has moved from a mechanism in the arsenal of foreign policy to an immigration control device.[10] Its effects are most substantially felt by those seeking to flee persecution, for whom the chance of obtaining a visa is extremely slim, whether because of state surveillance of foreign embassies and consulates in the country of persecution, an inability to get to the part of the country in which consulates are to be found on account of repressive measures within the state, or the inability to meet the standard requirements for a visa: that is, the intention to return to the country of origin at the end of the stay. Visas specifically to apply for asylum, while recognized in UK law where the person is applying outside his or her own country, are extremely rare and more a figment of judicial imagination than a tool of administrative action. In the situation of former Yugoslavia the consequences for asylum seekers were dramatic.

The policing of mandatory visa requirements is undertaken by the carriers, which face substantial fines if they transport persons without the required documents, including visas if these are mandatory. The efficiency of visa requirements as a tool to make arrival on the territory more difficult and as policed by the carriers can be seen from the numbers of asylum seekers arriving from former Yugoslavia in 1992 before the mandatory visa requirement was imposed (5635) and in 1993 when, although the war in Bosnia was at its height, the numbers of asylum seekers arriving in the UK dropped by almost 4000 (to 1830). As the efficiency of visa requirements began to bite properly, these numbers continued to drop until the Kosovo crisis and the increased arrival of asylum seekers from there on false documents.[11]

Dissuading spontaneous arrivals

During the Bosnia crisis and again during the Kosovo crisis, while obstacles were placed in the way of persons seeking to flee the region, if they got as far as the UK border the situation began to change. Once at the border the person would be able to apply for asylum but would risk being sent back to a safe third country through which he or she might have travelled *en route*. This scenario accounted for 430 refusals of asylum to FRY nationals in 1998.[12] If it was not possible to return the person to a third country then he or she would be admitted to the asylum determination procedure in the UK. For the Bosnians in particular, a policy which permitted the detention on arrival also acted as an important dissuading possibility, though this was less in evidence during the Kosovo crisis, a point to which I will return.[13] In both cases the UK government's approach was to seek to maintain the distance between the UK and Bosnia/Kosovo, and control carefully the linkage points so as to limit to the smallest number possible those asylum seekers from the region arriving spontaneously at the border. The priority was to maintain as much control as possible over the arrival of refugees, and if possible limit those arrivals to persons who had been selected for admission by the administration itself from the camps in the region.

One of the most dissuasive measures used by the administration to deter asylum seekers is their administrative detention in prisons or dedicated closed camps on arrival in the UK. This measure, the power of exercise of which rests with the Home Office and is unrelated to criminal procedures, or indeed safeguards, was defended by the government in respect of the Bosnian crisis as necessary to keep numbers down. By letter of 18 April 1994 the Conservative minister in power at the time advised in respect of 22 former Yugoslavs in detention pending the consideration of their asylum appeals:

The fact remains that the great majority of those seeking asylum here are not refugees as defined by the Convention, and many are seeking to circumvent immigration controls. A blanket policy of never detaining asylum seekers would encourage unfounded applications and undermine the position of genuine refugees.[14]

The vibrancy of the minister's defence of administrative detention is an indication of the degree of opposition which the government was coming under regarding its use. The use of detention reached a high in 1991 of 1690 detention orders being served, a figure which began to drop: 1992: 1470; 1993: 1240; 1994: 640; 1995: 650; 1996: 550.[15] By 1998–9 the situation was as shown in Table 4.3.

During the Kosovo crisis the use of detention in respect of Kosovars was not common.[16] This may have been the result of two factors: a heightened sense of responsibility for the plight of the refugees and the shift from direct administrative detention to prosecution which had occurred between 1994 and 1999 but was under attack in the courts. After 1994 the number of criminal prosecutions of asylum seekers for using false documents to enter the territory began to rise.[17] As most persons coming from refugee-producing countries were by now also mandatory visa nationals unable to board carriers to flee persecution because of the lack of a visa coupled with carrier sanctions, a substantial increase had been noted in the use of false documents by asylum seekers. What is less clear is the use of detention in respect of persons claiming to be Kosovars but suspected of being Albanians who were unable to produce sufficient documents to support their claim to origin in the Kosovo province. There are some reports that persons in this position were detained notwithstanding the well-publicized problem of Kosovars whose documents, if they were able to obtain any at all, had been confiscated by the Serb forces or irregulars before they managed to get out of Kosovo.

Table 4.3 Administrative detention of asylum seekers in the UK, 1998–9

Date	Detention under 1 month	Detention 1–2 months	Detention 2–6 months	Detention 6–12 months	Detention over 12 months	Total
31 March 1998	257	155	243	89	21	765
29 May 1998	223	136	280	96	23	758
28 July 1998	329	145	255	88	28	845
29 September 1998	193	150	287	98	31	759
30 November 1998	266	230	255	69	40	860
29 January 1999	126	154	370	75	41	766

Source: M. Watson and R. McGregor, *Asylum Statistics in the United Kingdom 1998* (London: The Stationery Office), issue 10/99 (27 May 1999)

Therefore the use of detention was tempered and given legitimacy on the basis of a criminal conviction for false document use.[18] However, by the time of the NATO bombing campaign the UK administration was in difficulties over this policy of prosecution of asylum seekers. A challenge in the courts had led to a Court of Appeal case which was nearing its conclusion and the possibility of a decision against the administration. In the case, the applicants, who had been charged and convicted of possession of false documents even though their possession was exclusively for the purpose of arriving in the UK to seek asylum, claimed that the prosecution was contrary to article 31 of the Geneva Convention, which prohibits contracting states from imposing penalties on asylum seekers on account of their illegal entry or presence on the territory.[19] At the oral hearing the judges had given an indication of some sympathy on legal grounds for asylum seekers claiming that the prosecutions were illegal. In the judgement which was finally handed down on 29 July 1999 the administration was indeed condemned and the delicate matter of damages for those wrongly imprisoned arose. Therefore, at the time of the bombing campaign, the administration was already alert to the difficulties it would shortly be facing regarding prosecutions (which generally resulted, on conviction, in detention) of asylum seekers for criminal offences relating to false documents used to gain entry to the state.

Reluctant resettlement

Moving, then, from the Kosovars who arrived at the border sponta-neously, what about those who arrived under the government's resettlement plan? On 2 April 1999, Germany, in its role as president of the Union, called on all the EU states to take their 'share' of the Kosovo refugees.[20] By 4 April the UN High Commissioner for Refugees (UNHCR) was urging states to offer a safe haven to refugees from Kosovo.[21] In that context Germany had offered as a first step that the Union would take 20,000, of whom 10,000 would be sheltered in Germany.[22] In response the next day, the British Home Secretary, Jack Straw, stated: 'We've already taken almost 10,000 refugees from Kosovo, the second highest number of any of our EU partners and we stand ready to take some thousands more.'[23]

The number, however, appears to have resulted from a quick count of all the FRY asylum applicants who had arrived in the UK from 1997 (1865), 1998 (7395) and over the first two months of 1999 (1260), which makes a total of 10,520.[24] Thus there was some confusion over the numbers which the UK had actually admitted as a result of the crisis and those who had arrived before the commencement of the bombing campaign and so, while undoubtedly in need of protection, could not be considered as having been admitted in response to the bombing campaign. In other words, the Home Secretary was making the first of what would be a continuing distinction between 'our' Kosovars – those who are already in the UK and were dealt with more quickly and generously as a result of the disaster in their province – and 'others' – those Kosovar asylum seekers in Macedonia, Albania or elsewhere who were of particular concern to the UNHCR to find resettlement countries. As regards these persons, the UK was not quick to offer resettlement possibilities: 'Home Secretary Jack Straw declined to say how many refugees would be heading for the UK, but said the government would not be skimping on the cost of helping the victims of "a terrible humanitarian disaster".'[25]

The following day the UNHCR by press release announced that in the preceding two weeks 'more than 400,000 people have fled or been expelled from Kosovo' to Albania, Macedonia or Montenegro.[26] This announcement was followed by silence from the UK on the numbers which it would take. By 18 April increasing pressure was being brought to bear on the UK to make a commitment. A UNHCR spokesperson singled out the UK, requesting that it keep its pledge to accept Kosovar refugees; the figure suggested was 5000, not substantial in the light of the overall crisis but nonetheless resisted by the UK government.[27] Two days later the Home Secretary announced that the first Kosovo refugees were being admitted to the UK: originally 120 in number, mainly women and children.[28] The first refugees actually arrived on 26 April, a total of 161. However, after that little happened. The German presidency of the Union began to accuse member states of a lack of enthusiasm in taking refugees – singling out the UK and France as particularly unresponsive to pleas.[29] The European Parliament also sought news of the humanitarian efforts of the member states sufficiently persuasively to put the UK Home Secretary on the defensive:

> The British government has been criticised in the last month for not assuming its responsibility in this area, but recently it has promised to take a larger share, with Home Secretary Jack Straw announcing that the UK would accept significantly greater numbers.[30]

As the only number of 'others' accepted by the UK so far in the crisis had been 161, 'significant' could have a wide interpretation.

The pressure continued to mount on the UK to make a more comprehensive commitment to the resettlement of refugees from Kosovo. Finally, by 8 May 1999 the UK had promised to take 1000 refugees a week, the first group of 300 scheduled to arrive on Sunday 9 May in Scotland.[31] In a press release from the UK's Home Office on 17 May, it was announced that the UK had received 1000 refugees since April, and over the subsequent ten days (i.e. between 17 May and 27 May

1999) a further 1500 persons would be evacuated from Macedonian camps.[32] However, despite the 1000 refugees a week promise of the UK government, according to the UNHCR on 31 May 1999 the UK had offered fewer than 2000 Kosovar evacuees asylum in the UK.[33] By the end of the Humanitarian Evacuation Programme, 4346 persons had been admitted to the UK under it: over half of them arrived during the final ten days of the bombing campaign. Just over four weeks elapsed from the UK's commitment to take 1000 refugees per week until the end of the bombing campaign. In numbers, then, the UK came close to fulfilling its commitment.

How does this compare with the UK's attitude towards the resettlement of Bosnians during that crisis? First, it must be remembered that the Bosnian war lasted from the autumn of 1992 until the Dayton Peace Accord in December 1995. Therefore, unlike the very short time scale of the NATO bombing campaign in Kosovo, there was a long, protracted war in Bosnia. The role of NATO was also very different in the Bosnian war: the international peace-making/peace-keeping effort was undertaken by the UN and not subject to the same severe criticism internationally as the NATO campaign in Serbia.

The UK Home Secretary announced at the end of November 1992 that the country would take 4000 refugees from former Yugoslavia. When pressed he clarified that the UK would offer asylum to 1000 former camp detainees and their dependants to be selected by the UN.[34] In the same announcement he stated that the UK had already taken in 40,000 former Yugoslavs in the preceding twelve months. This statement, while broadly true, gave a somewhat false picture of the UK's generosity towards refugees from Bosnia as it covered all parts of former Yugoslavia (possibly even from independent successor states of Yugoslavia) and all categories of entry, for instance as visitors and students long before the conflict started. To juxtapose this figure against that of admission of persons on humanitarian grounds might be considered somewhat disingenuous. In this respect the UK Minister's response on 5 April 1999 that the UK had already taken in 10,000 refugees from Kosovo, failing to clarify the time period over which these persons had been 'taken in' and the fact that all of them had arrived spontaneously and in spite of various government measures designed to impede their arrival, is completely in keeping, and indeed one could argue slightly more transparent than the 1992 statement.

By the November 1992 announcement and a later one of 6 August 1995, the UK government had committed itself to resettlement programmes for particularly vulnerable persons from former Yugoslavia and their family members. Under the first of these, by 21 April 1998, 976 principals and 1,239 dependants, had arrived. Under the second scheme, 453 persons, including dependants came to the UK. A third group of 68 sick and wounded ex-detainees arrived from Bosnia in September 1992 and exceptionally were permitted immediate family reunion, being joined by an estimated 120 dependants.[35] By 11 August 1993 the UK had to acknowledge that of the 4000 persons it had committed itself to receiving from the Bosnian crisis, only 700 had arrived in the UK. The delay was blamed on procedural requirements.[36] By the date of the Dayton Peace Accord the UK had finally managed to admit 2660 refugees under the resettlement programme. Again, the majority of these persons had been admitted towards the end of the period in question.

In comparison with the Kosovo crisis, then, the UK government during the Bosnian war was not only less generous and slower in coming up with a figure to place on the numbers it would resettle, but, in implementing the programme, managed to retain approximately 1400 empty spaces. As with the Kosovo crisis, however, the numbers were filled towards the end of the period, or indeed even afterwards. The approach, then, was similar. There are two categories of persons in need of protection: 'our' refugees, who are those persons already on the territory and seeking asylum at the time their country or province of origin becomes even more unsafe than it had previously been;[37] and 'others' – those outside the territory and whose access to the territory should continue to be impeded, be it by visa requirements and carrier sanctions or reluctance to commence serious resettlement programmes.

What comparisons, then, can be made between the two events? The first is that in overall numbers there is a remarkable symmetry. It is almost as if the figure of 4000 was more or less predetermined, though of course this would be unlikely in the light of the different ways in which the two crises developed. The time periods of the two crises, as I have already mentioned, were very different, as was the international framework. However, in both cases the UK's response was mixed: on the one hand those brave souls who had managed, notwithstanding the administrative efforts to place obstacles in their way, to get to the UK were then permitted to stay[38] and presented publicly as evidence of the UK's commitment to the international humanitarian effort. On the other hand, those persons outside the UK seeking to go there were subject to very slow procedures, political commitments which were vague and subject to reinterpretation, coupled with a burst of activity towards the end of the crisis period to permit a number of persons in need of protection into the country.

If the reaction of the UK administration, then, to the Kosovo crisis was predicated on how it had responded to the Bosnian crisis, its assessment of its own activity on the previous occasion must have been positive, as the same steps, approaches and results were followed the second time as the first, including ministerial responses to international criticism.

Notwithstanding the change of government in the UK which had occurred between the two crises, the administration appears to have approved of its record during the Bosnia crisis and sought to repeat it during the Kosovo crisis. A substantial difference, however, is that in the later case the UK actually came closer to filling its commitment on numbers. The immediate pressure brought to bear by EU partners may have contributed to this. So the lesson learned may have been by other member states: to put immediate and continued pressure on the UK to accept refugees for resettlement and not to accept vague indications.

Arriving in the territory

The second question which I am addressing in this chapter is what happened to Kosovar refugees when they arrived in the UK and how it compares with the treatment of Bosnians. This question must be understood in the light of the UK court's consideration of the case of a Mr Gashi. Mr Gashi was a Kosovar of Albanian ethnic origin. He applied for asylum in the UK. On 22 July 1996 the UK's Immigration Appeal Tribunal [IAT] (the second-tier immigration court in the UK) held that Mr Gashi and his co-appellant were both refugees on account of their race and the history of persecution of their race on that ground alone in Kosovo. In an unusual application of the ground of persecution for reasons of race alone, contained in the definition of a refugee in article 1(a) of the Geneva Convention,[39] the court astonished the administration. As the case proceeded to the higher courts, the UK government argued that the Secretary of State had been constrained to recognize as refugees every 'Kosovar' case by the decision in *Gashi*, even though he did not agree with it, while Germany (and other member states) could make their determinations on a case-by-case basis.

The Court of Appeal was singularly unimpressed by the difficulties of the UK Secretary of State in comparison with his European counterparts. It stated:

> There was nothing in the evidence to suggest that the Secretary of State himself or his officials had considered the discrepancy [between the number of Kosovar Albanians recognised as refugees in Germany in comparison with the UK] and decided that it could properly be ignored on these grounds. And, in any event, the argument is ill-founded as a matter of fact. The decision in *Gashi & Nikshiqi* is the governing English law on direct Kosovar cases, and deserves respect not just for the fact of the decision but also for the facts on which it proceeded. The IAT considered a large body of evidence about the position of Kosovar Albanians, including the United Nations resolution already referred to, and also received submissions from the UNHCR. Whilst it is theoretically possible that the facts of individual

cases falling within the general category surveyed by the IAT might properly yield the low recognition rates set out in the applicant's evidence, common sense suggests that that conclusion cannot be assumed without further enquiry.[40]

Therefore, between 1996 and 1999 the UK administration was under a duty, imposed on it by the UK courts, to recognize as refugees Kosovar asylum seekers of Albanian ethnic origin. But did it? The answer to that question is mixed, as the available statistics are not sufficiently broken down to clarify the position. Before looking at the statistics, however, some important distinctions need to be made. First, recognition as a refugee under the Geneva Convention is the best possible status which a refugee may have in UK law. Not only does it give an entitlement to social assistance benefits equal to those available to British and EU citizens, including access to education on a non-discriminatory basis, immediate family reunion with spouses and children, with a sympathetic approach to parents, but also it confers economic activity rights of all kinds and, as of a recent change in policy, very quickly a right of permanent residence. In 1998, 17 per cent of the decisions taken on asylum applications resulted in recognition as a refugee under the Convention.[41] For those asylum applicants where the UK authorities are not satisfied that there is a genuine fear of persecution on the grounds of race, religion, nationality, membership of a social group or political opinion but nonetheless it would be unsafe to send the person back to the country of origin as there is a real risk that he or she would suffer torture or inhuman or degrading treatment (contrary to article 3 of the European Convention on Human Rights and the UN Convention Against Torture), the administration gives a second-tier status: exceptional leave to remain (ELR). In this category the individual is entitled to social assistance benefits, but family reunion and a durable residence right are delayed. In 1998, 12 per cent of asylum decisions resulted in this grant.[42]

So what happened to refugees from the Kosovo crisis? They must be divided into two groups. First, those who arrived spontaneously in the UK and applied for asylum went into the normal asylum application queue, but their applications, particularly in May 1999, were expedited.[43] Second, those who arrived under the resettlement programme were treated differently and are not included in the statistics. I will return to the second group shortly; first, however, some further precision on the first group.

The available statistics do not include a separate category for Kosovars, only nationals of the FRY, which includes Serbia, Kosovo and Montenegro. However, the Statistical Office states in its explanatory memorandum, 'The majority of FYR applications are thought to be from Kosovars but we are currently not able to separately identify all cases.'[44] The figures for Bosnia and Herzegovina are now broken down separately and so for the

Table 4.4 Asylum applicants in the UK from Serbia, Kosovo and Montenegro

Year	Applications	Decisions	Refugee status	ELR	Refused
1996	400	555	70	40	445
1997	1865	1945	1355	210	380
1998	7395	1570	935	75	565

Source: M. Watson and R. McGregor, *Asylum Statistics in the United Kingdom 1998* (London: The Stationery Office), issue 10/99, 27 May 1999

Table 4.5 Asylum applicants in the UK from Bosnia and Herzegovina

Year	Applications	Decisions	Refugee status	ELR	Refused
1996	245	1170	865	285	20
1997	170	385	235	120	25
1998	160	95	45	20	30

Source: M. Watson and R. McGregor, *Asylum Statistics in the United Kingdom 1998* (London: The Stationery Office), issue 10/99, 27 May 1999

comparison are included. The statistics on treatment of applications from these persons for the period 1996–9 are shown in Tables 4.4 and 4.5.

It is not clear from the statistics whether the administration was following the court's judgement on Kosovars. From anecdotal information which is at least permitted by the statistical evidence, not all Kosovars were being recognized as refugees.[45] Until about mid-May 1999 it seemed that applicants were being recognized as a refugees on a rather random but individual basis. Then there was a rush of recognitions of Kosovars as refugees, followed by a complete stop in July 1999, whereafter some Kosovars were granted 12 months' exceptional leave to remain. Then, on 13 September 1999, the Home Secretary announced that no exceptional leave to remain would be granted automatically to Kosovars (though it is not entirely certain that such a grant had in fact been automatic). 'The Home Secretary said he was satisfied that the risk of persecution of the ethnic Albanian majority by the authorities of the Federal Republic of Yugoslavia has been removed by the establishment of a secure Kosovo by KFOR.'[46] The comparison with Bosnians is instructive. The division of persons recognized as refugees and those granted lesser statuses is clearly apparent but not necessarily explicable from the external situation. An assessment of the individual circumstances of applicants appears to be taking place for Kosovars notwithstanding the group decision on the basis of race provided by the courts.

Table 4.6 Yugoslav nationals applying for asylum at the UK border or in the country, 1996–8

Year	Total applications	Applied at border	Applied in country
1996	400	250	150
1997	1865	1260	605
1998	7395	2800	4590

A further problem is the treatment of persons in the queue. As a result of changes to the UK's legislation on access to benefits which preceded and then, after a court challenge, accompanied the Asylum and Immigration Act 1996, unless an asylum seeker sought protection at the port of entry he or she was refused access to social assistance benefits at the level of emergency benefits (90 per cent of that available to British citizens). Only after intervention by the courts were asylum seekers reinstated as entitled to a minimal form of social assistance which, in principle at least, excludes cash assistance.[47] This harsh regime also applies to persons from the moment they are refused asylum (though if they are granted a subsidiary status, benefits are awarded). Therefore those Kosovars who arrived spontaneously in the UK and sought asylum were divided into two groups as regards access to benefits: those who had applied at the border and those who applied after arrival. The former had access to social assistance benefits at a much higher level than the latter. The picture, in terms of numbers, again for nationals of Serbia, Montenegro and Kosovo, is shown in Table 4.6.

On the question of asylum applicants who apply at the border or within the territory, an issue considered earlier in this chapter must be taken into account, namely the difficulties of arrival at the territory and the risk of prosecution for arrival on false documents. Those asylum applicants who arrive on false documents which are not immediately detected risk a further check on the genuineness of their documents at the border when they apply for asylum. Therefore, while they may gain access to social assistance benefits by applying for asylum at the border, if they have arrived on false documents they run an increased risk of being subject to criminal prosecution for having done so. On the other hand, if their false documents are not detected on arrival at the border and they pass into the country, for instance on someone else's Italian identity document, and they subsequently apply for asylum from inside the territory, then because of the way in which the administration is arranged,[48] the chance of being subject to a criminal prosecution for having false documents diminishes dramatically.

What, then, of those Kosovars who were admitted under the terms of the resettlement programme? These persons were granted the status of temporary refuge,[49] stated specifically to be granted at the request of the UNHCR. Under its terms, the individual was granted permission to reside for a period of one year. Such a person was expressly notified that he or she had not been considered for refugee status under the Geneva Convention. The individual was automatically permitted to take employment or engage in self-employment. Additionally, the person was given access to the national health system and to the same social assistance scheme as British citizens. A new condition was applied, however, to these persons. The document evidencing the grant of status to them stated:

> You should fully understand that if, during your stay in the United Kingdom, you take part in activities involving, for example, the support or encouragement of violence, or conspiracy to cause violence, whether in the United Kingdom or abroad, the Secretary of State may curtail your stay or deport you.

The legality of this threat is questionable. By virtue of the absolute nature of article 3 of the European Convention on Human Rights as clarified by the European Court of Human Rights in *Chahal*,[50] even if a person is considered a security threat because of his or her political activities alleged to involve the promotion of violence, if there is a substantial risk that the person would face torture if returned to the country of origin, then forced return is prohibited.

How does this compare with the status granted to Bosnians arriving spontaneously and admitted under the programme? In fact the situation was virtually the same as regards a division between spontaneously arriving refugees and programme refugees. However the status granted to them was not differentiated in the same way. The Bosnians who were resettled were given the new status of 'temporary refuge', which had not previously existed. In respect of the Bosnian spontaneously arriving refugees, some of them were joined to the normal asylum queue awaiting a decision on their applications but others were granted a variety of short-term statuses which had the effect of delaying the date at which they applied for asylum and joined the main queue. However, up to 1996 the differentiation between access to benefits for individuals depending on where they applied for asylum and whether their application had been determined had not been successfully introduced. Accordingly, the financial difference for those persons whose applications were pending in the queue in comparison with those who were granted temporary refuge was not so dramatic. The standard of living for those in the queue and those admitted under a resettlement programme was similar.

There were wide variations, particularly during the initial stages of the Bosnian crisis, as to the status which applicants were given. As can be seen from Table 4.2, it was not until 1994 that even a few Bosnians were being given refugee status. Indeed, it was only after the Dayton Peace Accord had been signed at the end of 1995 that Bosnians began to be recognized as refugees in any particular numbers.

Again, the document issued to the Bosnians for temporary refuge indicated that the protection granted to them was at the request of the UNHCR. Also, the term and benefits of the grant were the same: temporary refuge, so defined, with relatively generous social benefits. However, no menace about political activity was included in the grant to Bosnians. On the other hand their status was in the first instance often limited to six months' residence. In practice, by 1995 legal advisers were reporting the 'upgrading' of Bosnians to full refugee status.[51] By October 1995 the administration were advising:

> we would not for the time being seek to refuse asylum applications from Bosnians solely on the basis that those who would face persecution for a Convention reason in that part of Bosnia from which they came would not be at risk of persecution if they returned to another part of the country.[52]

Finally, the UK government announced that the Bosnians admitted under the programme would be allowed to stay in the UK.

What conclusions, then, may be drawn from the treatment of the two groups of refugees after arrival in the UK? First, a strict parallel was applied as to their treatment: those arriving within the terms of the resettlement programmes were given a specific status, which was stated to be temporary in both cases. As regards the Bosnians, however, this status was also applied to some of those arriving spontaneously. This does not appear to have been the case in respect of the Kosovars. The extent to which the reception of Kosovars had been prescribed by the court's judgement on Kosovars as persecuted in FRY on the grounds of race within the meaning of the Geneva Convention is a matter of discussion. Certainly the government argued before the Court of Appeal that it had considered itself constrained in a way in which its EU partners had not been as regards the treatment of Kosovars. The anecdotal evidence, supported by the statistical information available, raises some questions about just how circumscribed the administration actually considered itself. The grant of inferior status to Kosovars after the court's judgement in *Gashi* appears substantiated as regards spontaneously arriving Kosovars and is the rule in respect of those included in the resettlement programme.

The refusal rate of Kosovars appears to be substantial; however, it should be remembered that many of the refusals are based on the grounds that there is a third country to which the person should apply for asylum, usually a country through which the individual has travelled on the way to the UK.[53] In respect of the Kosovars, the dispersal programme is also an issue of interest. Those refugees who arrived as part of the resettlement programme were placed across the country. The flights were mainly brought into Leeds, Bradford and Manchester airports, and people placed from there with different local authorities charged with their care. The perspective of these local authorities on the success of this dispersal programme will be interesting to follow, though it will be some time before even some preliminary conclusions may be drawn. In any event the programme has acted as a forerunner of a more general policy which the UK administration is seeking to implement in dispersal of asylum seekers.

The political context

The Kosovo crisis could not have arrived at a less propitious time from the perspective of the general debate on asylum seekers in the UK. The government was shepherding through Parliament a bill which had been introduced at the beginning of 1999, and at the date of writing has yet to be passed, designed to tighten up the asylum system and reduce the incidence of what the authorities consider abusive asylum applications. The discourse in Parliament has been dominated by the spectre of abuse. Among the key elements of the bill which had caused criticism are: a provision to legislate EU countries as safe; the diminution of social assistance benefits to all asylum seekers to a very low level, and excluding cash payments; provisions creating what non-governmental organizations consider untenable time limits on the processing of applications; an extension of powers of arrest, search and fingerprinting; and extension of provisions on detention of asylum seekers, although coupled with provisions on bail which had previously been considered inadequate;[54] the extension of carriers' liability to lorry drivers; and a diminution of appeal rights.[55]

Curiously, while the UK press has been generally unfavourable to asylum seekers and willing to run articles on 'bogus' asylum applicants, it has remained, in general, positive towards Kosovar asylum seekers.[56] Their plight was given a high profile in the press and generally deplored. The contrary perspective, of Kosovar asylum seekers as a negative influence, was left to the Serbian press. However, the question of the refugees did not figure as an important topic during the parliamentary debates on Kosovo. In the third debate, on 20 May, in the context of Foreign Office questions, little reference was made to the humanitarian dimension by reference to the refugees.[57] However, after the end of the bombing campaign and less than a month before the Home Secretary's announcement that he considered Kosovo safe for ethnic Albanians, in August 1999 a ferocious press and parliamentary discussion broke out about the inability of some of the towns on the south coast of the UK, in particular Dover, to cope with the numbers of arriving asylum seekers, in particular Kosovar Albanians. This was reported in the press as race related and targeted the arrival of refugees as bad for good race relations in the UK.[58]

The approach parallels that which obtained during the Bosnia crisis. The press coverage of the refugees was generally positive, though that in no way prevented the continuation of a more negative discourse on asylum seekers as 'bogus' in general. The existence in both cases of government programmes, irrespective of their effectiveness in resettling refugees, may have been an important factor in this positive approach. The leadership given by the government in favour of assistance during the humanitarian disaster appears to have muted opposition. Also, the involvement of British troops in both cases, in the region, whose purpose was, *inter alia*, to alleviate the suffering of those persecuted led to a positive representation of those in need of protection. A division was not made in the press between the deserving persecuted in Bosnia or Kosovo as against the undeserving who arrived and sought asylum in the UK.

Instead, a more fundamental division became apparent: refugees as worthy of protection and support where this is the object of government policy, as against refugees not worthy of support or tolerance where government policy is not engaged either at all or as directly. During the period of the Bosnia and Kosovo crises, both the government in Parliament and the media maintained an anti-asylum seeker discourse where those asylum seekers arrived spontaneously from countries where the UK was not engaged in such high-profile military or peace-keeping operations. However, in respect of former Yugoslavia the debate was decidedly different.

Conclusion

It is tempting to seek the conclusion that there is a relationship between the perception of refugees who enjoy the protection of public policy through their prior acceptance for admission by resettlement programmes as against those who, contrary to the wishes of the authorities, arrive spontaneously seeking asylum. However, such a division does not seem to be justified. Those Kosovo or Bosnian asylum seekers who arrived spontaneously were subject to different and less advantageous legal rules, but they were not singled out by the press as undeserving. Therefore the level of administrative discretion in operation does not appear to have been a key factor in the public perception of their need or worth.[59] Instead, a more comprehensive approach to the acceptance of Kosovar and Bosnian refugees appears to have been at play: where a positive public commitment to their plight is evidenced, this is respected by the press and their portrayal at the national level has been welcoming. This would appear to indicate that where there is public leadership in favour of asylum seekers and refugees, the discourse of 'bogus' and 'scroungers' as epithets appropriate for people in search of international protection loses its attraction.

Acknowledgements

I wish to express my sincere thanks to Catriona Jarvis, Special Adjudicator, Immigration Appeals, London, for her extremely helpful comments and corrections to the drafts of this chapter, and to Robin Ghosh of Kingsley Napley for his assistance in the preparation of the chapter. All errors are of course my own responsibility.

Notes

1. This took place in three steps: first a group of 68 sick and wounded ex-detainees in September 1992; then, by announcements of 30 November 1992 and 6 August 1995, a further 976 and 453 principals respectively were admitted, accompanied or joined by their dependants.
2. By the end of December 1992 there were already 5400 applications for asylum from nationals of the Federal Republic of Yugoslavia (FRY) awaiting an initial decision. In 1992 there were 5635 new applications for asylum from nationals of former Yugoslavia and 1830 in 1993. In 1998 the numbers rose to 7980. The total number of decisions taken on the cases of nationals of former Yugoslavia were: in 1992: 127; 1993: 180; and 1998: 1835 (M. Watson and R. McGregor, *Asylum Statistics in the United Kingdom 1998* (London: The Stationery Office), issue 10/99 (27 May 1999)).
3. 'The Home Office reduced contract payments to Siemens Business Services by £4.5 million [7 million euros] for delays at the Immigration and Nationality Directorate (IND) and fined it a further £66,000 [100,000 euros] for the passport problems. The delays resulted in a massive backlog of asylum and refugee cases, and the issuing of passports was held up by so much that some people missed holidays. The chaos at the IND was demonstrated by the fact that until October 1998 it had processed up to 3,000 applications a month. This dropped to 995 in January 1999. By then, the queues of personal callers to the IND's Lunar House headquarters stretched for hundreds of yards every morning. Many telephone calls went unanswered and sacks of letters were left unopened around the offices.' – 'Computer firm fined £4.5m over passport bungle chaos', *Daily Telegraph*, 6 September 1999. Also see 'Passport Agency escapes heavy payout for bungling', *Guardian*, 6 September 1999.
4. See the dramatic rise in May 1999 of recognition as refugees of spontaneously arriving Kosovar asylum seekers in Table 4.1. Not least was this the result of

the creation of a special unit within the administration in May to deal with Kosovar applications.

5. *Fairer, Faster, Firmer: A Modern Approach to Immigration and Asylum*, Cmnd 4018, White Paper, The Stationery Office (27 July 1998).

6. *Besnik Gashi* v. *Secretary of State for the Home Department* CA 25 March 1999; the Court of Appeal confirmed the adjudicator's determination of 1996 (unreported).

7. *Control of Immigration: Statistics United Kingdom 1995, 1996* (London: HMSO, 1995 and 1996).

8. In practice there was some flexibility allowed to the rule but only after the British embassy in Vienna refused to process applications by Bosnians, a decision which caused the Mayor of Vienna to suggest that if the Bosnians had been Her Majesty's corgis they would have received better treatment (reported in the *Sunday Times*, 22 November 1992).

9. For example, mandatory visas were introduced for Algerians on 1 April 1990 even though the numbers of asylum seekers from that country were low: only 25. The justification for the introduction of visas was immigration related.

10. For further discussion on this from a European perspective, see A. Cruz, 'Visa policy under the first pillar: a meaningless compromise', in M. den Boer (ed.) *Schengen, Judicial Co-operation and Policy Co-ordination* (Maastricht: EIPA, 1997), p. 218.

11. In 1998, 6338 persons (all nationalities) were detected arriving at UK ports on false documents. The numbers of persons from former Yugoslavia given notice of illegal entry (the administrative response, *inter alia*, to attempted entry on false documents) jumped from 140 in 1996 to 265 in 1997 and 2320 in 1998 (Home Office Research, Development and Statistical Directorate, letter to Kingsley Napley, 7 September 1999).

12. For more details, see note 44.

13. 'Turning a Bosnian crisis into a very British bungle', *Sunday Times*, 22 November 1992.

14. Letter from Charles Wardle, Under-Secretary of State for the Home Department, to Alistair MacKenzie, Refugee Legal Group.

15. *Control of Immigration: Statistics United Kingdom 1995, 1996*.

16. According to the Home Office Research, Development and Statistics Directorate, as at the end of July 1999 4 such persons were in detention. Letter to Kingsley Napley 7 September 1999.

17. *R.* v. *Uxbridge Magistrates Court & onr ex parte Adimi* CA, 29 July 1999: www.casetrack.com.

18. On this point, see Lord Justice Simon Brown in *ex parte Adimi*: 'As already stated the United Kingdom has done nothing to comply with [article 31 of the Geneva Convention – see further below]. It cannot be suggested – indeed I do not think it is suggested – that compliance is achieved merely by pointing as the respondents [the government] do to:-

(a) the possibility, on certain facts, of raising a substantial defence of necessity or duress of circumstances – see *R* v. *Adbul Hussain* [1999] Crim LR 570. This defence applies only in cases of imminent peril or serious injury to the defendant and is manifestly narrower than that afforded by Article 31.

(b) the defendant's right to invite the court to stay the prosecution on grounds of abuse of process. To this I shall return.

(c) the fact that the Code for Crown Prosecutors, issued by the DPP [Department of Public Prosecution], under s. 10 of the Prosecution of Offences Act 1985, requires prosecutors to decide, once a case passes the evidential test of realistic prospect of conviction, if a prosecution is needed in the public interest. The history of these prosecutions and others like them suggests that whether the offence was committed in the context of escape from persecution, or whether or not an asylum claim has been made, plays not the least part in determining the public interest. On the contrary, as appears from the terms in which characteristically these defendants come to be sentenced, the very fact that false documents are presented by refugees in flight appears to count against them. A report by Liz Hales, published by the Cambridge Institute of Criminology, cites as a typical comment by Magistrates: "This serious offence is becoming too prevalent and it is in the public interest that you are sent to prison." '

19. Article 31(1) of the Geneva Convention: 'The Contracting States shall not impose penalties, on account of their illegal entry or presence, on refugees who, coming directly from a territory where their life or freedom was threatened in the sense of Article 1, enter or are present in their territory without authorisation, provided they present themselves without delay to the authorities and show good cause for their illegal entry or presence.'

20. 'Bonn tells EU: Take your share of refugees', *Daily Telegraph*, 2 April 1999.

21. UNHCR press release, 4 April 1999: 'UNHCR urges the world to receive Kosovo refugees as exodus grows'.

22. *Ibid.*

23. BBC News On-Line Network, 5 April 1999.

24. Home Office Immigration Research and Statistics Service, RSD 31/08/99; annex to letter from the Service to Kingsley Napley, 7 September 1999.

25. BBC News On-Line Network, 5 April 1999.

26. UNHCR press release, 6 April 1999: 'United Nations High Commissioner for Refugees chairs emergency Mmeeting on Kosovo refugees'.

27. 'Britain "must take in 5,000"', *Daily Telegraph*, 18 April 1999.

28. 'UK politics: Kosovo refugees to arrive in UK', BBC News On-Line Network, 20 April 1999.

29. 'Bonn tells Britain to take more Kosovars', Daily Telegraph, 1 May 1999. See also Koser, Chapter 2 (Germany) and van Selm, Chapter 3 (The Netherlands) in this volume.

30. 'Kosovan refugees – the EU must do more', *EP News*, p. IV, May 1999.

31. 'UK preparing for refugee influx', BBC News On-Line Network, 8 May 1999.

32. Home Office Press Release 149/99: 'Kosovan arrivals to UK stepped up', 17 May 1999.

33. UNHCR News: Refugee Daily, 1 June 1999: www.unhcr.ch/news/media/daily.htm

34. 'Britain takes 4,000 more refugees from Yugoslavia', *The Scotsman*, 1 December 1992.

35. Home Office Research, Development and Statistics Directorate, 1998 *Asylum Bulletin* (London: The Stationery Office, 1999), para. 14.

36. 'The Foreign Office UN department receives the UNHCR documents and passes them to the Overseas Development Administration. [The Foreign Office] circulates the documents to the [UK] spending departments [i.e. Health and Social Security]. If they say yes, the Foreign Office pass the decision to the UNHCR in Geneva, who pass it on to their people in Zagreb' – *Independent*, 'War victims trapped by red tape: UK's quota for "refugees" unfilled as rescue for Irma remains critical', 8 November 1993.
37. It is for this reason that I am not willing to classify these persons as refugees *sur place*. That concept as it appears in the Geneva Convention is reserved for persons who are present on the territory of a foreign state at the time when they become refugees as a result of an event in their country of origin or habitual residence. In the case of both Bosnia and Kosovo, many of the people already on the territory of the UK at the beginning of the armed conflicts were already refugees as a result of pre-existing persecution.
38. Subject, of course, to efforts, which were taken in respect of a small number, to return them to a safe third country through which they had arrived in the UK.
39. Article 1A: 'For the purposes of the present Convention, the term "refugee" shall apply to any person who:

    . . .

    (2). . . owing to a well-founded fear of being persecuted for reasons of race, religion, nationality, membership of a particular social group or political opinion, is outside the country of his nationality and is unable, or, owing to such fear, is unwilling to avail himself of the protection of that country; or who, not having a nationality and being outside the country of his former habitual residence as a result of such events, is unable or, owing to such fear, in unwilling to return to it.'
40. *Besnik Gashi* v. *Secretary of State for the Home Department* CA 25 March 1999.
41. Watson and McGregor, *Asylum Statistics in the United Kingdom.*
42. *Ibid.*
43. 'The United Kingdom continues to give substantive consideration to asylum applications lodged by nationals of the Federal Republic of Yugoslavia and has recently set up a specialist team within the Immigration and Nationality Directorate to expedite the processing of such asylum applications.' *Ibid.*
44. *Ibid.*
45. See minutes of the Refugee Legal Group, London, 1998.
46. Home Office press release: 'Change of policy in respect of citizens from the Federal Republic of Yugoslavia', 277/99, 13 September 1999.
47. *R.* v. *Secretary of State for Social Security, ex parte JWCI & Ors*, CA, 1997.
48. On entry, the applicant is making an application to a distinct part of the administration: the Immigration Service, decentralized to all the ports of entry. After entry into the territory the applicant is making an application to the singular administration, which has a tendency to be monolithic.
49. A status with this name was first created for the Bosnians.
50. (1996) Judgement 15 November 1996: 70/1995/576/662.
51. Minutes of the Refugee Legal Group, 9 January 1995.
52. Letter from IND to Bindman & Partners, 2 January 1995.

53. In 1997, of 550 FRY nationals refused asylum in the UK, 370 were refused on this ground; a further 30 applications were refused on the basis of failure to provide evidence to support the asylum claim within a reasonable period (non-compliance). In 1998, of 705 refusals, 430 were based on the 'safe third country' ground and 135 on non-compliance (Watson and McGregor, *Asylum Statistics in the United Kingdom*).
54. The bill introduces a presumption in favour of bail, but this is followed by a long list of exceptions.
55. Immigration Law Practitioners Association, briefing on the 1999 Immigration and Asylum Bill, 22 February 1999, and Inter-agency report by Alison Harvey, Medical Foundation for the Care of Victims of Torture, and Mike Kaye, Refugee Council, 22 August 1999.
56. 'UK crisis brings challenge for UK press', BBC News On-Line Network, 2 April 1999.
57. Kosovo: *Hansard*, 18 May 1999.
58. P. Foster, 'Race attack fear in "refugee" town', Electronic Telegraph (www.telegraph.co.uk), 4 August 1999; D. McGrory, 'Refugee tide causes waves of unrest', *The Times*, 5 August 1999; also see BBC South East interviews with the Home Secretary and A. Widdecombe, Shadow Secretary of State, in the week of 4 August 1999.
59. By this I mean that the discretion available to the administration when choosing individuals to whom to offer protection from a pool of persons in a refugee camp in a third country is larger than the discretion available to the same administration when faced with the spontaneous arrival of a refugee who is entitled to rely on the Geneva Convention to prevent his or her *refoulement* to the country of persecution, at least until a substantive decision has been taken on the application.

Bibliography

Books

M. den Boer, *Schengen, Judicial Co-operation and Policy Co-ordination* (Maastricht: EIPA, 1997).

Reports

Control of Immigration: Statistics United Kingdom 1995, 1996 (London: HMSO, 1995 and 1996).
Hansard, 18 May 1999.
Harvey, A. (Medical Foundation for the Care of Victims of Torture) and Kaye, M. (Refugee Council), unpublished inter-agency report, 22 August 1999.
Home Office press release 149/99, 17 May 1999.
Home Office press release: *Change of Policy in Respect of Citizens from the Federal Republic of Yugoslavia*, 277/99, 13 September 1999.

Home Office Immigration Research and Statistics Service, RSD 31/08/99; annex to letter from the Service to Kingsley Napley, 7 September 1999.

Home Office Research, Development and Statistics Directorate, *1998 Asylum Bulletin* (London: HMSO, 1999).

Immigration Law Practitioners Association, *Briefing on the 1999 Immigration and Asylum Bill,* 22 February 1999.

Refugee Legal Group: Minutes, London, 1998

UNHCR press release, 4 April 1999.

UNHCR press release, 6 April 1999.

Watson, M. and McGregor, R., *Asylum Statistics in the United Kingdom 1998* (London: The Stationery Office), issue 10/99, 27 May 1999.

Primary sources

Fairer, Faster, Firmer: A Modern Approach to Immigration and Asylum, Cmnd 4018, White Paper, The Stationery Office, 27 July 1998.

Web site

www.casetrack.com

CHAPTER FIVE

Sweden: the Kosovars and refugee policy changes – 'Isn't it best for everyone if they stay close to home?'

ELISABETH ABIRI

Introduction

The 1990s was a decade of change. For Sweden it was also a decade of hard awakenings. A long period of peace and democracy, together with economic prosperity and increasing welfare arrangements, had per-haps lulled Sweden into believing that it could remain untouched by international events. After the fall of the Berlin Wall, the well-known political division between East and West disappeared, leaving neutral Sweden without a map by which to navigate. Change became the rule of the game. For the first time in ages it dawned upon Swedes that change might not always be on their terms. In fact, change may be instigated by processes out of domestic control, something that makes it far less amenable to planning. Change was becoming globalized.

Sweden's entwinement with the surrounding world had become tangible already in the mid-1990s through the spontaneous arrival of asylum applicants. Refugee flows from the Middle East, mainly from Iran, Iraq and Lebanon, arriving in Sweden were neither instigated by domestic processes, nor open to planning in any real sense of the word.

This chapter argues that Swedish policy towards the Kosovo refugee crisis in the spring of 1999 was a test case for the non-arrival approach of the new refugee policy in effect since 1 January 1997. The case is contrasted with the Swedish policy towards the war refugees from Bosnia and Herzegovina in 1992–3 before the policy change in question took place. The contexts within which these policy responses were carried out are compared. It is argued that although there are some manifest differences between the Sweden of 1992 and that of 1999, these differences cannot by themselves explain the changes in Swedish refugee policy. The changes are rather the result of a securitization of Swedish migration policy that developed during the 1990s.

Sweden in the early 1990s: the domestic context to the reception of the Bosnian refugees

When refugee policy changes are on the political agenda, the need for change is commonly explained by corresponding changes in the overall domestic context. Thus, a hardening of a country's refugee policy is described as necessary since X, Y and Z has changed. Let us first take a look at the Swedish domestic context at the time of the reception of the Bosnian refugees.

Political configuration

At the end of 1990 the emergence of a new political party, 'New Democracy', had stirred up the Swedish political landscape. As in the cases of other European parties of discontent, 'New Democracy' found its major support among those opposed to immigration and people lacking faith in traditional party politics and politicians. Established as late as December 1990, the party was estimated to have gained the support of as much as 11.7 per cent of the electorate at the end of May the following year, only four months before the election in September 1991.[1] If the outcome of the election reflected this poll, New Democracy would hold the balance in Parliament, something that the other political parties wanted to avoid at all costs.

Not surprisingly, the official debate prior to the election in 1991 came to a large extent to be focused on refugee and immigration policy. All other parties marked the distance between themselves and the 'populist' New Democracy. The Liberals took an especially hard stand on the issue and emerged as the strongest advocate for a continued generous refugee policy.

After the election, which the Social Democratic Party (Socialdemokratiska Arbetarpartiet) lost, the Moderate Party (Moderata Samlingspartiet) formed a new government together with the Centre Party (Centerpartiet), the Liberal Party (Folkpartiet Liberalerna) and the Christian Democratic Party (Kristdemokratererna). As a concession to the Liberals, the new Prime Minister, Carl Bildt, announced that there was no longer any need for the more restrictive praxis that had been in effect since December 1989. The Liberal Party was also put in charge of refugee and immigration policy.

Economic factors

During the beginning of the 1990s the growing budget deficit was the focus of all policy-making regardless of the field in question. In order to regain the market's confidence in Sweden's finances, quite severe economic measures were taken in every area of the national budget. For the first time a trend towards ever-expanding health and social welfare arrangements was reversed, something that may explain the deep impact this recession had on Swedish society, even though the Swedish welfare state remained one of the most extensive in the world. The relative deprivation, almost invisible to the rest of the world, is thus an important factor not to be disregarded. The first years of the 1990s also brought another important change to the country, which for decades had had 'full employment' as the goal for its labour market policy. Unemployment rose dramatically from the 'normal' 1.4 per cent in 1990 to 10.7 per cent in 1993.[2]

International cooperation and coordination

Sweden applied for membership of the EU as early as 1991 but did not become a member until 1 January 1995.[3] Consequently, Swedish refugee policy was not dependent on any formal cooperation or membership at the time of the arrival of the Bosnians. The cooperation with the countries of the EU on refugee issues was, however, highly prioritized well before 1995. It was in fact Swedish officials who initiated a new, more organized form of cooperation among the industrialized countries on concrete refugee policy matters such as information exchange, and intensified the work towards a convention of country of first asylum.[4] This cooperation, initiated in 1985, is known as 'The Intergovernmental Consultations on Asylum, Refugee and Migration Policies in Europe, North America, and Australia' (IGC).

Furthermore, Sweden has always been a strong supporter of the work carried out under the auspices of the United Nations High Commissioner for Refugees (UNHCR) and has also been one of the main financial contributors to that organization's annual budget through the years. In 1992 Sweden's contribution to the UNHCR was close to US$92m (85.2 million euros). Sweden was also one of the first states to accept an annual quota of refugees. The yearly quota at the beginning of the 1990s was fixed at 1250 persons.

Refugee policy

At the beginning of the 1990s, applicants for asylum could be a given permanent residence permit on any of four grounds: as 'Convention refugees', in accordance with the Geneva Convention; as *'de facto* refugees';[5] as 'war rejecters',[6] or on 'politico-humanitarian grounds'.[7] Permanent residence permits were generally granted to the immediate family (the nuclear family), defined as the husband/wife and unmarried children under the age of 20 and to older parents (over 60) with all their children living in Sweden. An exception could also be made for so-called 'last link' cases, when a person did not have any close relatives left in the country of origin, or in the country of first asylum. Even though the wording of the Aliens Act did not explicitly so state, all individuals given asylum were in principle granted permanent residence permits. This principle had been agreed upon in 1984 and was based on the explicit view that, regardless of whether a person eventually would go home (repatriate) or not, a permanent residence permit was needed to give the person the security necessary to start life over again in a new country.

When Yugoslavia disintegrated and people started to flee the region, the Swedish government had already declared that the increasing number of asylum applicants was becoming too large to handle in an acceptable way. In 1989 the number of applications rose to just over 30,000, a noticeable increase from a level of around 20,000 in 1988. This 50 per cent increase led the Social Democratic government to issue an emergency decision in December 1989 to limit the granting of asylum to individuals who could be defined as 'Convention refugees'. According to the Social Democratic government, the number of claims for asylum was beyond the capacity of the Swedish state to handle. The opposition was divided on the issue. Critics maintained that this kind of emergency legislation gave the impression that the country was indeed 'swamped' with asylum applicants when in fact it was not. The number of arrivals that can be defined as being 'being beyond the capacity of the state' is of course a matter of opinion, especially in cases where the receiving state is able to stop the arrival of asylum applicants if it sees fit. As mentioned above, this more restrictive praxis remained in effect until autumn 1991, when it was removed by the new non-social democratic government.

Swedish policy towards the Bosnian refugees

When people started to flee the war and the 'ethnic cleansing' in former Yugoslavia, Swedish immigration and refugee policy was the subject of a heated and polarized political debate. The number of asylum seekers had been rising throughout the 1980s and showed no tendency to decline. Not only had the previous government decided to limit arrivals and acceptance rates, all official predictions were that refugee flows towards Western Europe would keep increasing:

Europe will be exposed to growing immigration pressure. … The population movements of the next twenty years cannot be met by the instruments that were created to handle the situation in post-war Europe.[8]

Western Europe is exposed to heavily increasing immigration pressure … a pressure that the European states will not be able to handle separately.[9]

Individuals arguing for a generous refugee policy were immediately labelled 'professional debaters' or part of the 'moral elite' and thus persons who by definition did not understand how 'people' felt about the issue. A person who, on the other hand, argued for a more restrictive refugee policy was labelled 'populist' or 'xenophobic' and therefore not worth the time of the day.

The basic line in the Swedish refugee policy debate can be described in terms of cosmopolitanism ('empathy and assistance have no borders') or communitarianism ('we have to take care of our own people first'). This is a traditional dividing line in refugee policy debates that is by no mean specifically Swedish. The situation at the beginning of the 1990s did, however, provide new bases for both arguments. The economic difficulties and the unemployment rate were hard to accept as a fact of life. The fact that all prognoses were that the situation would become even worse before it would get any better did, of course, add fuel to the communitarian argument. On the other hand, the war in former Yugoslavia was horrific in its consequences. Women, men and children were driven from their homes, raped or brutally killed because of their ethnic identity. It appeared obvious that these human beings were in desperate need of protection, something that strengthened the cosmopolitan argument.

The country of first asylum

The principles of the country of first asylum and carrier liability did not decrease the number of asylum applicants arriving in Sweden as they were meant to, even though they had been in practice since the 1980s. First, it was hard to establish whether the principle of the country of first asylum could be applied or not, since the number of asylum applicants without travel documents increased. Second, even it were possible, the transit countries did not agree to become first countries of asylum. Consequently, as the conflict in the Balkans unfolded, the number of asylum applicants arriving in Sweden increased.

The big increase, from just over 27,000 in 1991 to 84,000 in 1992, was received with mixed emotions. On the one hand, the need for people to leave the brutal ethnic cleansing in Bosnia was hard to deny even for the majority of the 'restrictionists'. On the other hand, the majority of the asylum applicants came from Kosovo, rather than Bosnia, a fact that gave new fuel to the debate on the 'genuineness' of asylum applicants. These asylum applicants from Kosovo were generally treated with suspicion, and the majority of them were also denied asylum.[10] In October 1992 the Minister of Immigration, Birgit Friggebo, announced that the government would introduce a visa requirement for Yugoslav citizens. 'The government is now focusing on the real protection need, on human beings who are escaping violence, persecution and terror,' she stated, implying that this was not the case with the Kosovars.[11]

The influx had already, in June 1992, prompted the Minister of Immigration to appoint a committee to examine how the administration of 'extraordinary large inflows of relief seekers' could be facilitated.[12] In time, this led to the introduction of temporary protection as a legal status.[13]

The visa obligation put an effective end to the arrival of Kosovars, but because the situation in Bosnia had worsened, the number of asylum applicants did not diminish. In the late spring of 1993 approximately 1200–1700 Bosnians arrived per week. The majority of them came by bus, via Poland, Hungary and Slovakia. In June 1993 the Swedish Minister of Immigration announced the introduction of a second visa requirement, this time for citizens of Bosnia and Herzegovina. One of the arguments behind the visa policy change was that the acceptance of refugees was not the best way to deal with the situation in Bosnia Herzegovina.[14] An attempt to soften the humanitarian significance of the policy changes was made by a declaration that the majority of the 40,000 Bosnians awaiting decisions on their asylum applications in Sweden would be granted permanent residence permits. This decision was taken even though the government bill proposing the introduction of temporary protection was in preparation[15]

The official statement announced that Sweden was not able to cope with the influx, and that the transit countries did not take their responsibility seriously, since they were merely allowing asylum seekers to travel on to Sweden. According to Birgit Friggebo, the introduction of the visa obligation should be seen as a direct signal to these countries to change their policies.[16]

The need for a harmonization

The introduction of the visa obligation was formulated in a way that underlined the Swedish government's feeling that the country had admitted more than its share of the refugees as compared to some other states outside former Yugoslavia. This reference to the policies of other, 'comparable' countries has become increasingly common, always with the same conclusion: Sweden has done more than the others.

The Swedish emphasis on the importance of a harmonization of the

European countries' refugee policies increased dramatically after the events in the Balkans. Even though the need for a harmonized European refugee policy was mentioned as early as 1990, the change was nevertheless noticeable.[17] Since then the need for a harmonized European refugee policy has been emphasized whenever refugee policy matters have been up for discussion. In the government bill of 1996 it is stated that Sweden's ability to have a migration policy different from those of the other countries in the region had diminished.[18]

Even with the introduction of the visa obligation, the accumulated number of Bosnian refugees makes them the largest refugee group received in Sweden to date. Today Sweden hosts around 5 per cent of all Bosnians who crossed state borders on their flight. This is also a fact that is frequently referred to as a reason for not taking on such a responsibility in the Kosovo crisis: 'We have already done more than our share.'

Sweden in the late 1990s: domestic context to the reception of the Kosovars

With this development in mind it is interesting to see under what circumstances the Kosovo crisis took place, and whether this situation differs from the one in 1992–3.

Political configuration

The Swedish political landscape kept changing through the 1990s as more traditional parties changed in relative importance and weight in the political arena. The Social Democratic Party regained office in 1994 and was re-elected again in 1998. Even if it remains the largest political party, its support among voters has weakened considerably, while the Left-Wing Party (Vänsterpartiet) has grown stronger. The Moderate Party has increasingly developed into the only right-wing alternative as the support for the two other traditional non-socialist parties, the Liberal Party and the Centre Party, has fallen off. The Christian Democratic Party has, however, increased its support among the voters.[19] 'New Democracy' managed to stay in Parliament only between 1991 and 1994, as it was torn apart by internal conflicts.

Economic factors

The economic situation is considerably better at the end of the 1990s than it was at the beginning of the decade. The pace of economic growth has quickened. Balance is restored to public finances and the credibility of the monetary policy framework has strengthened, two main requisites to ease pressures on the financial markets and bring about lower interest rates.[20] The health and social welfare arrangements have not gone back to the levels of 1990, but some improvements have been made. The unemployment rate is still high compared to the 1.4 per cent of 1990, but has, nevertheless, decreased from 10.7 per cent in 1993 to 5.9 per cent in June 1999.[21]

International cooperation and coordination

The initial discussion on cooperation within the EU mainly focused on the influence Sweden could have on EU policy-making and vice versa. While EU advocates were eagerly describing how Sweden could improve the EU, opponents to Sweden's entry were equally conceited, focusing on how the membership would endanger Swedish social and environmental accomplishments. When it came to refugee policy changes, the Swedish Aliens Act already comprised many of the issues that the discussions on harmonization have centred on, for instance the principle of country of first asylum and carrier responsibility before the country became an EU member. Parliament approved Sweden's membership of the Schengen Group in spring 1998. Within the field of cooperation on immigration and asylum affairs Sweden has emphasized the issue of 'burden sharing' and the need to develop a distribution formula for refugee acceptance among the states of the Union.[22]

Even though the focus of Sweden's refugee policy as far as international cooperation is concerned lies at EU level, the country is still one of the largest contributors to the UNHCR, both in absolute terms and according to per capita income. However, the yearly contribution decreased during the 1990s. In 1999 Sweden's contribution to the UNHCR had from US$92m (85.2 million euros) in 1993 to US$44.3m (42 million euros or 370 million Skr). The number of quota refugees accepted has been around 1475 per year for the past four years.[23]

Refugee policy

Since the refugee policy reform, effective as of 1 January 1997, asylum applicants can be given residence permits on only two grounds. They can be given asylum as 'Convention refugees', in accordance with the Geneva Convention, or they can be given residence permit on grounds of their 'protection needs'.[24] Residence permits can still be granted to the immediate family, but the concept is more narrowly defined, referring now only to unmarried children under the age of 18 and other close relatives who were living in the same household prior to flight. Temporary protection has been introduced for situations of 'mass flight'.

This kind of protection can be given to a group 'in need of protection' for a defined time period regardless of whether the individuals in the group in question are entitled to asylum or not.

After the peak year of 1992 when Sweden received 84,000 asylum applicants, most of them from former Yugoslavia, the numbers gradually subsided from 37,581 in 1993 and 18,640 in 1994 down to 9047 in 1995, and fell further to only 5753 in 1996.[25] At the end of the 1990s, the numbers are back to around 10,000 asylum applications per year.[26]

Flight from Kosovo in 1999

It is clear that the situation in Sweden in 1999 when people fled Kosovo in tens of thousands each day was quite different from that of 1993. The number of asylum seekers had declined markedly and was back to the levels of the mid-1980s. The debate on immigration and refugee policy issues had not, of course, ended, but the context in which it took place was also markedly different from the one a decade before. At the beginning of the 1990s Sweden appeared to be in shock over the fact that racism, xenophobia, discrimination and segregation could appear in Swedish society. At the end of the 1990s, segregation between ethnic Swedes and so-called immigrants is still a large socio-political problem. The differences in unemployment rates indicate that the Swedish labour market is highly discriminatory towards certain groups of 'immigrants'. Racist violence and neo-Nazi groups are, alas, recurring features in Swedish society. The novelty of these phenomena has, however, faded and with it some of the sense of emergency. Sweden is in that sense more prepared to deal with these kinds of problems than it was at the beginning of the decade. The end of 'New Democracy' made the realization of the changed reality easier. In spring 1999 the Swedish economy was also in much better shape than it had been for a number of years. The prognoses were for a continued improvement.[27] There was also a genuine wish to help the Kosovars among the Swedish public. Aid organizations reported that they had never received such a good response to their calls for assistance as during the spring of 1999.[28]

The changing climate, however, did not have any impact on Swedish refugee policy in the direction of generous refugee reception. When the UNHCR urged the international community to give protection to one hundred thousand refugees, the Swedish government declared that it was willing to give temporary protection to 5 per cent of that number refugees, i.e. 5000 persons.[29] If the number is compared to the more than 47,000 Bosnians who were given permanent residence permits in 1993 and 1994 during more troubled domestic conditions, the decision

99

appears even more significant. Furthermore, the Swedish government decided that the reception of the 5000 Kosovars should be partly financed by funds dedicated to the reception of quota refugees. This policy change led to a last-minute cancellation of the reception of 425 Kurds from refugee camps in Iraq and Turkey. The Swedish Under-Secretary of State, Gun-Britt Andersson, declared that the original plan to give permanent protection to 1800 quota refugees during 1999 had changed. The number was reduced to 580.[30] This reduction of the previously agreed refugee quota was criticized by the UNHCR, which pointed out that Sweden was the only country that reduced the number of quota refugees because of the Kosovars.[31] Swedish officials replied: 'UNHCR should work on getting more countries to receive quota refugees, instead of complaining about Sweden.'[32]

The visa requirement for Yugoslavian citizens in force since the end of 1992 was never lifted. Today it is a part of the EU common visa policy. That the visa policy makes it *de facto* impossible for a person to apply for asylum in a country that requires a visa is very clearly shown in a written reply by the Minister of Immigration, Pierre Schori, to a question in Parliament:

> The possibilities for obtaining a visa are under the current conditions very limited. The reason is that the issuing of a visa is based on the condition that it concerns a temporary visit in Sweden and that you can assume that the visitor will leave the country when the visa expires. Under the current conditions you cannot assume that this is the case. Thus strong humanitarian reasons that are not caused by the current condition in the Federal Republic of Yugoslavia are required in order for a visa to be issued.[33]

Temporary protection

The question of permanent residence permits, once so central a feature of Sweden's humanitarian refugee policy, did not even arise with regard to the Kosovars. The 5000 who were transferred to Sweden were all given temporary residence permits for a period of eleven months. It was argued that to give permanent residence permits would in effect support the ethnic cleansing of Kosovo. The same argument was also used in relation to the question of whether the refugees should leave the camps in the immediate region or not:

> The main principle for Sweden and the international community at large is that those expelled from the Kosovo province should stay in its immediate surroundings. An important reason for this is to facilitate the refugees' return. The ethnic cleansing must not become permanent. The further away from the immediate surroundings you get, the more complications may arise at the prospect of returning.[34]

It is interesting to note that now the issuing of temporary protection is described as the most humanitarian approach to refugeedom.

The new logic of relationship between distance and degree of complications may also be questionable. Nevertheless it is the logic of the Swedish policy and also the official explanation for the change of focus away from the reception of refugees in Sweden to humanitarian assistance to those neighbouring countries that have been the main receivers of the refugee flows.

Humanitarian assistance as a part of refugee policy

According to the Swedish government, Swedish migration policy should be seen as an integrated whole which embraces refugee, immigration, integration and repatriation questions and which also includes foreign policy, security policy, trade policy and aid policy. Consequently, Sweden's policy in relation to the Kosovo question and reception in Sweden is characterized by notions of this comprehensive approach.[35]

The official web site of the Ministry of Foreign Affairs presented the Swedish policy towards the so-called Kosovo crisis. The new focus on humanitarian assistance is shown by the inclusion of a detailed list of Swedish humanitarian assistance in relation to the Kosovo refugees. According to this list, Sweden has dedicated 9 million euros (79.5 million Skr) to different humanitarian activities mainly carried out by different organizations within the United Nations and international and national non-governmental organizations. This sum includes the parts of the yearly contributions to the UNHCR and the ICRC (International Committee of the Red Cross) that have been redirected towards the Kosovars.

'This is our part of Europe's responsibility'

Another major part of the Swedish approach to the Kosovo crisis was the focus on multilateralism and international cooperation. The importance of dealing with the issue multilaterally through all the correct channels has been described as so great that actions by individual states were ruled out as being almost obstructive to the multilateral process. The importance of negotiation with other countries before making any final decision was more highly prioritized than the domestic demands for information about the official Swedish line of action. The Minister of Immigration made a special point of not making the number of refugees officially known to the Swedish public until negotiations on so-called burden sharing had been conducted within the EU and with the UNHCR.

The Swedish point of departure in the discussion on burden sharing was that the country had done more than its share during the Bosnian war. The Swedish Prime Minister, Göran Persson, declared, 'We in Sweden have earlier received a very large part of the refugee flows, a responsibility far beyond what any other country in Europe has taken on. We must keep this in mind when we discuss this acute situation.'[36] The failure of the EU to reach a common policy for the distribution of the refugees among themselves was therefore a great disappointment to the Swedish line.[37] Official statements declare that responses of the other countries of the EU have not been 'impressive', but that Sweden has accepted its responsibility to the full.

In the end, 3697 Kosovars were evacuated to Sweden before the evacuation programme was ended on 23 June 1999, thirteen days after the bombings ended. On 26 July 1999 the first Kosovars returned. A returning grant of 570 euros (5000 Skr) per capita or 3420 euros (30,000 Skr) per family was introduced to facilitate the repatriation of the refugees.[38] By March 2000, 1800 had returned to Kosovo. The Kosovars, whose 11-month residence permits have expired, are now entitled to apply for asylum on an individual basis. A government Bill delivered to Parliament in January 2000 proposed an extension of the period a person could be given a temporary residence permit, from 1999's 11 months to a period of up to two years. During this period the persons involved should not have the right to apply for asylum. Furthermore, they should neither be entitled to more than acute medical and dental care, nor be enrolled in any language programme, etc.[39] The Bill met with strong criticism both in public debates and in Parliament. When it became obvious that the Bill lacked parliamentary support it was withdrawn from Parliament at the beginning of March in the same year.

The securitization of refugee issues

When the Swedish policy towards the Bosnian refugee crisis is compared with that towards the later Kosovo crisis, it is clear that the differences cannot be explained simply by the domestic context at the time. The Kosovo crisis has rather been a test case for the new refugee policy that had evolved in Europe during the 1990s – a policy that the Swedish Social Democratic Party had been pushing for, nationally as well as internationally all through the 1990s.

After the Social Democrats regained office in the election of 1994, they appointed a Refugee Policy Commission to revise the refugee policy.[40] The mission of the commission was clear: to develop a 'more explicit policy with more efficient routines and at a lower cost'.[41] However, it is important that, except for a few additions, the 1994 commission's terms of reference corresponded to the terms of reference of another commission appointed by the Social Democrats back in 1990, something that indicates that the party had felt the need for a policy change at the beginning of the 1990s.[42]

The core concept of the terms of reference, the report and the reform itself was an 'integrated refugee and immigration policy', implying close coordination between traditional refugee and immigration policy-making and policy-making in the fields of foreign affairs and international aid. According to this definition of refugee policy, support for the struggle for human rights, measures to manage the economic and demographic imbalances, and promotion of trade with developing countries are also part of the refugee policy.

It seems that the Social Democrats wanted to get the proposed changes implemented as soon as possible. The decision to appoint the new commission came only two months after the election, and the commission report was to be completed as early as 1 July 1995. The report that formed the basis for the new refugee policy was entitled 'Swedish refugee policy in a global perspective' (*Svensk flyktingpolitik i globalt perspektiv*).[43]

The government bill that followed in 1996 took the commission's report as its point of departure.[44] It was approved in Parliament on 10 December 1996 with the support of the Moderate Party.[45] The changes became effective as of 1 January 1997.

The balancing act

The development of the new Social Democratic refugee policy can be described as an attempt to find a compromise between the cosmopolitan and the communitarian strand of the electorate. It is as if the politicians are trying to say 'Assistance has no borders and we will help people who are in a plight, but we will take care of our own people here', or, in the words of the former Minister of Immigration, Pierre Schori, 'To me it is not about showing solidarity either to the refugees or to the unemployed. It is about showing solidarity to both refugees and unemployed – or not to show solidarity at all.'[46] This balancing act between what the government bill of 1996 calls the 'humanity' and the 'legitimacy' of the migration policy is always present in immigration and refugee policy.[47] The relative weights of the two parts have, however, shifted over time. Since 'humanity' and 'legitimacy' are still important words in Swedish political discourse, it is especially interesting to see how the balance has changed.

The underlying change that enabled the refugee policy change has mainly taken place within two fields. On the one hand, the right to asylum has been reinterpreted and narrowed down. On the other hand, Swedish national security and threats towards this security have been reinterpreted and widened.

First of all, it is accepted that cross-border migration is not to be regarded as an acceptable way to change international conditions. This is clearly stated in the government bill, which explains that emigration of the kind that many Swedes undertook during the nineteenth century does not exist as an alternative anywhere in the world today: 'The earth is populated and land and other resources are to a large extent already claimed. Today the whole world repudiates colonialism.'[48] That the phenomenon of large-scale international migration is something quite different from the colonialism that was an intricate system to install European supremacy over the rest of the world is not mentioned. The statement is rather revealing as it exposes an underlying view of international migration as a phenomenon that if not restricted can get out of control.

The reinterpretation of the right to asylum

The texts of commission reports are always interesting since they are used to support the changes envisioned by the government. Even though a commission of inquiry is officially appointed to investigate the issue area in focus, its work is nevertheless anticipated to support the policy changes already sketched in the commission's terms of reference, something that the reports almost always end up doing. The work of the Refugee Policy Commission is no different in this regard.

The foundation of the new refugee policy was clearly elaborated in the commission's report. One of the goals of the refugee policy reform was to develop a policy that was able to reduce the number of asylum applications treated on Swedish territory. How this policy could be carried out successfully without violating the human right to seek and enjoy asylum from persecution in other countries was therefore a concern of the report. The report's overview of international instruments indicates that there is an active tendency to define international commitments as narrowly as possible. It was perceived as self-evident that refugees should be made to stay in the close vicinity of the country of origin.

> UN declarations are not legally binding on states and accordingly neither is the right to seek and obtain asylum. ... The international right to asylum is thus in principle constituted by a ban on states' deporting a person who is a refugee to his home country or to another country where he risks persecution, or from which he runs the risk of being sent back to the home country.[49]

> The Refugee Convention does not give refugees any right to permanent settlement in the country in which they have sought and obtained asylum.[50]

> Neither does the Refugee Convention give refugees any right to choose the country of asylum. Thus, a state may deport a refugee to another state in which satisfactory protection can be given. This is currently being done by

Sweden and other European countries in accordance with the principle that refugees shall be given protection in the country in which they first applied for, or could have applied for, asylum, the so-called principle of the country of first asylum.[51]

According to this narrow definition of the right to asylum, it can be said to be in line with Sweden's international commitment to let countries close to the source of flight take the pressure of different refugee flows. Whereas burden sharing on the European level refers to the distribution of refugees among various countries, on the international level the distribution of refugees is not considered a good solution. Here, burden sharing means humanitarian assistance to countries that host hundreds of thousands of refugees.

The report also redefines the prevention of the emergence of refugee flows so that it does not apply only to the countries of origin. The report also describes actions to be taken in the so-called countries of first asylum to enable them to carry their 'refugee burden' in order to prevent a second flight. The prevention of continued flight is important, and the report stresses the need for the international community to use a comprehensive approach to ensure that the countries of first asylum will give protection and assistance to the refugees. This can be done through a number of instruments, not only through conventional emergency material assistance. The report makes a number of suggestions of possible instruments:

> For instance, the prospects of favourable trade agreements or social and economic development aid (that is, besides the emergency aid to the refugees) may be important to persuade the country of first asylum to continue to pursue a humane policy.[52]

> ... in Croatia, demands can be made for refugees' reception to be upheld in accordance with existing international norms in order to improve the possibilities of reaching different agreements with the European Union.[53]

> At the same time, signals should be given concerning the relationships that exist between the resources in the form of development aid that the international community can give the country of first asylum and the costs potential donor countries incur if a large proportion of the refugees instead apply for asylum in these countries.[54]

It is quite obvious that the new Swedish refugee policy aims at using all measures to hand in order to reduce the number of people applying for asylum in Sweden.

The redefinition of national security

The wish to limit the arrival of asylum seekers was accompanied by a redefinition of Swedish national security in which refugees and asylum seekers – irregular migrants – were increasingly defined as a threat.

When the international security debate opened up to a wider spectrum of threats and a more broadly defined security concept, Sweden followed this new trend. For Sweden, a country that had built its security policy around the concept of neutrality among rival super-powers, bloc politics and the nuclear arms race, the need to revise the security policy was obvious. The end of the Cold War became the start of a restructuring of Swedish security policy. In this process migration and refugee flows became officially included as a concern of the country's security policy without any debate over the issue, either in Parliament or in newspaper editorials.

The first time refugee questions were officially introduced into the realm of security policy was at the end of 1992 when the Minister of Defence, V. Anders Björk, appointed 'The Threat and Risk Commission' (Hot- och riskutredningen) to 'investigate the stress and risks to peacetime society'. More directly, the task of the commission was to investigate the consequences of a number of plausible emergency situations that commission members could choose as they saw fit. They were, however, given clear guidance as regards the terms of reference, where Mr Björk mentioned a number of phenomena he thought should come into question for this kind of overview, among them 'an influx of refugees of such dimensions that the stress on different aspects of society can become dramatic'.[55]

The report, 'Mass flight of asylum and relief seekers to Sweden' (Massflykt till Sverige av asyl- och hjälpsökande), was ready in September 1993. In the report three different scenarios of mass immigration of refugees are presented. The first scenario pictured an event where political persecution in Russia leads to the arrival of 50,000 asylum seekers in Swedish ports during a single week. In the second scenario, political persecution in Russia is combined with severe material hardship, presented as leading to the arrival of 200,000 Russians over a period of four months. The third scenario presented an even grimmer picture, where a long period of severe hardship in combination with a serious accident in a nuclear plant outside Moscow leads over a six-month period to the immigration of 500,000 Russian relief seekers. In these kinds of sudden emergency situations, it is quite clear that the so-called total defence[56] has a number of roles to play: the civil defence organizations as the coordinators of activities and the military defence forces as the organizers of logistics. The link between security and refugees here has to do with the need to make use of the organizational capacity of the total defence forces in these kinds of emergencies.

It is important to note that this report was made at a time when the country was receiving the first asylum seekers from former Yugoslavia. It was quite obvious that the spectre of a possible refugee crisis was scaring the government. However, the fear of large-scale refugee flows had surfaced previously, during the winter of 1990–1. It is obvious that the three scenarios in the report are based on the issued raised that year.[57] It is also worth noting that national security concerns over long-term changes in the fabric of civil society, such as are raised with increasing frequency (e.g. Waever *et al.* 1993 [The Copenhagen School]) were not included in the terms of reference of the commission.

The 'new' security concept

A working committee dealing with renewal of Swedish security policy was appointed and in 1995 it issued its first major official document, 'Sweden in Europe and the world' (*Sverige i Europa och Världen*).[58] This report focused on the broader aspects of security and defence policy, and the goals for total defence. It is especially interesting since it paints the working committee's picture of the world in which Sweden will implement its renewed security policy. According to the report, the world is changing as a result of the end of the Cold War but also as a result of a number of global trends. Here, the globalization of technology, the economy and finance are mentioned as the most important of these trends, but demographic developments, the ongoing environmental deterioration, and the growing economic rifts between the North and the South are also mentioned as important. These changes are described as transnational in the sense that they mainly take place outside what the report calls 'normal international relations' and that they gradually change the basis for global security policy.[59]

In relation to these global trends the report introduces the notion of a wider security concept:

> The population explosion in some parts of the world, in combination with the lack of economic development, gives rise to migration pressure, political and social instability, and stress on the ecological system. This creates a negative circle that is becoming increasingly difficult to break. Environmental problems also emerge as a consequence of the ongoing industrialization in large parts of the world, not the least in the populous countries. The risk of a ruthless exploitation of non-renewable resources is great in both cases. *The wider security concept originates to a significant degree in these trends.*[60]

The working committee suggested that this wider security concept should be used as the point of departure for Swedish policy-makers when reforming Swedish security and defence policy. The concept itself, strangely enough, is never clearly defined.

There is, of course, never such a thing as a concept without a definition. A number of statements can be found in the text that together give a picture of the underlying definition used by the working committee. The concept is presented as self-evident, as part of a common trend that by default should make it unproblematic. It is stated that it is a common trend to talk about a wider concept of security. Another generally accepted part of the concept of security is, according to the report,

> the threats and risks that by themselves are of a transnational character and, in part, have to be handled in international cooperation, but in fact have more to do with national security interests in the sense of protection of the country and the population. This may apply to natural disasters, *large-scale refugee flows*, infrastructure disturbances or large-scale environmental accidents.[61]

This is a very interesting statement in the sense that it takes a number of issues commonly defined as transnational and/or international and 'renationalizes' them by defining them as national security interests. This is also the first time it is officially stated that Sweden should understand refugee flows as a threat both to the country as such and to the population. Since refugee flows still have a strong linkage to the human rights field, it must be considered a major step to change the refugee discourse from the area of human rights towards that of national security. Closer definitions of the kinds of threat refugee flows may pose are, however, lacking in the report. If you compare the quotations above, the first describes refugee flows as a part of a mix that threatens to lead to the exploitation of non-renewable resources, while the second describes refugee flows more widely as a threat to countries and their populations.

Sweden's security interests are defined on three levels: the global level, the European and transatlantic level and the immediate surroundings. This is somewhat confusing, since the subject of security (who or what is threatened?) keeps changing, and with it the character of the threat (how someone or something threatens someone or something). The only constant is the definitional vagueness of the subject of security and the character of the threats. These obscurities aside, what remains clear is the working committee's perception of refugee flows as a threat to a number of different units and in a number of different ways. In fact, refugee and migration flows keep recurring as a security threat all through the report. For instance, the report states:

> The rifts that exist between poor and rich may easily lead to domestic antagonisms and tribal rivalry, and foment extremist movements. In addition to the stress this may put on the population of the continent, it creates threats of large-scale migration, environmental deterioration, terrorism, etc. for the surrounding world.[62]

Here, large-scale migration from Africa is presented as a threat to the surrounding world. Under what circumstances and in what ways this migration would be a threat are, however, not described.

The report goes on:

> Unemployment, organized crime and new risks of serious internal social tensions, i.e. as a consequence of the large migration flows to Europe during recent decades, also constitute problems in the established democracies of Western Europe, and under unfavourable conditions may undermine the foundation of democracy.[63]

Here, however, the threatening effects on Western Europe are clearly stated. Migration flows have (together with other things not defined in the report) caused unemployment, organized crime and serious risks of internal social tensions to the degree that they may undermine the democratic foundation of the European states. This is a very strong statement.[64]

It is interesting to note that the securitization of refugee issues is visible also in the commission report on Swedish refugee policy mentioned above:

> Forced migration and refugee flows are, however, not only consequences of problems; they also cause problems, which not only are acute but also are of a more long-term nature. Large-scale population movements can in themselves threaten peace and security.[65]

The two 1995 reports on refugee policy and security policy respectively have been crucial instruments for changing the official discourse on refugees. Whereas the refugee report limits the links between refugees and human rights/international law, the security report establishes and consolidates links between refugees and national security. From being an issue most commonly framed in terms of human rights and international solidarity, refugee flows are now perceived as a presumptive destabilizing threat to Sweden, one that should be avoided, and not only for the benefit of the refugees.

Conclusion: keeping up appearances

The differences between the Swedish responses in the two cases in question can be understood if they are seen in the light of the securitization of Swedish refugee policy which developed during the 1990s.

Today, as indicated by the Kosovo crisis, refugee flows have been redefined as a phenomenon that is threatening the state and that therefore has to be kept outside its borders. This is, of course, in line with the overall policy of the EU. However, the securitization of Swedish refugee policy has its roots in the domestic situation.

At the same time human rights are still understood as an important part of Swedish official political discourse and its self-image.

The conflict between human rights and security is by no means new. Although there have been obvious changes in Sweden's refugee policy, it is therefore interesting to note that the official view and goals of the Swedish policy have remained the same over time. All committee reports (*betänkanden*), government bills (*propositioner*) and communications (*skrivelser*), no matter whether formulated by socialist or conservative governments, declare that the Swedish refugee policy is based on humanitarian principles, comprehensiveness, generosity, internationalism and humaneness.[66] On the other hand, refugee flows have always been part of Sweden's security concerns in a more traditional sense, where every person outside the country's borders can be a potential threat to national security in the form of a spy or a fifth column. This view of non-nationals was a strand of national security all through the Cold War and continues to be so to the present day.

Sweden is one of the international promoters of human rights-based policy-making. In 1993 the country was confronted by human beings from Bosnia who, through the act of applying for asylum, placed decision-making over their lives and well-being in the hands of the Swedish state. This confrontation has proved very uncomfortable for a country that prides itself on being a humanitarian state.[67] The difference between the promotion of human rights in theory and in practice is highlighted through the asylum decisions, something that in the long run may affect the country's self-image. It is almost impossible to preserve a positive image of a 'humanitarian super-power' and a strict refugee policy at the same time.[68] There has thus been a wish to escape these kinds of confrontations all together. Thus, the new Swedish refugee policy carried out in relation to the Kosovar refugees can best be understood as an attempt to avoid these kinds of confrontations. It seems that international solidarity is preferably practised from a distance.

Notes

1. According to the SIFO monthly electoral forecast 26 May 1991. New Democracy received 6.7 per cent of the votes in the election in September of the same year.
2. C. Nilsson, 'Nära 500 000 utan arbete' (Close to 500,000 unemployed), *Dagens Nyheter*, 10 August 1993.
3. At the time of application the European Union was, of course, still the European Community.

4. C. Keely and S.S. Russell, 'Responses of industrial countries to asylum-seekers, refugees and migrants', *Journal of International Affairs* 47 (2) (1994), 399–418.

5. The concept 'de facto refugees' was introduced in praxis during the 1960s. Their right to asylum was confirmed by law in 1976. However, they were not to be regarded as refugees de jure (G. Melander and P. Nobel, *Handbok i invandrarrätt* (Manual of immigration law) (Uppsala: Carmina, 1984), pp. 35–7).

6. War rejecters' (krigsvägrare) right to asylum was also introduced in praxis during the 1960s and confirmed by law in 1976. The concept refers to a person who runs a manifest risk of being enrolled in active military service in a war *between* states. The praxis developed as a way to give asylum in Sweden to Americans enrolled for military service in the Vietnam War.

7. Often described as individuals who have escaped 'war or other warlike conditions such that they risk being affected without being part of the fighting forces'. In fact people in this category have not had a legal right to asylum, but residence permits *could* be granted on humanitarian grounds.

8. Commission terms of reference, Dir. 1990:42, *Utredning om förutsättningarna för och inriktningen av en sammanhållen flykting- och immigrationspolitik* (Inquiry into the requirements for and direction of an integrated refugee and immigration policy).

9. Commission terms of reference, Dir. 1993:1, *Översyn av invandrarpolitiken samt invandrings- och flyktingpolitiken* (Revision of the immigrant policy and the immigration and refugee policy).

10. During the years 1992–5 66,452 persons from Yugoslavia (Serbia, Kosovo and Montenegro) applied for asylum in Sweden. The absolute majority of them were Kosovars. Of these, 46,960 persons were denied asylum (SIV (Swedish Board of Immigration) yearly statistics).

11. K. Eneberg, 'Flyktingströmmen har minskat' (The refugee flow has decreased), *Dagens Nyheter*, 15 October 1992.

12. Commission terms of reference, Dir. 1992:51, *Översyn av vissa delar av utlänningslagsstiftningen m.m.* (Revision of certain parts of the Aliens Act, etc.).

13. Government bill, Prop. 1993/94:94, *Mottagande av asylsökande m.m.* (Reception of asylum applicants, etc.). Temporary protection should, however, only be used for persons in search of protection from conflicts and crises of short-time duration, and the notion of temporariness should not apply to persons with the right to asylum.

14. The act of giving asylum to people fleeing Bosnia could indeed be of indirect assistance to the persecutors, for whom the creation of refugees was a goal in itself, and a part of a strategy of ethnic cleansing. The people who fled the civil war had, however, made their choice: the personal costs of maintaining a ethnically mixed society were much too high.

15. For an analysis of the Swedish decision to grant the Bosnians permanent residence permits, in contrast to the other West European countries, see M. Appelqvist, *Responsibility in Transition: A Study of Refugee Law and Policy in Sweden* (Umeå: Umeå University Press, 1999), part III.

16. K. Eneberg, 'Nya regler för bosnier på flykt' (New regulations for fleeing Bosnians), *Dagens Nyheter*, 22 June 1993.
17. Commission terms of reference, Dir. 1990:42, *Utredning om förutsättningarna för och inriktningen av en sammanhållen flykting- och immigrationspolitik* (Inquiry into the requirements for and direction of an integrated refugee and immigration policy).
18. Government bill, Prop. 1996/97:25, *Svensk migrationspolitik i globalt perspektiv* (Swedish migration policy in a global perspective).
19. The difference between the elections of 1988 and 1998 is a good illustration of the changes. The figures for the 1988 election: Moderate Party 18.3 per cent; Centre Party 11.3 per cent; Liberal Party 12.2 per cent; Social Democratic Party 43.2 per cent; Left-Wing Party 4.5 per cent; Environmental Party 5.5 per cent; Christian Democratic Party 2.9 per cent; others 1 per cent. The figures for the 1998 election: Moderate Party 22.9 per cent; Centre Party 5.1 per cent; Liberal Party 4.7 per cent; Social Democratic Party 36.4 per cent; Left-Wing Party 12.0 per cent; Environmental Party 4.5 per cent; Christian Democratic Party 11.8 per cent; others 2.6 per cent (SCB, *Allmämma valen, del 1* (General Elections), 1988 and 1998).
20. OECD, *Economic Survey on Sweden 1998*, Paris: Organisation for Economic Co-operation and Development.
21. SCB, *Allmänna valen, del 1* (General Elections), 1998.
22. The issue has yet to be solved, as was demonstrated in relation to the Kosovars.
23. SIV (Swedish Board of Immigration) press release, 16 July 1999.
24. A person with a 'protection need' is defined as (a) a person who has a well-founded fear of severe punishment (the death penalty or bodily punishment) or torture or other inhuman or degrading punishment if returned home; (b) a person who is in need of protection as a result of an armed conflict (between or within states), or who cannot return home because of an environmental disaster; (c) a person who has a well-grounded fear of persecution on the grounds of his/her gender or homosexuality.
25. In fact the figure for 1996 is the lowest figure since the official statistics on asylum seekers started in 1984.
26. All statistics come from the Swedish Board of Immigration.
27. M. Björklund, 'Statsfinanserna: högtryck över Sverige' (The finances of the state: high pressure over Sweden), *Dagens Nyheter* 21 May 1999, and M. Björklund 'Konjunkturen: högtryck över svensk ekonomi' (The state of the market: high pressure over the Swedish economy), *Dagens Nyheter*, 23 June 1999.
28. Web site www.svt/radiohjalpen/index, and J. Gustafson and A. Eberhardson, 'Enormt stor vilja att bistå människorna på Balkan' (Immensely great desire to assist the people in the Balkan), *Röda korsets tidning* no. 2, 1999.
29. It is important to keep in mind that while it is 5 per cent of the number requested by the UNHCR, it is only 0.6 per cent of all Kosovars who fled Kosovo during spring 1999.
30. E. Andersson, 'FN kritiserar svensk flyktingpolitik' (UN criticizes Swedish refugee policy), *Svenska Dagbladet*, 6 May 1999.

31. The decision was also criticized by the other political parties with the exception of the Moderate Party: S. Baltscheffy and I. Hagberg, 'Stopp för flyktingar får hård kritik' (Stop to refugees receives severe criticism), *Svenska Dagbladet*, 7 May 1999.

32. *Ibid.*

33. Skriftligt svar av statsrådet Pierre Schori på fråga av Barbro Westerholm (fp) om kosovoalbanska flyktingar och visumtvånget (Reply by cabinet minister Pierre Schori on a question by Barbro Westerholm (Liberal Party) concerning the Kosovo refugees and the visa requirement), question no. 1998/99:547 (Prot 1998/99:95).

34. *Ibid.*

35. Web site www.ud.se.

36. O. Billger and C. Axelsson, 'Sverige öppet för fler Kosovoflyktingar' (Sweden open to more Kosovo refugees), *Svenska Dagbladet*, 7 April 1999. It is, of course, not true that Sweden has received more refugees than all other countries in Europe. It appears as if, first, the Prime Minister is referring to the EU member states, and second he is measuring the reception rate in refugees per capita rather than in absolute terms or in relation to the GDP.

37. M. Holmberg, 'Kriget i Jugoslavien: EU oenigt om flyktingpolitik' (The war in Yugoslavia: EU in disagreement over refugee policy), *Dagens Nyheter*, 8 April 1999.

38. Swedish Board of Immigration press release, 16 July 1999.

39. Government Bill, Prop. 1999/2000:42, *Utlänningar i massflyktsituation, sociala förmåner mm* (Aliens in situations of mass flight, social benefits, etc.).

40. It is considered usual to appoint a commission whenever a reform of any significance is considered, regardless of whether the reform involves policy, legislation, or simply administrative changes. For an informative description of this kind of structured consultation, see H. Heclo and H. Madsen, *Policy and Politics in Sweden: Principled Pragmatism* (Philadelphia: Temple University Press, 1987), pp. 9–15. The Refugee Policy Commission replaced another commission, the Immigrant and Refugee Commission, appointed by the non-socialist government in 1993. The discontinuation of the Immigrant and Refugee Commission was motivated by its excessively wide mission: to revise refugee and immigration policy as well as immigrant policy (minority policy). Although the government in the new terms of reference (Dir. 1994:129) stated that in fact there was a clear connection between immigrant and immigration policies, it nevertheless felt that the urgent need of immigration and refugee policy reform made it necessary to deal with the two areas separately.

41. Commission's terms of reference, Dir. 1994:129, *Översyn av invandrings- och flyktingpolitiken* (Revision of the immigration and refugee policy).

42. Commission's terms of reference, Dir. 1990:42, *Utredning om förutsättningarna för och inriktningen av en sammanhållen flykting- och immigrationspolitik* (Inquiry into the requirements for and direction of an integrated refugee and immigration policy).

43. Commission report, SOU 1995:75, *Svensk flyktingpolitik i globalt perspektiv* (Swedish refugee policy in a global perspective).

44. Government bill, Prop. 1996/97:25, *Svensk migrationspolitik i globalt perspektiv* (Swedish migration policy in a global perspective).

45. Minutes of plenary session, Prot. 1996/97:42, 10 December 1996.
46. Official print, Ministry of Foreign Affairs, UD information, *Tydlighet och humanitet: ledstjärnor för svensk flyktingpolitik* (Clarity and humanity: guiding lights of Swedish refugee policy), no. 6, June 1998.
47. Government bill, Prop. 1996/97:25, chapter 12:7.
48. *Ibid.*, chapter 6:1.
49. Commission report, SOU 1995:75, *Svensk flyktingpolitik i globalt perspektiv* (Swedish refugee policy in a global perspective), p. 45.
50. *Ibid.*, p. 45.
51. *Ibid.*
52. *Ibid.*, p. 82.
53. *Ibid.*
54. *Ibid.*, p. 83.
55. Commission's terms of reference, Dir. 1993:4, *Utredning om påfrestningar och risker i det fredstida samhället* (Investigation into the stress and risk of peacetime society).
56. The concept 'total defence' is used as an inclusive concept that embraces all parts of Swedish defence, from the military to the Swedish Agency for Civil Emergency Planning (ÖCB).
57. Reports in the daily news media paid much attention to the deterioration of the Soviet Union and the mass migration that looked likely to become a reality any day. The daily newspapers wrote about experts in the West who estimated that hordes of 20–50 million people could be set in motion, fleeing from civil unrest, starvation and unemployment. (See, for example, G. Johansson, *Expressen*, 8 June 1990, and Hård, *Expressen* 19 November 1990) The risk of a Soviet refugee flow towards Sweden was estimated as so high that the Director of the Swedish Board of Immigration arranged a meeting with the directors of the regional branches of the Board, the Rescue Service, the coastguards, the National Police Corps and the National Board for Health and Welfare in order to prepare a nationwide emergency plan to deal with the potential mass emigration of Russians (*Expressen*, 21 November 1990).
58. Commission report, Ds 1995:28, *Sverige i Europa och världen* (Sweden in Europe and the world).
59. *Ibid.*, pp. 7–8.
60. *Ibid.*, p. 8, emphasis added.
61. *Ibid.*, p. 114, emphasis added.
62. *Ibid.*, p. 11–12.
63. *Ibid.*, p. 17.
64. An attempt to categorize these different threat perceptions and security concerns has been made by B. Hettne, and E. Abiri, 'The securitisation of cross-border migration: Sweden in the era of globalisation', in D. Graham and N. Poku (eds) *Redefining Security: Population Movements and National Security* (London: Praeger, 1998).
65. Commission report, SOU 1995:75, *Svensk flyktingpolitik i globalt perspektiv* (Swedish refugee policy in a global perspective), p. 60.
66. E. Abiri, 'The changing praxis of "Generosity": Swedish refugee policy changes during the 1990s', *Journal of Refugee Studies* (forthcoming 2000).

67. E. Abiri, 'Thinking the separated together: migration and security in a North–South perspective', in D. Graham and N. Poku (eds) *Migration, Globalisation and Human Security* (London: Routledge, 2000). The epithet 'moral super-power' has from time to time been used to describe both by Swedish politicians and academics, mockingly or proudly depending on the user. The Swedish Minister of Immigration, Pierre Schori, proudly described Sweden as a 'humanitarian super-power' in relation to the actions to help the Kosovo refugees (interview in *Aktuellt*, the public TV network news, 5 April 1999).

68. A number of cases brought to public attention, e.g. the *Sincari* and *Shakeri* cases, have also clearly shown how human rights are interpreted differently depending on who you are and how strong your legal ties to the country are.

Bibliography

Books and journal articles

Abiri, E., 'Thinking the separated together: migration and security in a North–South perspective', in D. Graham and N. Poku (eds) *Migration, Globalisation and Human Security* (London: Routledge, 2000).

Abiri, E., 'The changing praxis of "Generosity": Swedish refugee policy changes during the 1990s', *Journal of Refugee Studies* (forthcoming 2000).

Applequist, M., *Responsibility in Transition: A Study of Refugee Law and Policy in Sweden* (Umeå: Umeå University Press, 1999).

Heclo, H. and Madsen, H., *Policy and Politics in Sweden: Principled Pragmatism* (Philadelphia: Temple University Press, 1987).

Hettne, B. and Abiri, E., 'The securitisation of cross-border migration: Sweden in the era of globalisation', in D. Graham and N. Poku (eds) *Redefining Security: Population Movements and National Security* (London: Praeger, 1998).

Keely, C. and Russell, S.S. 'Responses of industrial countries to asylum-seekers, refugees and migrants', *Journal of International Affairs* 47 (2) (1994), 399–418.

Melander, G. and Nobel, P., *Handbok i invandrarrätt* (Manual of immigration law) (Uppsala: Carmina, 1984).

OECD, *Economic Survey on Sweden 1998* (Paris: Organisation for Economic Co-operation and Development, 1998).

Newspaper articles

Andersson, E. 'FN kritiserar svensk flyktingpolitik' (UN criticizes Swedish refugee policy), *Svenska Dagbladet*, 6 May 1999.

Baltscheffy, S. and Hagberg, I., 'Stopp för flyktingar får hård kritik' (Stop to refugees receives severe criticism), *Svenska Dagbladet*, 7 May 1999.

Billger, O. and Axelsson, C., 'Sverige öppet för fler Kosovoflyktingar' (Sweden open to more Kosovo refugees), *Svenska Dagbladet*, 7 April 1999.

Björklund, M. 'Konjunkturen: högtryck över svensk ekonomi' (The state of the market: high pressure over the Swedish economy), *Dagens Nyheter*, 23 June 1999.

Björklund, M. 'Statsfinanserna: högtryck över Sverige' (The finances of the state: high pressure over Sweden), *Dagens Nyheter*, 21 May 1999.

Eneberg, K. 'Flyktingströmmen har minskat' (The refugee flow has decreased), *Dagens Nyheter*, 15 October 1992.

Eneberg, K. 'Nya regler för bosnier på flykt' (New regulations for fleeing Bosnians), *Dagens Nyheter*, 22 June 1993.

Friggebo, B. and Westerberg, B., 'Viseringsbeslutet var korrekt' (The visa decision was correct), *Dagens Nyheter*, 18 March 1994.

Gustafson, J. and Eberhardson, A., 'Enormt stor vilja att bistå människorna på Balkan' (Immensly great desire to assist the people of the Balkans), *Röda korsets tidning* no. 2, 1999.

Hård, C. 'Norrbotten rustar för sovjetisk flyktingvåg' (The northern region is preparing for a Soviet refugee flow), *Expressen*, 19 Nov 1990.

Holmberg, M. 'Kriget i Jugoslavien: EU oenigt om flyktingpolitik' (The war in Yugoslavia: EU in disagreement over refugee policy), *Dagens Nyheter*, 8 April 1999.

Johansson, G. 'Inbördeskrig och massflykt hotar Sovjet' (Civil war and mass flight threaten the Soviet Union), *Expressen*, 8 June 1990.

'Krismöte om massinvandring' (Emergency meeting on mass immigration), *Expressen*, 21 November 1990.

Nilsson, G. 'Nära 500 000 utan arbete' (Close to 500,000 unemployed), *Dagens Nyheter*, 10 August 1993.

Statistics

SCB (1988) Allmänna valen, del 1 (General Elections)

SCB (1991) Allmänna valen, del 1 (General Elections)

SCB (1998) Allmänna valen, del 1 (General Elections).

SCB (1999) Labour Force Survey (press release July 1999).

SIFO monthly electoral forecast, 26 May 1991.

SIV (Swedish Board of Immigration) official yearly statistics.

Commissions' terms of references

Dir. 1990:42, *Utredning om förutsättningarna för och inriktningen av en sammanhållen flykting- och immigrationspolitik* (Inquiry into the requirements for and direction of an integrated refugee and immigration policy).

Dir. 1992:51, *Översyn av vissa delar av utlänningslagsstiftningen m.m.* (Revision of certain parts of the Aliens' Act, etc.).

Dir. 1993:1, *Översyn av invandrarpolitiken samt invandrings- och flyktingpolitiken* (Revision of the immigrant policy and the immigration and refugee policy).

Dir. 1993:4, *Utredning om påfrestningar och risker i det fredstida samhället ...* (Investigation into the stress and risk of peacetime society).

Dir. 1994:129, *Översyn av invandrings- och flyktingpolitiken* (Revision of the immigration and refugee policy).

Commission reports

Ds 1995:28, *Sverige i Europa och Världen* (Sweden in Europe and the world) (Stockholm: Fritzes).

SOU 1993:89, *Massflykt till Sverige av asyl- och hjälpsökande* (Mass flight of asylum and relief-seekers to Sweden) (Stockholm: Fritzes).

SOU 1995:75, *Svensk flyktingpolitik i globalt perspektiv* (Swedish refugee policy in a global perspective) (Stockholm: Fritzes).

Government bills

Prop. 1990/91:195, *Flykting- och immigrationspolitiken* (Refugee and immigration policy).

Prop. 1993/94:94, *Mottagande av asylsökande m.m.* (Reception of asylum applicants, etc.).

Prop. 1996/97:25, *Svensk migrationspolitik i globalt perspektiv* (Swedish migration policy in a global perspective).

Prop. 1999/2000:42, *Utlänningar i massflyktsituation, sociala förmåner mm* (Aliens in situations of mass flight, social benefits, etc.).

Minutes of plenary sessions

Prot. 1996/97: 42, 10 Dec 1996.
Prot. 1998/99:95, 18 May 1999.

Other official printed sources

UD info (1998) 'Tydlighet och humanitet: ledstjärnor för svensk flyktingpolitik' (Clarity and humanity: guiding lights of Swedish refugee policy), no. 6, June 1998.

Television broadcasts

Interview with the Minister of Immigration, Pierre Schori, in *Aktuellt* (the public network news) TV1, the 9.00 p.m. broadcast, 5 April 1999.

Interview with Ian Wachtmeister in *Aktuellt*, TV1, the 9.00 p.m. broadcast, 2 February 1998.

Web sites

www.ud.se, July 1999, the official site of the Swedish Ministry of Foreign Affairs, web pages entitled 'Kosovokrisen: allmänt om mottagande i Sverige av personer från Kosovo' (The Kosovo crisis: general information on the reception in Sweden of persons from Kosovo) and 'Sveriges humanitära insatser i samband med Kosovokrisen' (Sweden's humanitarian actions in relation to the Kosovo crisis).

www.svt.se/radiohjalpen/index.htm, 5 July 1999, the site of the aid organization Radiohjälpen.

CHAPTER SIX

Austria: reception of conflict refugees

IRENE STACHER

Introduction

The twentieth century was an era of great refugee movements in Europe. As a result of war, internal political conflicts, forced movements, politically organized massacre and 'ethnic cleansing', tens of millions of people were forced to flee, seeking protection elsewhere in, or beyond, their country of origin. In the first half of that century, during and after the two world wars, Austria became a country of origin and destination for hundreds of thousands of refugees.[1]

The East–West confrontation that began in the 1950s introduced a new refugee era. Austria, like all Western European states, signed the 1951 Geneva Refugee Convention, which particularly affected those refugees leaving the Eastern bloc who could not or would not return to their countries of origin. This system functioned very well in the Cold War years because Austria was generously prepared to admit refugees from the communist states of Eastern Europe.

Because of the East–West division, almost all people leaving Eastern Europe were considered in the West to be political refugees. In Austria the admission of these refugees was also positively anchored in the public's conscience. Austria granted asylum to thousands of refugees. However, the majority of those refugees were offered what amounted to temporary protection because at that time most of them headed for other Western states, where they received permanent asylum status and were economically integrated into the respective country's workforce. However, this Cold War-era 'temporary protection' was based not on specific legal provisions, but on political decisions taken in the knowledge that Austria represented the door to security and a place of transition to other Western states for many refugees from the Eastern bloc countries. This was therefore a form of short-term protection prior to resettlement.

Resistance to the generous admission policy became prevalent in the 1980s as refugees who either did not fit into this anti-communist framework or came from the Third World started to arrive. Parallel to this, the number of migrants leaving their countries of origin for economic reasons began to increase. Thus, the asylum question in Austria, as in other Western states, was often at the heart of domestic political controversies. As a consequence, the term 'refugee' gradually gained a more negative connotation and, in many cases, led to xenophobic and racist inclinations initiated by far-right groups. The early 1990s saw the creation of a more restrictive asylum and migration policy, as will be described below. In spite of this, the admission of high numbers of conflict refugees from Bosnia and Herzegovina and from Kosovo did not lead to controversial debates. Indeed, the generous reception of hundreds of thousands of refugees during the Cold War had had a positive impact on public opinion and presumably influenced the positive approach of Austrian society towards new waves of war refugees from former Yugoslavia.

The largest refugee wave in Europe in the second half of the twentieth century developed after the dissolution of Yugoslavia. Although Western European states proved to be relatively prepared to grant temporary protection, the political climate after the Cold War had undergone a fundamental change with regard to refugees. While those fleeing the violence in former Yugoslavia corresponded to public notions of genuine refugees in need of protection, only a small number of people from these war-torn areas were granted asylum based on the 1951 Geneva Refugee Convention. Receiving states did not consider that state persecution made Bosnians leave. Rather, general violence was regarded as the reason for leaving the country. As stated elsewhere in this volume, the introduction of temporary protection as an instrument for coping with mass influxes of 'refugees' presented a departure from earlier forms of practice. But now temporary protection had become focused much more on return than on resettlement, which had been the previous Austrian experience. Indeed, the resettlement of 'refugees' from Austria to other Western states was no longer guaranteed, increasing the 'burden' on Austria. The large wave of 'refugees' from former Yugoslavia was limited to a few countries, leading to a European and international debate on solidarity and on the instruments available for the temporary admission of large numbers of 'refugees' fleeing conflict. At the time of the NATO intervention in Kosovo, as was discussed in the Introduction to this volume, European Union (EU) states still did not have a functioning harmonized system of 'burden sharing' and temporary protection at their disposal.

In this chapter, and as distinct from other chapters, I will first develop in some depth the historical context within which 'refugee' protection in Austria is viewed. Throughout this historical discussion, reference will be made to the influence of racism and xenophobia and right-wing extremism on asylum and immigration policies. Continuous reference will also be made to Austria's position of neutrality during the Cold War, and to its gradual involvement in European integration, leading to membership of the EU. The history is particularly important in the Austrian case for the insights which handling of the Hungarian exodus of 1956 and that from Czechoslovakia in 1968 can give when considering the approach to reception of Kosovars. In this sense, Austria has learned important lessons not only from the Bosnian case (which is also dealt with in other chapters) but also from a longer past as a transit country offering short-term protection to refugees.

The reception of refugees in Austria after the Second World War

In the first decade after the Second World War, agreement was reached on both the essential supranational agreements for the protection of political refugees and the foundation of Austria's legal understanding of human rights regulations. Apart from the European Convention on Human Rights, the most important legal instruments were the 1951 Convention relating to the Status of Refugees (the Geneva Convention) and the 1948 Universal Declaration of Human Rights.

Austria can be considered a country of asylum: it has hosted and integrated hundreds of thousands of refugees. Between 1945 and 1989 Austria was, owing to its geopolitical position, one of the main intake and transit countries for refugees from Eastern and Central Europe. These refugee waves were largely caused by political crises in communist countries. Admission of these refugees was closely linked to the prevailing Cold War logic. Approximately two million persons found shelter in Austria before leaving for other Western receiving states. Although many West European and other countries were prepared to receive thousands of them, many refugees remained in Austria, where generous integration possibilities were offered. In the period 1950–90 about 350,000 foreigners were naturalized and acquired Austrian citizenship.[2]

In late 1956, as a result of political events occurring in Hungary, over 180,000 refugees entered Austrian territory. Austria was prepared to grant these refugees temporary protection, although, one year after the signing of the state treaty giving independence to Austria, the declaration of perpetual neutrality and the pull-out of the Allied occupation forces, the country was still preoccupied with its political and economic stabilization. However, because of its clearly Western orientation, Austria reacted especially sensitively to the events in Hungary.[3]

Austria's initial burden as a result of the mass influx of Hungarian

120

refugees in November 1956 was beyond reasonable proportions. As refugees continued to pour in and with the Austrian government facing grave difficulties in accommodating them in transit camps and providing food, clothing and medicine, the government appealed to the United Nations and the Western countries for rapid help. Within a matter of days, a total of 25,000 refugees were resettled in the USA, Canada, Switzerland, Argentina, Australia, West Germany, France, the UK, Italy, The Netherlands, Norway, Sweden and New Zealand. The Austrian case clearly sets the example that it was sufficient for Austria to request 'quick action to provide a solution' in order to convey the message that Austria could not provide a durable solution for all the refugees and that international assistance through resettlement was necessary.[4] Indeed, European 'burden sharing' came into effect at this juncture. Nevertheless, approximately 20,000 Hungarian refugees were granted permanent asylum in Austria and, over time, integrated as citizens.

During and after the Prague Spring of 1968, about 162,000 people from Czechoslovakia entered Austria and were given temporary protection. The post-war economic problems had, by then, been overcome, and the Austrian economy was experiencing an upward trend. Hence aid for thousands of refugees was organized quickly and in a non-bureaucratic fashion. In Vienna and other federal provinces emergency shelter was constructed. Although there are no exact numbers for those who continued westward, we can assume that many Czech and Slovak refugees travelled to other Western states, where they would be welcomed, as those countries were also experiencing an economic upturn. The economic situation in Austria enabled many trained and qualified employees who did not request asylum to be quickly integrated into employment.[5]

In the 1970s Austria also took in, on a contingent quota basis, refugees from non-European crisis areas. In 1972, 200 people from Uganda, displaced by President Idi Amin, were granted asylum and were integrated. As a result of political events in Latin America 200 people from Chile in 1974 and 250 people from Argentina in 1977 were granted asylum status. In addition, Chinese refugees trying to get to the USA were resettled from Cuba, as were Kurdish refugees from Iraq, while Indonesian asylum seekers were also admitted into the Republic of Austria.[6]

Towards the end of the Cold War asylum era

In 1981–2 approximately 250,000 people left Poland after the imposition of martial law. About 150,000 entered Austria, with most of them heading later for other Western countries. However, more than 33,000 Poles applied for asylum in Austria. The refugee waves from Poland were the last before the opening of the Iron Curtain. Shortly thereafter, a political debate took place in Austria on the revision of asylum legislation and the practice of admission.

After the mass influx of Polish asylum seekers at the beginning of the 1980s, the total number of asylum applications decreased again to 6314 in 1982 but rose rapidly towards the end of the 1980s to 21,882 in 1989, 22,789 in 1990 and 27,306 in 1991. The late 1980s therefore saw increased pressure on the Austrian migration and asylum system. There were, in fact, several interrelated reasons for this. First, as the influx of spontaneous labour migrants (including family members) increased, the system for organized recruitment from abroad of the 1960s and 1970s no longer functioned adequately. Second, the increase of illegal migrants from Central and Eastern Europe, in combination with the large number of asylum seekers who reached Austria in the late 1980s and early 1990s, and who were unable to continue to overseas countries as before, influenced the decision of the Austrian government to make a thorough review of the post-war system for regulating immigration. Finally, the changes in the East, together with the need to revise the Austrian aliens legislation as a result of the EEA (European Economic Area) negotiations, led to an overhaul of Austrian immigration policy, resulting, in the early 1990s, in a government package. This package included the Law on the Reception of Asylum Seekers (*Bundesbetreuungsgesetz*) in August 1991, the Asylum Law (*Asylgesetz*) in June 1992, the Law Regulating the Entry of Foreigners (*Fremdengesetz*) in January 1993, and a new law on residence permits (*Aufenthaltsgesetz*) in July 1993. This whole legislative framework was characterized by an increasingly restrictive asylum policy and new immigration rules which allowed for a new system to plan, on a quota basis, the annual intake of immigrants.[7]

This more restrictive immigration policy was also a consequence of far-right and populist movements in Austria. The new package came under fire from the United Nations High Commisioner for Refugees (UNHCR), the Green Party and humanitarian organizations, as a result of which the 1991 asylum law was amended in 1997. The new law (Asylum Law 1997) provides for an independent asylum tribunal (UBAS) which is the instance of final appeal for asylum seekers, and other stipulations to safeguard the right of asylum seekers. Moreover, the migration policy, according to the new Aliens Law 1997, focuses on the integration of immigrants into Austrian society.

In spite of the restrictive nature of the Austrian immigration policy and the support it received in broad public opinion, which was less open towards the influx of foreigners than in the Cold War era, Austria opened its doors to thousands of refugees from former Yugoslavia in the early 1990s. For historical, geopolitical and geographical reasons the Austrian population felt engaged in the situation of Croatian and Bosnian 'refugees'. This led to widespread support and a generous reception for them. The positive experience of reception, integration and transition of large numbers of refugees during the Cold War had clearly influenced public opinion on the emotional level. Moreover, because of the guest-worker tradition of Yugoslav labour in Austria, which began in the 1960s, there was an important network of family ties in Austria before the war. In 1991 some 197,900 people from former Yugoslavia were living as guest-workers or as family members in Austria.

Population displacements due to political conflicts in former Yugoslavia

Austria, like many other European states, responded to the initial mass flight from former Yugoslavia by creating a special legal basis for the admission and residence of conflict refugees, as a progressive interpretation of the 1951 Geneva Refugee Convention was not considered appropriate in the case of mass arrivals from former Yugoslavia.[8]

Reception of refugees from Croatia

With the advent of war in the territories of former Yugoslavia, Austria was confronted once again with a significant influx of refugees. In the summer of 1991 war 'refugees' from Croatia started to arrive in great numbers, and approximately 100,000 Croatians entered and transited Austria. About 13,000 refugees from Croatia were granted temporary status in Austria. Most of the 100,000, however, returned to Croatia after a few months.

As Croatia had not yet been recognized as an independent state, the entry of Croatians into Austrian territory was possible in line with the Austrian–Yugoslav Agreement on Visa Policies of 1965 – which gave a right to entry and residence for three months. The legal basis for the reception of the war 'refugees' was provided for by the new law on the reception of asylum seekers (*Bundesbetreuungsgesetz*), which had entered into force in August 1991. The main purpose of the new law was to create a new decentralized, flexible and modernized system for the reception of asylum seekers. This new law was also implemented later for temporarily displaced persons from Croatia and from Bosnia and Herzegovina with only small deviations.

The case of Bosnia and Herzegovina

The war in Bosnia and Herzegovina led to massive population displacements. About 1.1 million persons were displaced in the country and some 1.2 million left Bosnia and Herzegovina (BiH) for other countries. About

123

half of these went to Western Europe. The distribution of refugees from BiH in Western Europe turned out to be strikingly uneven. About 95 per cent arrived in just six Western European countries: Austria (about 95,000), Denmark (18,000), Germany (approximately 345,000), The Netherlands (23,500), Sweden (more than 60,000) and Switzerland (nearly 27,000). Meanwhile France received about 15,000, Norway 12,000, the UK only 6000, Italy 8000, Spain 2500, and Portugal 60 persons. The figures alone demonstrate the lack of a common European approach. Europe did not have at its disposal either cooperative structures for mass influxes of refugees or effective burden sharing, and the uneven burdens have led to tensions between EU countries.

Austria's reception of refugees from Bosnia and Herzegovina

Austria was one of the first Western European countries to be confronted with the mass influx of refugees from Bosnia and Herzegovina. From the beginning there was a political willingness to grant protection: public opinion towards the 'refugees' was positive and the private donations and offers for help were accordingly generous.

Since 1992 a total of some 95,000 'refugees' from BiH have sought refuge in Austria. Most of them were granted temporary protection and received official assistance. The largest inflow occurred in 1992, with some 50,000 persons fleeing to Austria. As a result of the active integration programme of the Austrian government, by July 1999 about 70,000 persons previously under temporary protection had been granted long-term residence permits and are integrated in Austria. Only about 700 Bosnian refugees were still under the prolonged temporary protection regime in Austria in 1999. From April 1992 to April 1998 a total of 1277 persons from BiH were recognized as Geneva Convention refugees. Some 10,000 persons returned on a voluntary basis to BiH and some 10,000 resettled to other countries.

The entry into Austria and the residence provisions for refugees from Bosnia and Herzegovina[9]   The first displaced persons resulting from the war in BiH arrived at the Austrian border in April 1992. Austria responded to the mass flight situation by creating a special legal basis for the admission and residence of the externally displaced persons as described above. Consequently, these 'refugees' were initially subject to existing agreements reached decades earlier between the Republic of Austria and the Socialist Federal Republic of Yugoslavia (SFRY), as well as new laws enacted in response to the mass movements from the conflicts in former Yugoslavia.

In 1992, when thousands of externally displaced persons from BiH sought refuge in other European countries, the Austrian government granted admission to Austrian territory by pragmatically continuing to apply the Austrian–Yugoslav Agreement on Visa Policies 1965, described above in the context of Croatia. Upon further review of the legal stipulations of this law, the Austrian authorities decided to offer a prolongation of the visa-free residence period from three to six months.

In July 1993, for the first time the legal framework for a temporary protection status (TPS) was established in Austria, when a time-limited right of residence without an individual eligibility procedure was introduced into the Austrian legal system by the enactment of the Residence Law. Section 12 of this law enables the federal government to pass decrees

> during times of heightened international tension, armed conflict or other circumstances that endanger the safety of entire population groups … and to order that directly affected groups of aliens who can find no protection elsewhere shall be accorded a temporary right of residence in the federal territory.

A decree concerning Bosnian displaced persons was immediately issued.[10] Citizens of BiH who had to leave their country of origin owing to armed conflict and were not able to find protection in another country were granted *en masse* a time-limited right of residence until 30 June 1994 provided that they had entered Austrian territory before 1 July 1993. Section 12 of the Residence Law was also applied after 1 July 1993 to persons who had entered Austria before 1 July 1993 and had identified themselves at the border control. In the following months and years the time limit was continuously extended: first for every half-year, then for a full year, and finally for seventeen months until 31 July 1998. In 1998 the decision was taken to lift temporary protection ultimately on 31 July 2000.

The integration of refugees from BiH into the Austrian labour market was facilitated by a decree issued by the Ministry for Labour and Social Affairs providing for possibilities to work, initially in specific employment categories and later in the private sector. In July 1992 the Minister for Labour and Social Affairs issued an ordinance designed to allow municipalities or humanitarian organizations to employ foreigners from regions of armed conflicts for a three-month period. In further ordinances the time limit was deleted, and the preferential treatment as regards labour permits (*Beschäftigungsbewilligung*) for displaced persons from Bosnia and Herzegovina over newly arriving 'normal' third country-nationals was expressly stated.

By the end of 1994 some 20,000 Bosnians had found a job and by end of 1996 the number was already more than 30,000. Although the majority of displaced persons from BiH were subject to section 12 of the Residence Act, the residence of a number of Bosnians was regulated under other legal provisions. Persons under temporary protection do not need to go through individual eligibility procedures. However, they may still apply for asylum with the Federal Asylum Agency (*Bundesasylamt*). Those citizens of BiH who applied for asylum were subject to the Asylum Law of 1991, which granted a temporary right of residence during the asylum proceedings (section 7 of the Asylum Law 1991), provided the applicant satisfied the following criteria: (a) direct arrival from a country of persecution, and (b) the submission of the application for asylum within one week of entry. In total, 4,477 persons from Bosnia and Herzegovina applied for asylum in Austria between 1 May 1992 and 8 April 1998, of whom 1277 persons had been granted asylum by the beginning of 1998.

The Austrian relief programme for refugees from Bosnia and Herzegovina
At the request of the Ministry of the Interior, the Austrian government agreed on 22 April 1992 to establish special assistance for displaced persons from BiH jointly financed and administered by the federal and provincial governments, with additional assistance in implementation from non-governmental organization. This aid programme, called the *Bund–Länder Aktion*, started on 1 May 1992 and provided necessary relief for refugees from the Bosnian conflicts. The *Bund–Länder Aktion* registered 91,400 displaced persons. It was also successful in incorporating several social aspects, including employment opportunities, education, social assistance, medical aid and insurance, and unemployment, maternity and paternity benefits.[11]

In accordance with Austrian education law, all children from BiH in Austria were integrated in state schools after the autumn of 1992 and were able to obtain bilingual instruction if necessary. Furthermore, languages courses were organized by the Austrian federal government together with the *Länder*, and in order to promote vocational training for young people from Bosnia, the federal government in March 1993 issued an ordinance of preferential treatment. Apprenticeship programmes required that non-nationals obtain a work permit (*Beschäftigungsbewilligung*) subject to the Law on the Employment on Non-Nationals.

Return of refugees from Bosnia and Herzegovina

The signing of the Dayton Agreement at the end of 1995 theoretically opened the way for the return of considerable numbers of refugees and displaced persons to their places of origin. However, given the slow pace of general implementation of the agreement in 1996, a certain pessimism spread during that year with regard to return prospects. As the general situation in BiH improved in 1997, returns from abroad increased in number while the internally displaced continued to move back to their places of origin. More than 25 per cent of all internally displaced persons had, by the summer of 1999, returned to their places of origin, and about 40 per cent of all refugees in Western Europe have now returned to the Federation area of BiH. However, returns of Serbian refugees presently in Yugoslavia (250,000) and of Croatian and Bosnian refugees in Croatia (255,000) have been minimal, and likewise returns of Croatians and Bosnians to the Serb entity and of Serbs to the Federation area have been very low.[12]

About 10,000 Bosnian refugees from Austria returned to BiH. Their repatriation was carried out on a voluntary basis. On 3 November 1994 a working agreement between the governments of Austria and Bosnia and Herzegovina was signed, concerning, *inter alia*, the provision of information to Bosnians living in Austria about their potential repatriation. Moreover, different projects were offered by the Austrian government, focusing on vocational training and improving professional skills in order to facilitate reintegration in BiH. The federal government initiated a special programme of financial support for the return of displaced persons under paragraph 12 of the Residence Law. Voluntary return should thereby either be based on projects funded by the EU, the Federal Chancellery or private institutions, or on an individual financial allowance of ATS 1,500 (109 euros) in the case of return.

Mass displacements from Kosovo at the end of the 1990s

Kosovo has a long tradition of labour migration to Western European countries. Between 1960 and the beginning of the 1980s about 150,000 Kosovar Albanians left as guest-workers for Western Europe, mainly for Switzerland, Germany and to a lesser degree for Austria. However, with increasing restrictions on immigration in these countries, many Kosovars made greater use of the asylum system as an entry channel. From 1985 to 1990 about 250,000 Kosovars applied for asylum in Western Europe. Although most of the asylum applications were rejected, the return of the rejectees could not be realized, owing to difficult negotiations with Belgrade on readmission agreements and their implementation. This led to an increase of the total Kosovar population in Western Europe to about 500,000 at the beginning of 1998, representing about 25 per cent of the total population of Kosovo. Although Germany, Switzerland and Sweden accounted for 85 per cent of the total Kosovar population in Western Europe, some 13,000 Kosovo Albanians were in Austria.

Emigration from Kosovo up to 24 March 1999

In the spring of 1998 the escalation of the conflict in Kosovo caused an increase in both internal displacements of the Kosovo population and emigration to neighbouring countries and Western Europe. Although most refugees from Kosovo found shelter in neighbouring countries, the influx of Kosovar Albanian asylum seekers in wider Europe increased sharply. Though Switzerland and Germany were traditional destination countries for Kosovar Albanians, Austria experienced a large increase of asylum claims in 1998. The number of asylum applications from the Federal Republic of Yugoslavia (FRY) rose from 90 in January to 210 in March and 1260 in September 1998 (September saw the highest number in 1998). The total number of asylum claims lodged in Austria in 1998 amounted to 6647, compared to 1084 in 1997. Table 6.1 shows the number of asylum applications by Yugoslav nationals submitted in Austria.

Mass displacement after NATO military intervention

The first three months of 1999 showed little change in the trend of asylum seekers from FRY to Austria, as the political, economic and humanitarian situation was still critical. In fact, numbers remained relatively high even during the negotiations for a peace treaty in Rambouillet, before the NATO military intervention.

Table 6.1 Asylum applications by Yugoslav nationals in Austria, 1998

Month	Applications
January	90
February	130
March	210
April	240
May	250
June	440
July	630
August	790
September	1260
October	1160
November	820
December	63
Total	6650

Source: UNHCR

Note: No distinction is made in official government statistics regarding ethnic origin, but it is implied that owing to the nature of this ethnic conflict, a large majority were from Kosovo.

Following the NATO air strikes starting on 24 March and ending on 12 June 1999, mass displacements from Kosovo to neighbouring countries developed dramatically. During the period of NATO attacks, the asylum applications from Kosovar Albanians in other European countries also increased sharply. A noticeable increase in the numbers of those seeking protection in Austria is demonstrated in Table 6.2. In Austria the number of asylum seekers went up in April and even more in May 1999, when the number compared with that for March had nearly doubled.

Austrian measures to cope with mass displacements in and from Kosovo

After the massive outflow of refugees from Kosovo following the beginning of NATO air strikes, the UN High Commissioner for Refugees, Sadako Ogata, on 26 March called on all neighbouring countries to keep the doors open for refugees from Kosovo. At the beginning of April 1999 the number of Kosovo refugees sheltering in the neighbouring countries amounted to about 400,000. As the mass outflow from Kosovo continued, the situation in the region deteriorated, owing to overcrowded refugee camps and poor infrastructure. It became clear that Western countries had to offer protection for refugees from Kosovo, as the region was no longer in a position to cope with the mass influx.

On 6 April 1999 UNHCR held a crisis meeting in Geneva concerning Kosovo. On that occasion the USA, Turkey, Sweden, Norway and Austria declared their willingness to evacuate Kosovar refugees from the neighbouring countries. Most EU states did not make any resettlement pledges, as the EU Ministers of the Interior were to meet the next day. On 7 April 1999 the Justice and Home Affairs (JHA) Council agreed that refugees from Kosovo were in need of protection:

Table 6.2 Monthly asylum applications by Yugoslav nationals in Austria, 1999

Month	Number
January	565
February	615
March	516
April	700
May	1340
June	1470
Total (6 months)	5206

Source: Austrian Ministry of the Interior

Despite the consensus that in principle protection should be given as extensively as possible within the region, the Council recognised that it might, for humanitarian reasons and to avoid the destabilisation of the main receiving countries in the region, prove necessary in the future to afford displaced persons protection and assistance outside the region of origin on a temporary basis for Kosovo refugees.[13]

The German EU presidency evoked the EU discussions on a burden-sharing system based on voluntary pledges for resettlement, and declared the willingness of Germany to receive 10,000 refugees. Austria decided to evacuate 5000 persons, and more pledges came from various other EU countries. Some EU member states, however, maintained that resettlement would be equivalent to assisting Yugoslavia's strategy in the mass expulsion.

Because of the lack of a common European position to handle the problem of Kosovar refugees, Austria did not take any decision concerning the admission of displaced persons from the conflict area until the EU Justice and Home Affairs Council meeting of 7 April 1999, when the agreement was reached that a certain number of displaced Kosovar Albanians should be evacuated from the region (mainly Macedonia) and be given temporary protection in European host countries. However, during the phase of mass flight from Kosovo from the end of March until beginning of June 1999, individual asylum applications lodged by Kosovar Albanians were generously handled and many persons from Kosovo were granted asylum (under the terms of the Geneva Convention) on grounds of suffering state persecution as members of an ethnic group. In 1999 about 2500 Kosovar Albanians were granted Convention status in Austria.

The refugee evacuation programme   Austria, in conjunction with several other EU member states, conducted an evacuation programme to take in a specific number of Kosovar refugees to alleviate the crowded conditions in many of the Macedonian refugee camps. The Austrian evacuation project lasted from 15 April to 8 June, and a total of 5115 Kosovar Albanians were accepted into Austria from Macedonian refugee camps.

Refugees were registered by a team of up to thirteen people from the Austrian Ministry of the Interior stationed in the Macedonian capital of Skopje, and working in cooperation with the UNHCR and the Macedonian authorities. The actual registration was largely conducted with the assistance of UNHCR and the International Organization for Migration (IOM) in the Macedonian refugee camps Stankovec I, Stankovec II and Čegrane.

Identity documents were issued by the Austrian team to those who were to be temporarily evacuated to Austria. The evacuation process was carried out with a total of 32 charter flights. Of the 5115 people evacuated, 2121 were children (309 of whom were under the age of 2 and 1812 under the age of 15). The distribution of Kosovo refugees under temporary protection is, worked out according to the population in each province as a percentage of the total Austrian population, as follows: Burgenland 3.85 per cent, Salzburg 6.46 per cent, Carinthia 7.87 per cent, Lower Austria 20.21 per cent, Upper Austria 18.65 per cent, Styria 17.15 per cent, Vorarlberg 2.08 per cent and Vienna 19.37 per cent.

The reception and right of residence in Austria for the evacuated Kosovar refugees was legally based on paragraph 29 of the Aliens Act 1997, providing temporary protection.

Temporary protection status for Kosovar Albanian refugees

The legal provision for a temporary right of residence was introduced into the Austrian legal system for the first time by the enactment of section 12 of the Residence Law 1993, and was applied in the case of refugees from Bosnia and Herzegovina as described above. This special provision on temporary protection is now section 29 of the new Aliens Law 1997, and enables the federal government to pass decrees during times of armed conflict or other circumstances that endanger the safety of entire population groups and to provide temporary right of residence in the federal territory.

On 27 April the Austrian government passed a decree on the basis of paragraph 29 of the Aliens Act 1997 that provides in article 1 for the right of residence for Kosovar Albanian refugees. The decree is binding until 31 December 1999.[14] According to the decree, temporary protection status (TPS) is granted to the following groups of persons from Kosovo who had to leave their country of origin owing to armed conflict and were able neither to return nor to find protection elsewhere:

1 Kosovo Albanians who have been evacuated from Macedonia within the internationally coordinated action (preference is given to persons who have relatives in Austria);
2 Kosovar Albanians, including spouses and minor children, who arrived before 15 April 1999 and who cannot return to Kosovo owing to the conflict. This does not apply to persons who have other residence titles;
3 Kosovo Albanians, including spouses and minor children, who have, according to the Austrian Interior Ministry security directorate, entry permits for the following reasons:
   • being the parent of minor children who are in Austria according sections 1 and section 2;

- being the minor child of parents who are in Austria according sections 1 and section 2;
- being a close relative of Kosovo Albanians who possess a residence title in Austria and whose livelihood is secured;
- being the spouse or minor child of a Kosovar Albanian who is entitled to stay in Austria according to section 15 or section 19 of the Asylum Law.

Paragraph 2 of decree section 29 provides for an increase in the annual quota for residence permits for family reunification for Kosovar Albanians who submitted applications before 15 April 1999, and who have joined their families in Austria. The additional quota is 895 for the year 1999.[15]

Temporary protection, as per paragraph 3, section 29, of the Austrian Alien Law, requires the documentation of this act in the refugees' passports or travel documents. Proof of this granting of temporary refuge is to be in the form of an EU sticker in the passport. Should the refugee not possess a legal, valid passport, a picture identification card will be issued in which the temporary residence status is to be documented.[16]

Joint federal and provincial relief programme (Bund–Länder Aktion)
Upon request from the Ministry of the Interior, the Austrian government agreed to establish special assistance for 'refugees' from Kosovo who are granted temporary protection according to section 29 of the residence law. The relief programme started on 1 April 1999 for a period of temporary protection relating to section 29, which is expected to be until 31 December 1999. The programme, called *Bund–Länder Aktion*, provides refugees from Kosovo with special assistance and is jointly administered by the federal and the provincial governments. Two-thirds of the expenses are to be paid by the federal government, one-third by the provincial governments. By 10 July 4880 people were registered in the relief programme for Kosovar Albanians. This programme includes the evacuation from Macedonia, the registration and the admission of the refugees, as well as the arrangement of housing facilities and food, which are organized in publicly owned or private accommodation (e.g. with family members). Moreover, medical aid and other supplies have to be provided, according to the regulations of the social welfare legislation and medical insurance is required for each person in the relief programme. Furthermore, information programmes, German-language courses and specific treatment for traumatized groups are organized. The Ministry for Education has organized special bilingual classes for Kosovar Albanian children.

The federal–provincial relief programme provides assistance for voluntary return as soon as the security situation in Kosovo allows for return. The return programme includes the travel arrangements (travel documents, travel tickets, transit arrangements in Macedonia, transfer from Macedonia to Kosovo). Originally a lump-sum payment of DM 430 (220 euros) for adults and DM 140 (72 euros) for children was also offered. Later, a flexible scale was used, ranging from 218 to 654 euros, dependent on the damage inflicted on the person's house in Kosovo.

Austria's camp in Shkodra   In response to the mass suffering of refugees, several international relief and aid organizations constructed camps in the border regions of Macedonia and Albania in order to provide these people with basic needs such as water, food and shelter. One of Austria's relief organizations, Nachbar in Not, in cooperation with the Austrian Broadcasting Corporation, Caritas, the Red Cross and other organizations, became one of the first groups to offer relief to the Kosovar Albanian refugees in the region. The relief programme of Nachbar in Not was mainly financed by private contributions from the Austrian people. One of the greatest contributions to help alleviate the problem of accommodation came in the form of a refugee camp in the Albanian town of Shkodra. The Austrian camp in Shkodra was designed to take in approximately 5500 refugees. The total number of refugees sheltered there reached about 3700, most of them from the Kosovar region of Ishtok. The Shkodra camp also offered medical stations for several thousand refugees. In early July 1999, when the conditions for return to Kosovo had improved significantly and most of the refugees had left the camp, Shkodra camp closed.

Improved situation in Kosovo   As the political situation in Kosovo improved, approximately 200 Kosovar Albanians (most of them from the group which had been evacuated from Macedonia, but also a smaller group of persons in the asylum procedure) expressed the desire to return to their homes. The Austrian Ministry of the Interior requested the IOM to organize the return home of those refugees wanting to return. The IOM then took over the organization of booking flights to Skopje, organizing reception at Skopje airport and travel arrangements into Kosovo with personal escorts. The Austrian Ministry of Interior issued an 'EU *laissez-passer*' passport for those refugees without proper travel documents. The IOM arranged a permit for crossing the Yugoslav–Macedonian border into Kosovo with the Macedonian authorities.

By 1 July 1999 about 11,000 refugees from Kosovo were under protection in Austria, 5105 people had a temporary protection status under section 29 after evacuation from Macedonia and nearly 6000 had other residence titles, most of them in connection with asylum procedures. Despite the changed political situation in Kosovo, the Austrian government did not take any decision about lifting the temporary protection provisions for Kosovar Albanian refugees, nor are there plans for the forced return of Kosovar Albanians.

Conclusion

Since the Second World War Austria has granted permanent or temporary protection to over 500,000 refugees from conflict areas; moreover, a total of approximately 2 million found shelter in Austria before resettling in other countries. However, between the influx of 180,000 refugees from Hungary in 1956-7 and the granting of temporary protection for about 11,000 Kosovar Albanian 'refugees', the national and international conditions for admission of refugees had changed significantly. A radical change began in the early 1990s when the bipolar structure between the Western and communist worlds disappeared. The repression exercised by authoritarian communist regimes was then removed as the main cause of flight to the West. The past decade was, however, marked by different nationalistic conflicts which resulting in the persecution and expulsion of thousands of victims through the actions of state-sponsored and non-state actors. In the 1990s Austria and other Western European states were thus countries of refuge for 'war refugees', mainly from former Yugoslavia. Moreover, the number of individual asylum applications from Eastern Europe, Asia and Africa began to rise in the same period.

Because of this completely changed situation, new cooperation structures on migration and asylum policy issues began to develop among Western European states. Austria joined these new cooperation efforts towards a harmonized migration and refugee policy in the EU. But as early as the beginning of the 1990s, prior to Austria's accession to the EU in 1995, Austria formulated new and significantly stricter migration and asylum policies. Additionally, Austria, in cooperation with other EU countries, introduced a number of changes in legislation – for example, the principles of a safe country of origin and safe third country in asylum law and the Dublin Convention.

The Austrian strategy with regard to the 1992 admission of conflict 'refugees' from Bosnia and Herzegovina and the 1999 measures towards Kosovo's 'refugees' show quite different approaches which to some extent emerged from the efforts of cooperation within the framework of the EU. In 1991, when the war in former Yugoslavia broke out, owing to the lack of harmonized European strategies and lacking national instruments for mass influx, Austria as a non-EU member state acted under the application of the existing national legal instruments and the relevant governmental ordinances to cope with the admission of approximately 95,000 displaced persons from Bosnia and Herzegovina. In relation to other states in Western Europe Austria proportionally admitted and integrated the highest number of refugees from Bosnia and Herzegovina. Unlike in previous crises the resettlement or redistribution of refugees among Western countries was no longer a viable solution (earlier Australia, the USA and Canada took in several hundred thousand refugees from Austria within the framework of migration quotas). The admission and integration of Bosnian refugees, aside from several warnings of foreign infiltration from right-wing political parties and labour market considerations from the unions, occurred without any notable security problems or socio-political conflicts.

Between 1992 and 1998–9, Western European states united to seek basic cooperation in the area of asylum policy. With regard to refugees from Kosovo, Austria had already applied the principle of safe third countries and the conclusion of readmission agreements. Because of the implementation of the bilateral and multilateral agreements, Kosovar Albanian refugees, especially those who came through Hungary, were turned back at the Hungarian border and possibly re-routed to other countries.

Although there was neither an EU policy of burden sharing nor a general rule of temporary protection in force at the outbreak of military conflicts in Kosovo, Austria's policy for the protection of refugees from Kosovo was in line with that of other EU member states. At the beginning of the mass flight from Kosovo, temporary protection was considered, in unanimity, under a joint scheme adopted by international organizations and the main countries of admission. However, a policy of evacuation was only introduced when the admission of hundreds of thousands of refugees in the neighbouring areas threatened to lead to a humanitarian catastrophe and political destabilization.

In total, approximately 6600 people from the Federal Republic of Yugoslavia applied for asylum in Austria in 1998 and 5205 (90 per cent of them ethnic Albanians) applied in the first six months of 1999. During the mass displacements of March to June 1999 Austria generously granted asylum according to the 1951 Geneva Convention. About 2500 Kosovar Albanians have been granted asylum. Austria participated relatively generously in the evacuation action by admitting 5115 people and applying the legal provisions for a temporary right of residence and the relief programme for war-displaced Kosovar Albanians.

The reception of war refugees from Kosovo was again well received by the public and has not led to any major political confrontations or debates on security issues. Since neither the mass influx of refugees from former communist countries nor the acceptance of nearly 95,000 Bosnian refugees has been seen as a security threat or as having had negative effects on Austrian national interests, the generous admission of war refugees from Kosovo was not perceived as a problem. The Austrian population generously offered assistance and reacted compassionately, as they had done in previous cases of mass influx of war refugees.

Although far-right parties refer to immigration problems and the risks for Austria's safety and its economic, social and cultural development, in political debates – especially during election campaigns – the admission of war refugees from Bosnia and Herzegovina and from Kosovo has not been an anti-immigration issue.

The Austrian media, particularly the populist daily papers with a large circulation, presented the influx of Kosovar Albanian refugees not as a risk for Austria but rather as a challenge for the Austrian population. Thus, large sums of private donations were collected, which were transferred to Albania and Macedonia to keep relief activities there going.

Acknowledgements

I would like to express my gratitude to Mr Alexander Mirescu for his assistance in the preparation of this chapter.

Notes

1. S. Sassen, *Migranten, Siedler, Flüchtlinge: von de Massenauswanderung zur Festung Europa* (Frankfurt am Main: Fischer Taschenbuchverlag, 1996).
2. F. Löschnak, *Menschen aus der Fremde: Flüchtlinge, Vertriebene, Gastarbeiter* (Vienna: Verlag Holzhausen, 1993), p. 2.
3. B. Zierer, 'Willkommene Ungarnflüchtlinge 1956?', in G. Heiss and O. Rathkolb (eds) *Asylland wider Willen* (Vienna: Jugend & Volk, 1995), p. 163.
4. G.J.L. Coles, 'Temporary refuge and the large scale influx of refugees', in *Australian Yearbook of International Law* (Canberra, 1981), pp. 191f.
5. V. Vales, 'Die tschechoslowakischen Flüchtlinge 1968–1969', in Heiss and Rathkolb (eds) *Asylland wider Willen*, pp. 172–8.
6. H. Alizadeh, *Österreichische Flüchtlingspolitik der 70er* (Vienna: Jugend & Volk, 1995), pp. 188–92.
7. J. Widgren, *A Comparative Analysis of Entry and Asylum Policies in Selected Western Countries* (Vienna: ICMPD, 1994), p. 16.
8. ICMPD (International Centre for Migration Policy Development), *Registration for TPS: On the Creation of an EU-wide Registration System for Persons under Temporary Protection following Mass Influx* (Vienna: ICMPD, 1999), p. 20.
9. The information on Austria's reception of refugees from Bosnia and Herzegovina is a summary of the analysis provided by N. Marschik in ICMPD, *Registration for TPS*, final report and annexes.
10. *Bundesgesetzblatt* (BGBl), 1993/402. This decree was enacted on 25 June 1993, although its legal basis – section 12 of the Aliens Law – entered into force only on 1 July 1993.

11. See ICMPD, *Registration for TPS*, p. 23.
12. See J. Widgren, 'Rückkehr nach Bosnien-Herzgowina: Lektionen für eine europäische Migrationspolitik, 4 (1999),' *Internationale Politik* 31–8.
13. *Migration News Sheet*, May 1999, p. 5f.
14. BGBl.II, 1999/133.
15. *Ibid.*
16. *Wiener Zeitung*, 'Österreich Aufenthaltsrecht für vertriebene Kosovo Albaner', 21 April 1999.

Bibliography

Books and journal articles

Alizadeh, H., *Österreichische Flüchtlingspolitik der 70er Jahre* (Vienna: Jugend & Volk, 1995).

Coles, G.J.L., 'Temporary refuge and the large scale influx of refugees', *Australian Yearbook of International Law* (Canberra, 1981), pp. 189–212.

Heiss, G. and Rathkolb, O. (eds), *Asylland wider Willen* (Vienna: Jugend & Volk, 1995).

Kjaerum, M., 'Temporary protection in Europe in the 1990s', *International Journal of Refugee Law* 5 (1994), 444–56.

Löschnak, F., *Menschen aus der Fremde: Flüchtlinge, Vertriebene, Gastarbeiter* (Vienna: Verlag Holzhausen, 1993).

Migration News Sheet, May 1999.

Sassen, S., *Migranten, Siedler, Flüchtlinge: von der Massenauswanderung zur Festung Europa* (Frankfurt am Main: Fischer Taschenbuchverlag, 1996).

Selm-Thorburn, J. van, *Refugee Protection in Europe: Lessons of the Yugoslav Crisis* (The Hague: Martinus Nijhoff, 1998).

Stacher, I. and Martijn Pluim, M., 'The Kosovo crisis: a new migration challenge for Europe', in IOM/ICMPD, *Migration in Central and Eastern Europe* (Geneva: IOM, 1999), 51–65.

Vales, V., 'Die tschechoslowakischen Flüchtlinge 1968-1969', in G. Heiss and O. Rathkolb (eds) *Asylland wider Willen* (Vienna: Jugend & Volk Edition, 1995), pp. 172–81.

Widgren, J., 'Rückkehr nach Bosnien-Herzegowina: Lektionen für eine europäische Migrationspolitik', *Internationale Politik* 4: 31–8 (1999).

Zierer, B., 'Willkommene Ungarnflüchtlinge 1956?', in G. Heiss and O. Rathkolb (eds) *Asylland wider Willen* (Vienna: Jugend & Volk, 1995), pp. 157–71.

Reports

ICMPD, *Registration for TPS: On the Creation of an EU-wide Registration System for Persons under Temporary Protection following Mass Influx* (Vienna: ICMPD, 1999).

International Organization for Migration/ICMPD, *Migration in Central and Eastern Europe* (Geneva: IOM, 1999).

Kälin, W., 'Reconciling temporary protection with refugee and human rights law', in *Towards a Concept of Temporary Protection* (Bern: UNHCR, 1996).

Widgren, J., *A Comparative Analysis of Entry and Asylum Policies in Selected Western Countries* (Vienna: ICMPD, 1994).

Newspaper articles

'Österreich Aufenthaltsrecht für vertriebene Kosovo Albaner', *Wiener Zeitung*, 21 April 1999.

CHAPTER SEVEN

Italy: Gateway to Europe, but not the gatekeeper?

CHRISTOPHER HEIN

Introduction

Italy was in various ways closer to the crisis in Kosovo than any other of the countries dealt with in this book. Kosovo is in the almost immediate geographic neighbourhood of Italy, separated only by the narrow Adriatic Sea and small strips of Montenegro or northern Albania. Most of the NATO aircraft which took part in the bombing campaign set out from Italian territory, especially from the Aviano base in north-east Italy, on their way to Belgrade and other Serbian cities. Local people were eyewitnesses to the military activities on a daily basis. Missiles and bombs were found in the fishing grounds of the Adriatic Sea. Some Italian fishermen were injured and for a time fishing became dangerous and was forbidden in certain zones. For several months the civil airports of the Puglia region, Bari and Brindisi, were closed for security reasons. Frequent news stories appeared about alleged Serbian military aircraft crossing the sea, destined for Italy.

The geographic situation also made Italy the principal first country of arrival for Kosovar refugees within the European Union (EU). Daily arrivals in rubber dinghies and fishing boats crossing the channel of Otranto from Albania were reported for weeks and months in the media. The dramatic circumstances of these arrivals, the number of people, including children, killed or injured during the trip, and the frequent incidents in which smugglers threw refugees overboard, all created an extremely alarmed atmosphere.

From March to June 1999 Italians lived with the fear that the war could spread to directly involve Albania and Montenegro, just a few kilometres away from Italian territory, and with the fear that the NATO shield would not prevent Serbian forces or terrorists from making revenge attacks on Italy. There was also the fear that the immense business of smuggling tens of thousands of refugees from Albania to the Italian coast could extend also to the trafficking of weapons and drugs. The internal debate on Italy's participation in NATO warfare brought the government close to collapse. At the same time, the pictures broadcast daily of atrocities committed inside Kosovo and the physical exodus of masses of terrified people into Albania and Macedonia provoked an unprecedented wave of humanitarian solidarity, independent of political opinions or convictions.

In this chapter explanations are offered for the various phases of political and public reaction to the arrival of Kosovar refugees, in the framework of the experiences with immigrants and refugees within Italy over the past ten years. The particular situation of Italy within the EU's asylum policy is highlighted. Particular attention will be given to the concept of temporary and 'humanitarian' protection. The context is sketched through an analysis of Italy's development from a country of emigration to one of immigration. It is shown that Italy has not yet created a role for itself as an asylum country, in spite of the increasing number of 'refugee' arrivals. The majority of these refugees either transit Italy or resort to the apparently easier immigration channels, including the hope of falling under a general amnesty after a period of illegality. For this reason, the chapter concludes, resort to Convention status in the case of mass influxes would not be the most pragmatic way to achieve a legal status for those in genuine need of protection in Italy. Rather, temporary protection on an *ad hoc* basis seems to be the optimal solution for the Italian state, society and for the refugees, at least in the absence of a protection-maximizing EU-level approach.

Evolution from emigration to immigration country

To understand Italy's current asylum policy it is important to recall that for a period of 150 years until the mid-1970s Italy was an emigration country and that over the years around 27 million Italians have gone abroad, mainly for economic reasons.[1] Up to the early 1950s South America, the USA, Canada and Australia were the main destination countries for Italian emigrants. More recently migrants went as 'guest-workers' to European countries, especially Germany, Belgium, Switzerland and France. It is only over the past twenty years that Italy has developed into an immigration country, receiving migrants and refugees mainly from Eastern Europe, the Balkans, North Africa and the Philippines. Today there are still traces of a widespread mentality in public opinion as well as in political and administrative circles which considers Italy to be a small, overcrowded country where – in principle – there is no space for people from abroad (except tourists, of course).

From the end of Second World War until recent times, Italy has been mainly a transit country for refugees. During the Cold War period there was tacit agreement in the West that Italy, like Austria and Yugoslavia, was to be considered as a country of first safe haven for refugees from the Eastern bloc. A number of states, especially the USA, Canada, Australia and New Zealand, but initially also Scandinavian countries, offered generous resettlement opportunities to almost all the refugees arriving in Italy in that period.

This scene changed dramatically with the fall of the Berlin Wall and all its consequences. However, what has not changed so quickly is the mentality developed over many years which says, in a nutshell, 'Please come in, but please don't stay.'

At the same time, important parts of society, some church-linked, some not, have been promoting a fundamental change of attitude (and were doing so even before 1989). In these circles the increasing number of immigrants and refugees has been regarded as a positive element for the development of the country, and the ethical duty to receive them and to help them in the difficult process of enduring integration has always been stressed.

From its first legislation on foreign workers in 1986 to the present day (October 1999), Italy has adopted a policy of periodically regularizing illegal foreigners present in the country. In four different exercises of this 'labour amnesty', almost 1 million illegal foreigners have been converted into legal immigrants and represent today the majority of the non-Italian population with a legal status in Italy.[2] In comparison with this figure, and also when compared with other European countries, the number of recognized refugees and of those who have been admitted on the basis of family reunion is fairly small. As a matter of fact, an unknown number of *de facto* refugees prefer to make use of the regularization opportunity or to wait for the next exercise of this kind, rather than undergo the tiresome and uncertain asylum procedure.[3] This particular situation also explains the low figures in the asylum statistics. A similar story holds for family members of migrants or refugees, who also resort easily to illegal entry and residence while awaiting regularization, rather than attempting the official, but difficult, family reunification process.

These factors may also explain why it is that in Italian public opinion asylum has rarely been an issue of debate and interest, whereas immigration has been a constant theme. Only in very recent times can a more widespread understanding of the concept of refugee protection be observed. The dramatic circumstances under which thousands of Kurds and Kosovars have arrived and continue to arrive on the southern coast, along with the daily news reports on the situation in the areas of origin of these refugees, and, not least, the debate about the asylum request of the Kurdish PKK (Kurdish Workers' Party) leader, Abdullah Ocalan, in November 1998, have contributed to making headway into what generally is perceived as a kind of immigration quagmire, in which no distinction is made between the causes of arrival of foreigners and their different needs.

The legal framework

Until the 1990s Italy had two limited means of granting asylum. One, the 1951 Geneva Convention, was restricted by adherence to the geographical limitation. The other, the broad constitutional right to asylum, was unused, owing to the absence of an apparatus for its implementation. These two sources of refugee protection, and the changes the 1990s have brought to them both, will be assessed in this section, forming a background to the empirical nature of the situation surrounding the protection of Bosnians and, later, Kosovars in Italy.

From Italy's ratification of the 1951 Geneva Convention in 1954 up to 1990, when the so-called 'Martelli Law' entered into force, the right to asylum was effectively governed by the Convention itself and by a letter of understanding between the Italian government and the United Nations High Commissioner for Refugees (UNHCR). Italy had signed the Convention with the geographical limitation clause and with reservations to articles 17 and 18 regarding the right to work. As a consequence, only foreigners from Europe could apply for refugee status, leaving, until 1990, the whole responsibility of protection and assistance for non-European refugees in Italy in the hands of the UNHCR, which conducted a recognition procedure under the terms of its own mandate.

The provision of the constitution of 1948, which guarantees the right of asylum to foreigners who cannot exercise in their own countries the fundamental rights enshrined in the Italian constitution (article 10, paragraph 3), had no practical effect in the absence of implementing legislation. This constitutional right to asylum is unique in Europe in that it does not use the term 'persecution' to define a person's need of protection, but considers the impossibility of the effective exercise of fundamental rights as the principal basis for determining a protection need. Italy's own constitution is taken as the measure of the rights which should be exercised in any country of origin of asylum seekers. This extremely broad definition, which is explained by the experiences of many 'fathers of the constitution' who had been forced into exile under Mussolini's fascism, made it difficult to enact constitutional asylum through precise legal provisions for a long period of time.

Both the application of Convention status and the use of the constitutional right to asylum have undergone changes in the 1990s. As far as the Convention is concerned, law no. 39 of 1990, the Martelli Law, which constituted the first comprehensive Aliens Law, brought changes for protection in the only article dedicated to refugees. The geographical limitation and the reservations to the 1951 Convention were lifted. In addition, a minimum basis of rules on admission of asylum seekers, recognition, appeal procedures and an assistance mechanism were set out in that article. This law still, in 1999, governs all these aspects of protection, along with a number of decrees and administrative circulars which define the details on procedure and assistance.

During the 1990s, major refugee emergency situations have revealed the inadequacy of the existing legislation for dealing with these caseloads and forced the government and Parliament to adopt a series of *ad hoc* rules regarding specific refugee groups, and to develop, on a case-by-case basis, the concepts of humanitarian status and temporary protection outside the 1951 Convention and the established procedures. Emergency measures have to a great extent overruled the 'normal' ways of obtaining protection and assistance.

Meanwhile, an important ruling of the Italian Supreme Court (*Corte di Cassazione*) in 1997 has changed the legal scenario with regard to constitutional asylum. According to the court, article 10 of the constitution provides for a subjective right of the person, immediately applicable also in the absence of enforcement legislation and distinct from refugee status under the 1951 Geneva Convention. A new procedure for obtaining the recognition of the right to asylum was set by that ruling: the asylum seeker can make his or her claim directly to the civil court. One of the first cases to be dealt with under this procedure was the claim of Abdullah Ocalan, leader of the Kurdish PKK party, who had requested the constitutional right to asylum while staying in Italy at the end of 1998. The civil court of Rome ruled in October 1999 in favour of the applicant, in spite of the fact that he had in the meantime been forcibly returned to Turkey from Kenya, jailed and sentenced to death. Ocalan's simultaneous claim for recognition of Convention refugee status had, prior to this ruling, not been decided upon by the Central Commission on Recognition of Refugee Status (CCRRS) in substance, but rejected on the basis that the applicant could not be heard by the Commission owing to his absence from the country.

In 1997 the government presented a draft bill on 'the right to asylum and humanitarian protection' to Parliament. The bill was approved by the Senate in November 1998 with numerous amendments which the Italian Refugee Council and other non-governmental organizations (NGOs) had advocated. The text finally came under debate at the first chamber of Parliament (*Camera dei Deputati*) in late 1999. After more than fifty years, the draft bill aims at enforcing the constitutional asylum right by establishing one single status and one single procedure for both Convention and constitutional refugees.[4]

In March 1998 a new Aliens Law (law no. 40/98) entered into force. The

UNHCR and non-governmental organizations (NGOs) had successfully advocated that two separate pieces of legislation be drafted, separating immigration and asylum, expecting, however, that the two draft laws would be approved simultaneously. However, various emergency situations prevented the more rapid adoption of the asylum bill. The Aliens Law includes a provision on temporary protection which the government thought would be better placed in the immigration framework rather than in that of asylum. Moreover, the Aliens Law provides for the issuance of a humanitarian residence permit in cases where there are 'serious reasons, in particular of humanitarian nature or resulting from constitutional or international obligations' (article 5, paragraph 6). The CCRRS, when rejecting a claim, frequently recommends that the aliens police issue such a permit to the applicant, in the light of the situation he or she would face if returned to the country of origin. The humanitarian residence permit, issued for a period of one year and renewable, also includes the right to work, in line with details formulated in relevant administrative circulars. With regard to family reunion, the 'humanitarian refugee' has in general to fulfil the requirements of non-EU citizens in Italy.

Humanitarian status and temporary protection

Italy's asylum statistics over the past decade show clearly the very limited quantitative importance of the application of the 1951 Geneva Convention and the related procedure for recognition of refugee status, in comparison with the number of refugees who have found protection in the form of 'humanitarian residence permits'.

It is estimated that no more than 20,000 Convention refugees live in Italy. A total of 52,500 people have applied for Convention refugee status over the past ten years (1989–98). During the same period 8000 Somalis, 18,000 Albanians who arrived in 1991, 70,000 citizens from former Yugoslavia, 15,000 Albanians who arrived in 1997 and 25,000 persons from Kosovo have obtained a humanitarian status under legislation designed particularly for these groups. Approximately 10,000 refugees from other countries, mainly Kurds from Turkey and Iraq, have obtained a similar status under the provisions of the Aliens Law after rejection of their claims for Convention refugee status. Thus a total number of approximately 146,000 people have been granted supplementary forms of protection. However, many of these are no longer residing in Italy: they have either reached, irregularly, other European countries, especially Germany and Switzerland, or returned voluntarily to their home countries. Others have transformed their status to that of immigrants under the various regularization exercises during this period, and now show up in the immigration rather than in the asylum statistics. Therefore, it is virtually impossible to determine how many refugees or *de facto* refugees are actually living in Italy under the various statuses.

The resort to *ad hoc* measures to provide some kind of protection outside the frame of the 1951 Geneva Convention, the Martelli Law and the normal recognition procedures started in March 1991 when, in just a few days, some 27,000 Albanians crossed the Adriatic Sea to the Puglia region. Their claims for Convention refugee status were, in an extremely accelerated procedure, rejected, with the exception of some 900 cases. However, the general opinion was that they could not or should not be forcibly returned to Albania. A similar influx in August 1991, after the first democratic elections in Albania, met a different response: all were rejected immediately and returned to their home country, which was now considered 'safe'.

Similarly, refugees from Somalia, not recognized under the terms of the 1951 Convention and considered by CCRRS as victims of civil war, and not individually persecuted, obtained humanitarian status under a special decree in September 1992.[5] In September 1992 law no. 390/92 provided for the issuance of a humanitarian residence permit to all persons originating from the former Yugoslav republics.

The sudden arrival at the Puglia coast of some 16,000 Albanians in March 1997 provoked an intensive debate about how to deal with this situation. Their departure had clearly been caused not by persecution in Albania but by total civil disorder and generalized violence in the country. For the first time in Italy, the term 'temporary protection' was used in an *ad hoc* decree, which provided for a humanitarian residence permit, without the right to work, for a limited period of three months, later extended till November 1997. After that, very few Albanians were, in fact, forcibly returned, since those who had found work or a job offer were allowed to remain as immigrants, and others could claim a prolonged need of protection.

Finally, in May 1999, the government applied the temporary protection clause of the 1998 Aliens Law in favour of refugees from Kosovo until 31 December 1999, with the possibility of extension after that date.

It is evident that the vast majority of refugees who arrived and remained in Italy in the 1990s obtained protection without being recognized as refugees under the 1951 Convention. With respect to persons fleeing from the major crisis areas, it may be said that almost all the respective caseloads have been dealt with by the various *ad hoc* measures. From a statistical point of view the application of the Refugee Convention has been the exception, and other forms of protection the rule.

This is surprising when one considers that in the cases of refugees from former Yugoslavia and those from Kosovo at least, there has been the option of either making an individual refugee claim or the granting of temporary protection. Unlike many other countries, Italy has never frozen the examination of individual asylum applications. What is more, in some instances the material assistance provided to persons with a humanitarian status was even better than that for asylum seekers and recognized Convention refugees.

With regard to the level of rights, in several situations, specifically with regard to Albanians, Somalis and refugees from former Yugoslavia, during an initial period the status of the people concerned has been highly precarious. There was an obligation to renew the residence permit after three months, with no access to higher education and no right to family reunification. Only after living in such a fragile situation for a certain period of time, between one and two years, and after strong advocacy work by NGOs, were the level of rights and the duration of the residence permit increased by administrative decrees or circulars. This scenario will be returned to in discussion of the Bosnian case and the lessons learned below.

During the second, more secure period of protection, there was the full right to wage-earning employment, self-employment and access to university education. With regard to family reunion, until the Aliens Law of March 1998 even Convention refugees had no privileged legal treatment. Their status was, in this regard, the same as that of immigrants and non-EU nationals in general. Only the reform of the immigration legislation provided for the right to family reunion under the same conditions as for EU citizens.[6] However, in the case of refugees from former Yugoslavia and from Kosovo, some efforts were made to facilitate the arrival of close family members by accepting the applicants' declaration on the family link instead of insisting on documented evidence.

To summarize, the frequent resort to the introduction of group-specific regulations on humanitarian protection was caused by the following elements. The first was the sudden arrival of considerable numbers of persons fleeing their homeland under dramatic circumstances and arriving as (very visible) 'boat people' on Italy's Adriatic coast, as was the case for Albanians in 1991 and 1997 and Kosovars in the spring of 1999. In these situations the government considered that the normal machinery of status determination could not cope with such numbers and/or there was no point in taking individual decisions on refugee claims in view of the group nature of the causes of flight. Second, humanitarian status was introduced in order to create a legal basis for residence in the country of those persons who were not determined to be Convention refugees, but who nevertheless could not be sent back. This applied in particular to refugees from Somalia and from the Turkish and Iraqi areas of Kurdistan who arrived in considerable numbers, but over an extended period of time. The third element was the supposed temporary character of protection needs, in particular with regard to Albanians in 1997 and Kosovar Albanians in 1999, where immediate protection and assistance provided under a temporary regime was deemed to be the adequate answer, rather than Convention refugee status. Finally, the absence of a comprehensive and organic asylum law required legislative interventions on a case-by-case basis, especially in situations which public opinion also perceived to have the nature of an 'emergency'.

Reception of refugees during the Bosnian war

According to estimates, a total of about 90,000 refugees from Croatia, Bosnia and Herzegovina, Serbia and Macedonia were received in Italy during the period from 1991 to early 1996. Out of this total figure, 70,000 refugees have been granted a humanitarian residence permit. More than 8000 Roma from Bosnia, Serbia and Macedonia have never succeeded in obtaining such a permit even if they were, in principle, entitled to it. They have been prevented from regularizing their sojourn even after years in Italy on the basis of real or alleged records of (petty) crime, their refusal to contact the authorities and, quite simply, the widespread negative or even hostile attitude towards 'gypsies'.

Some 5000 former Yugoslav refugees joined family members and obtained a residence permit for family reunion. Others made use of the possibility of regularizing their situation as migrants under a 'labour amnesty' law. Others transited through Italy *en route* to various destinations, mainly in Western Europe. Only a few hundred made a refugee claim under the 1951 Geneva Convention and were recognized as Convention refugees in Italy.

During the first months of the conflict in former Yugoslavia, from 1991 to May 1992, the 'ordinary' asylum request constituted the only means of obtaining a legal status. When the number of asylum seekers from the former Yugoslav Republic increased, Italy was among the first countries to adopt special legislation providing for the issuance of humanitarian residence permits. Even prior to the UNHCR recommendation of July 1992 regarding temporary protection, a decree-law of 27 May 1992 opened the possibility for issuing humanitarian entry visas at the borders. Law no. 390 of September 1992, which converted the governmental decree into parliamentary law, addressed the need to provide humanitarian aid in the war-affected areas and at the same time the matters of the status of and assistance to persons arriving in Italy from those areas.

The term *sfollati* (displaced person) is used, reflecting the prevailing opinion that their protection need, and therefore status, was based on their displacement for war-related reasons and not on persecution on ethnic and religious grounds.

Law no. 390 established first of all the principle that all *sfollati* have the right to enter the territory without filing individual asylum requests. Parliament amended the governmental draft by introducing the clause 'without distinction whatsoever according to nationality, ethnic group or religion'. The application of the law revealed that this clause was not superfluous or rhetorical, but of great importance, especially with regard to Roma and Sinti, as indicated above.[7]

Even if the term is not explicitly mentioned, law no. 390 is meant as a measure of 'temporary protection'. During a first phase, residence permits were issued for a period of only three months, with no right to work or to family reunion. Only after strong interventions from NGOs, and in view of the continuation of the conflict, to which no end seemed to be in sight, was the status of the displaced persons improved, in 1993-4, by the extension of residence permit to one year, 'automatically' renewable and comprising the right to work under conditions equal to those applying to Italian citizens, the right to higher education and the right to family reunification. The option to request Convention refugee status was given at all times, but very few made use of it, most preferring the faster way of obtaining protection and assistance as *sfollati*.

The means of arrival from Croatia first, and Bosnia and Serbia afterwards, was totally different from that of Kosovar refugees later on. There were no, or very few, boat people yet. Refugees arrived via the land border with Slovenia or by regular ferry boats to Ancona, Trieste and other Adriatic seaports. In some instances, sealed overcrowded trains transited through Slovenia and arrived at Trieste. The question of evacuation from Bosnia was not really on the agenda. Governments and public opinion followed wholeheartedly the UNHCR policy of 'protection *in loco*' and welcomed the establishment of UN protected (or 'safe') areas on Bosnian territory. Italy participated in a small evacuation programme for medical reasons. Injured or sick persons were airlifted to Falconara on the Adriatic coast and residence permits were granted on medical grounds.

Meanwhile, several thousand refugees were brought to Italy under private initiatives. Local associations and groups of families organized a kind of spontaneous evacuation and guaranteed assistance and lodgings for these persons. Law no. 390 provided the legal basis for this operation, which anyway was 'tolerated' by the authorities. Facilitating the arrival of undocumented foreigners is a crime under the ordinary laws relating to aliens, but the transfer of refugees from former Yugoslavia was, even if not in line with official government policy, dictated by overriding humanitarian concerns. Moreover, it did not cost the state anything since the whole operation was financed privately.

Fewer than 3000 refugees were actually assisted directly by the Ministry of the Interior in collective centres in northern Italy. The vast majority were hosted privately through NGO networks or assisted by municipalities. In a few instances the government accorded local authorities a financial contribution for promoting the integration of groups of Roma from Bosnia and Serbia.

With the changing scenarios of the war, it was felt necessary, in 1994, to define more clearly the term *sfollati* and to stop the policy of indiscriminate leave to enter Italian territory. An ordinance of July 1994 excluded citizens of Macedonia and Slovenia from the benefits of law no. 390. The same act established an interesting model of legal transfer to Italy: the UNHCR agreed to issue a 'protection letter' to those refugees or internally displaced persons who could not be adequately protected in the area. On this basis, the nearest Italian consulate could then issue a 'protection visa' and arrange for resettlement to Italy. However, for a number of bureaucratic and procedural reasons, the model was actually applied in very few cases.

Law no. 390 had also established a round table on the coordination of aid to Yugoslav refugees, for both displaced persons inside the region and those present in Italy. Chaired by the Minister of Social Solidarity, participants in the round table included various ministries, international organizations such as the UNHCR and International Organization for Migration (IOM), local authorities, trade unions and NGOs. For four years this coordinating effort managed to resolve not only questions of logistics and the distribution of humanitarian relief items, but also questions of the protection of refugees, including the 'smooth' cessation of humanitarian protection after the Dayton Agreement of December 1995. After Dayton, the Ministry of Foreign Affairs entrusted the IOM to conduct a study on the refugees' willingness to return voluntarily. The most frequent reply was 'In principle yes, but not yet.'

Until mid-1997, humanitarian residence permits were renewed without any particular conditions being attached, and even issued to persons who had arrived after the Dayton Agreement. An ordinance of the Prime Minister of July 1997 allowed the extension of the permits for another year, but declared law no. 390 no longer applicable for new arrivals.[8] Finally, another ordinance of August 1998 declared the cessation of humanitarian protection, offering the following three alternatives: an asylum claim under the terms of the 1951 Geneva Convention; conversion of the humanitarian residence permit into an immigration permit valid for two years on condition of showing evidence of a job offer; or a permit on humanitarian grounds based on aliens laws no. 40/98 for persons unable to work for personal, health or age reasons.[9]

In other words, there has never been a question of forced return to Bosnia, Serbia or Croatia from Italy, except for those former refugees who for one reason or another had been unable to obtain a residence permit under law no. 390 before 1997 – and these were mainly people of Roma origin.

Reaction to the Kosovo refugee crisis: keeping them there or bringing them in?

The exodus from Kosovo and the arrival of Kosovar Albanians in Italy did not start in March 1999. In the second half of 1998, asylum seekers from Kosovo were already the biggest national group among asylum seekers in Italy.[10] However, the public paid little attention to the events in Serbia, and the arrival of people from Kosovo was not yet perceived as an 'emergency'.

During the winter of 1998-9, rumours intermittently spread that many thousands of Kosovars had gathered at the Albanian coast, especially at Vlore, waiting only for the right moment to cross the Adriatic. Arrivals at Puglia's coast do not depend only on the situations in the various countries of origin of asylum seekers who transit through Albania, and on the financial means for paying the smugglers; they also, and in fact largely, depend on weather conditions. It has been observed, over the years, that the number of arrivals, whether Kurds, Albanians or Kosovars, increases sharply in the month of March when the sea is calm.

In 1999 March also saw the failure of the Rambouillet peace talks and the start of the NATO bombings on 24 March. During the first two weeks after that date, many of those Kosovars who had previously sought refuge in Albania crossed the Adriatic by small boats organized by smugglers. On average some 200 people, 40 per cent of whom were minors, arrived every night on the beaches of the southern part of the Puglia region. An unknown number of refugees were killed when crossing the Otranto Channel, thrown overboard by the smugglers in order to reduce the weight of the boat and to be faster in escaping from the vessels of the Italian coastguard. Others arrived with serious illnesses and injuries. Still others were rescued by Italian vessels on the high seas. The Italian mass media reported daily on these incidents, together with the news concerning the bombing of Serbian cities and the mass deportations from Kosovo. Until early April politicians close to the government, and even the Prime Minister, were publicly raising the question of legal and protected transferral of refugees from Albania to Italy, stressing, however, that such a move would require prior agreement on the distribution of the refugees within the framework of the EU.

Following contingency planning, 25,000 bed-places were prepared at a former military airport in the northern part of the Puglia region for the reception of refugees via Albania on a large scale. NGOs had strongly advocated such a legal transfer operation from Albania, considering this the only effective alternative to the criminal smuggling of persons and the intolerable circumstances under which the spontaneous arrivals of refugees across the Adriatic had previously taken place.

However, in early April the government suddenly changed its attitude: it dropped any idea of such a plan and publicly promoted and strongly defended the solution of 'reception in the region'. The following arguments were used in support of this policy. First, any relocation of Kosovars would mean support for ethnic cleansing. Every effort had to be made to keep the Kosovar Albanians in Kosovo or at least as close as possible to the province. Second, in view of the government's conviction that the war would be of short duration and that the NATO bombing would have an immediate effect on the government of the Federal Republic of Yugoslavia and the Serbian militia in Kosovo, a quick and easy return of refugees should have priority, whereas relocation to Italy or other countries would make rapid repatriation difficult. Third, the Albanian government had formally expressed the wish to keep all Kosovar refugees in Albania, stressing the natural hospitality the Albanian population would give to 'their' people fleeing or deported from Kosovo.[11] Fourth, humanitarian aid to refugees could be provided at far less cost and for more people in Albania in comparison to the expense which would have occurred in Italy or in other Western countries.

In a meeting with the Italian Refugee Council on 23 April, the Minister of the Interior stated these arguments and also informed those present that Italy was trying to promote 'reception in the region' through bilateral relations with Bulgaria, Greece and Romania. The government was resolutely opposed to the perceived creation of a pull factor which the Italian preparation for the large-scale reception of Kosovar refugees would cause. This was also the reason for hesitation with respect to introducing a temporary protection regime.

At the same time, Italy actually made a great effort to build up reception centres in Albania, starting with two camps in Kukës, in the immediate proximity of the Kosovo border. The government publicly accused the UNHCR of not having made an adequate emergency response in Albania. The government supported a private fund-raising operation called *Arcobaleno* (Rainbow), which collected some 130 billion lire (67 million euros) in a short period of time, destined mainly for assistance programmes in Albania, in addition to the direct contributions of the Italian central government and the authorities of the Italian regions.

However, and in spite of these efforts, refugees continued to arrive daily by sea, and even the deployment of Italian police in Albania did not bring much of a reduction in the steady flow.

The UNHCR had already, on 6 April 1999, launched an appeal for humanitarian evacuations from the Former Yugoslav Republic of Macedonia (FYROM). Italy finally joined the many other countries heeding this appeal only on 4 May, announcing an initial quota of 10,000 persons. This delay in participating in the programme may be explained by the fact that by joining the programme Italy had to admit that 'reception in the region' was not working and that at least some of the above-mentioned arguments against evacuation from any of the neighbouring countries could not be maintained in view of the humanitarian catastrophe in FYROM, from where relocation was imperative in order to save lives and in order to keep the Macedonian borders open for new arrivals.

However, it remains true that no similar situation occurred in Albania, and it is fortunate also that the concerns expressed by the UNHCR regarding the safety of tens of thousands of refugees in camps located only a few kilometres from the Kosovo–Albania border proved unfounded.

For the reception of refugees evacuated from Skopje, the former NATO nuclear missile base in Comiso, Sicily, was transformed into a refugee camp for 5000 people. The total number of people transferred was 4700, some 90 per cent of whom repatriated voluntarily immediately after the end of the war, between mid-June and mid-July. A planned second phase of airlifting from Skopje was not carried out since the outflow from Kosovo had in the meantime come to an end.

While fully supporting the UNHCR's view that all refugees from Kosovo qualified for refugee status under the 1951 Convention, NGOs in Italy strongly advocated the use of a temporary protection mechanism for practical reasons.[12] It was clear that the administrative set-up of the regular determination procedure could not be adapted quickly enough to face this new challenge. The asylum seekers would have been left for a long time without work permits and without the possibility of family reunion. Also, the situation with regard to health assistance, badly needed by many refugees, would have been more precarious under the legal status of asylum seeker. After a lengthy decision-making process, a prime ministerial decree introducing temporary protection for all persons originating from the 'war-affected Balkan areas' finally entered into force on 26 May (decree of 12 May 1999).[13] Participation in the humanitarian evacuation programme was fundamental in this regard: those evacuated needed a legal status immediately.

The decree allowed for the issuance of a humanitarian residence permit, including a work permit, for an initial period until 31 December 1999, and the right to receive governmental assistance in collective centres at least up to that date. All those affected can alternatively opt for an individual refugee claim, but if they do, they have to go through the normal recognition procedure and would lose the right to assistance in government-run centres. Also, the residence permit would be valid only within Italy. Very few persons actually opted to apply for Convention refugee status.

In fact, a considerable number of Kosovar refugees had used Italy only as a transit country in order to reach Switzerland, Germany or, to a lesser degree, other Western European countries. Normally, the amount of money paid to the smugglers in Albania covers a journey to the final destination, including assistance with the illegal crossing of the borders to Switzerland, France or Austria. According to estimates, between 70 and 80 per cent of all Kosovar asylum seekers in Switzerland have arrived through Italy. The main reason for this phenomenon is the fact that almost all of them have relatives, or at least friends or neighbours, settled in other countries, while there has never been a Kosovar Albanian community established in Italy.

Even if returned by the Swiss authorities to the Como area of northern Italy, many hundreds or maybe thousands of refugees have tried again and again to pass the border until finally succeeding in entering far enough into Swiss territory to avoid rejection. Some 150,000 Kosovar Albanians are residing in Switzerland as immigrants, often second or third generation, and a further 50,000 have been admitted as refugees or asylum seekers. This community evidently represents a very strong pull factor for reaching Switzerland for those obliged to flee Kosovo. This was similar to experience with regard to Kurdish asylum seekers, especially from Turkey, who, also for family or community reasons, had shown no intention whatsoever to remain in Italy and rather preferred to pay more money to smugglers and to undergo additional risks in order to reach their family members in other countries.

Italy has often been accused of not controlling its sea borders sufficiently and of being too permissive with respect to the crossing of internal EU borders (with Austria and France) or that with Switzerland. These accusations have diverted attention from the real problem in the case of Kosovars, Kurds or other asylum seekers crossing the Adriatic from Albania. Increased control would mean *refoulement* and violations of international obligations regarding rescue at sea. Albania cannot yet be regarded as a 'safe third country', and the bilateral readmission agreement between Italy and Albania does not seem to cover asylum seekers originating from third countries, but only Albanians. Increased control would result in an increase of accidents like that on Good Friday 1997 when more than 80 Albanians died at sea as result of a crash between an Italian military navy vessel and a smugglers' boat.

With regard to increased vigilance at the internal EU or Swiss borders, it is obvious that even a barbed-wire fence along the whole border would not prevent people from trying to reach their families in other countries. And barbed-wire fences at internal borders would anyway not really seem to be in line with the concept of free circulation of persons within the EU (or Schengen) territory.

Thus, the unequal distribution of Kosovo refugees between the various Western European countries is not in the first instance caused by different policies, different reception facilities and different assistance schemes, but is rather to be seen as a late consequence of labour immigration or guest-worker policies adopted by a number of countries, especially Germany and Switzerland, some decades ago and which have, over the years, created large communities of persons whose co-nationals are now escaping as refugees from the same countries. Any effort to reach an agreement on responsibility sharing has to take this background into account.

Under Italian law there is no possibility of limiting the right of asylum seekers, refugees or humanitarian refugees to free movement within the country. But even if there had been the possibility of confining refugees within a particular province or municipality, it is more than doubtful that this would have had an impact on the movement towards other countries.

The surprisingly fast and massive movement of voluntary return immediately after the settlement of the conflict in Kosovo through UN Security Council Resolution 1244 does not contradict this argument: immediate return was requested mainly by those refugees who were evacuated from Macedonia and not by those who had arrived spontaneously in Italy through Albania. The evacuated refugees had far fewer family links in Italy or in other European countries and thus were not affected by the same 'pull factor'. All they wanted was temporary protection and to return to Kosovo as soon as possible. The 'migration element' which is very frequent in situations of mass exoduses of refugees was very much stronger among those who had arrived in Italy with a clear idea of reaching other and more distant destinations than among those rescued in Skopje and transferred to Sicily.

Public opinion reacted most favourably to the plight of refugees from Kosovo and to Italian participation in the humanitarian evacuation programme. While not seriously putting in doubt the orientation of the government towards 'reception in the region', and especially the aid provided to refugees in Albania, and thus not supporting openly the NGOs' request for the protected transfer of a certain number of refugees from Albania, hundreds of municipalities, local associations and single families offered accommodation for those who had arrived spontaneously on the Puglia coast. However, the authorities made no effort to coordinate this offer and to put in place something similar to the round table which had successfully functioned during the Bosnian war. Again there was clearly the wish not to give the impression of being prepared for the humanitarian reception of refugees on a large scale. The Minister of the Interior provided large centres of first reception and emergency assistance without a programme for a country-wide distribution of refugees and of accommodation in medium-sized or small centres under more humane conditions. A step in this direction was instead made by an *ad hoc* consortium of NGOs and trade unions, with the Italian Refugee Council as lead agency, benefiting from an EU programme for reception facilities for Kosovar refugees under the Joint Action of 23 April 1999. For the first time in Italy, under the project called *Azione Comune*, a system of reception at the national level has been developed whereby, thanks to close cooperation between NGOs, trade unions, the Ministry of the Interior and municipalities, refugees and asylum seekers are hosted in a large number of small and medium-sized centres or obtain rental assistance for private housing over a limited period of time. Some 1000 Kosovar refugees are expected to benefit from this new model, which includes not just accommodation and food but also a series of parallel interventions such as language courses, social and legal counselling, psychological assistance and professional training.

Unlike many other NATO countries, during the whole period of the war Italy had a strong anti-war and anti-bombing movement, criticizing, in particular, Italy's active participation in military action. Even within the governing coalition there were parties who took part in this movement, including the Greens and Italian Communists, who threatened several times to leave the government and/or to withdraw parliamentary support for it in the event of prolonged air force activity. Thus, the government had its own strong reasons for wanting, on the one hand, to bring the conflict to an early solution and, on the other, to demonstrate to the public a strong commitment to assisting the victims of the conflict. A lot of attention was given to the first arrival of evacuees in Comiso, Sicily. The various government-run reception centres were frequently visited by members of the government and even the Prime Minister. If up to March 1999 Kosovar refugees arriving at the coast were labelled as *clandestini* (clandestine immigrants), after 24 March the prevailing term was 'solidarity'. However, as we have seen, the government made every effort to explain that solidarity was better demonstrated in Albania with strong Italian involvement in terms of funds, logistics and personnel, most voluntary, rather than by assisting refugees on Italy's own territory.

Shortly after the end of the conflict in Kosovo was officially declared, the number of Kosovar Albanians arriving in Italy diminished sharply, and at the same time a new caseload of refugees appeared on the southern coast formed by the new victims of the peace settlement: Roma and Bosniaks, along with a relatively small number of Serbs. During the months of July and August more than 4000 Roma arrived by sea, this time mainly via Montenegro. Initially, they could opt for temporary protection or for recognition as Convention refugees. At the end of July, however, the Minister of the Interior declared publicly that in view of the end of the conflict and of the presence of international security forces in Kosovo, there was in principle no need for protection any more. In the face of heavy reaction, including from the UNHCR, against this statement, the government restated the continuing possibility of individual asylum claims and guaranteed admission to all those who claimed to be refugees, regardless of their ethnic origin. But by administrative circular of 5 August from that date temporary protection was no longer available for new arrivals. Again, most of the Roma population tried, normally successfully, to reach other countries, especially Germany. Others, in view of the fact that the special reception facilities under the temporary protection regime were no longer available, 'disappeared' somewhere within Italy and contributed to the increase of the so-called 'nomad camps' around the big cities. Some hundreds of Roma, however, are also hosted in the centres under the *Azione Comune* programme.

It is too early to say whether Kosovar Roma will, as a rule, be recognized as Convention refugees since, owing to the large increase in the number of asylum seekers in 1999 to some 35,000 persons, it will take at least one year to have their claims decided by the Central Commission – and probably many of them will no longer be in the country by that time.

Temporary protection continues to be applied for those who had already obtained a humanitarian residence permit before 5 August. At the time of completion of this manuscript (October 1999), the question arose as to whether the period would be extended after the end of the year, at least until the spring of 2000, as recommended by the UNHCR.

European integration process and security concerns: where is Italy's place?

Unlike the situation in a number of other member states, virtually nobody in Italy questions attempts to strengthen the EU and develop a high degree of integration. While monetary union was being constituted, during which period Italy's membership of in the first group of participating countries was doubtful, the mass media used the bizarre term 'enter Europe' as if Italy previously had been located in a different continent. Taxpayers did not protest against the introduction of a special contribution destined at reducing the state's debt: the prospect of 'entering Europe' merited some sacrifice.

There was no need for a referendum on the ratification of the Maastricht or the Amsterdam Treaties, but if such a referendum had been held, an overwhelming majority would have voted in favour. A constant fear of being excluded from an inner circle of EU countries, whether regarding the Schengen group or being part of the first group of countries opting for monetary union, has characterized the mood of recent years. The same frame of mind affected Italy's position in the harmonization of immigration and asylum policies. The transfer of some responsibility to Brussels and Strasbourg is perceived as purely positive, with a corresponding constant fear of not being in line with European orientations, including security concerns expressed by partner states. The existence of 8000 km of external borders, two-thirds of which are exposed to actual or potential crisis areas in the Balkans and North Africa, leads to enormous preoccupation with immigration control and the control of internationally organized trafficking and smuggling of arms, drugs and people.

Security concerns had priority in the Italian 'non-paper' for the European Council's extraordinary summit in Tampere in October 1999. In Tampere Italy claimed that the partner countries should share the financial burden caused by the need to strengthen vigilance of Italy's borders. Even the European Refugee Fund, at the last moment not formally established by the Council, should have served this purpose, in the view of the Italian government.

There is clearly a link between the type of emergency situations with which Italy has been faced, as described in this chapter, and the concept of responsibility sharing between the member states of the EU, a link which has been unsuccessfully stressed on several occasions by the Italian government. As early as 1991, long before burden and responsibility sharing was on the EU agenda as a topic of the harmonization process, Italy tried to 'distribute' the Albanians arrivals among the EU (then EC) partner states. It seems that only Luxembourg accepted 50 (!) persons for a form of resettlement. Countries such as Germany have certainly, on such occasions, presented their own asylum statistics showing more than a hundred times as many asylum seekers as those registered in Italy. The mass *refoulement* of Albanians in August 1991 has sometimes been explained by the poor response Italy had received from its EU partner countries some months earlier. During the extraordinary European Council summit in Tampere in October 1999, Italy claimed a common responsibility among the EU countries for the vigilance and control of its external sea borders, trying to obtain financial recompense for what it perceives to be a geographical accident for which Italy cannot be held responsible. But again the commitment of the Tampere summit in this regard is very low profile, and again the German government has a point when it refers not only to the relatively high figures for asylum seekers in Germany but also to the undoubted fact that many of them have transited Italy prior to their arrival in Germany.

In this context reference should be made to Italy's dissatisfaction with the clause of the Dublin Convention which determines, in general, that the country of first (irregular) arrival is responsible for examining an asylum application. It is feared that once the initial difficulties with the application of the Dublin Convention are overcome and the EURODAC Convention on finger-printing of all asylum seekers is enforced, a great number of people will be returned to Italy under 'Dublin' terms.

'Security', however, has become the principal topic in the internal political debate. Government and opposition are in severe competition as to which is taking security risks more seriously into account. The alleged involvement of a foreigner in a murder or a robbery is sufficient to nourish this debate again and again. Control of external borders, illegal immigration, organized crime and petty crime in the cities: in the public and political debate these are all part of one package into which, more and more, the refugee and asylum question risks being integrated.

This is also reflected in the present parliamentary debate on the draft bill on asylum and humanitarian protection. Following the London Resolutions of December 1992 and the Resolution on Minimum Standards for Asylum Procedures of June 1995, for the first time in Italy a pre-screening procedure for manifestly unfounded refugee claims will be introduced into Italian law. Here again, the concern is not only to sort out speedily those foreigners who may misuse the asylum procedure for immigration purposes, but also to create an allegedly efficient means of detecting criminals, terrorists, and so on, at an early stage of the procedure, with the possibility of their immediate return to whence they came.

European asylum approaches have a direct and immediate impact on the internal discussion. It is not exaggerated to believe that the government would be rather happy to do without a national asylum law and to wait for legislative measures taken by the EU on the basis of article 63 of the Amsterdam Treaty.

If in some other countries, especially Northern European ones, there is a frequent expression of concern that European harmonization could lower standards, in Italy standards in many aspects of refugee law and refugee reception would probably improve as a result of such a process. This optimism is especially justified when taking the relevant part of the Tampere conclusions into account. Italy belongs to that group of countries which need an input from partner states and from the EU as a whole in order to develop into an asylum country. But this process is not without risks. Often in the past, hostile or even *refoulement* measures regarding asylum seekers have been prevented only by what could be termed a certain *laissez-faire* approach. In the current national social and cultural context, an exaggeratedly legalistic approach could improve the level of guarantees and legal certainty in some people's favour but could well damage many others.

Conclusions

Of utmost importance for the future development will be the question of the extent to which security considerations are put on the priority list and overwhelm human rights and humanitarian considerations and obligations. The transformation from an emigration to an immigration country, which has occurred over the past fifteen years, and not without trauma for society, has not been accompanied by a transformation from a pure transit country for refugees into a true asylum country. The fact that two draft bills, one on immigration and one on asylum presented almost simultaneously to Parliament have not had the same speed of approval may be symptomatic in this regard.

The arrival and presence of refugees have been perceived as issues linked to particular crisis situations widely reported in the media, such as those in Albania, Kurdistan, Bosnia and Kosovo. Again symptomatic is the *ad hoc* legislative reaction, stepping from one of these 'emergencies' to the next one. Moreover, public attention has been concentrating, in recent years, on the dramatic circumstances of the arrival of boat people rather than on the legal status and the welfare of refugees later on. The arrival of about a thousand Kurds on overcrowded vessels provoked enormous media coverage as well as parliamentary debates. Similar media coverage and parliamentary attention are almost totally lacking with respect to the draft legislation on asylum. Temporary protection therefore has not only been a legal response to a given situation but has to be regarded as the only realistic way of dealing with refugee questions in general. Refugees have been perceived as one small section of the immigrant population and, except in times of 'emergency', no great difference is perceived between the two groups.

A final paradox lies in Italy's commitment to the promotion of human rights, very visible in its international relations, for which the patient and decisive promotion of the institution of an international penal tribunal may be cited as an example. This commitment is not equally visible when it comes to the protection of refugees. Labour market constraints, the lack of accommodation facilities, the fear of importing criminality and poor welfare resources are factors that, on the whole, carry more weight than do humanitarian traditions.

However, Italy is still in the midst of a process of becoming an asylum country, which means a country prepared, from a cultural, legislative and structural point of view, to receive, if the case arises again, a significant number of refugees like those produced by the Kosovo crisis in the first half of 1999. The rapidity with which this process develops, as well as the guiding values and policy principles, will to a great extent depend on the future orientation of the EU as a whole.

Notes

1. A short overview of Italian immigration with statistical details can be found in: *Immigrazione, Dossier statistico* (Rome: Caritas di Roma, 1994).
2. These exercises were: (a) law no. 943/86; (b) law no. 39/90, the 'Martelli Law';

(c) law-decree no. 489/95, the 'Decreto Dini'; and (d) the Prime Minister's decree of 16 October 1998.

3. *De facto* refugees means here those foreigners who had to leave their own countries under refugee or refugee-like situations.

4. It is interesting to note that the text of article 2 of the draft bill says, 'The right to asylum is guaranteed to foreigners or stateless persons who cannot or do not want to avail themselves of the protection of the State in which they are a citizen or an habitual resident, due to their being effectively prevented from exercising the democratic liberties guaranteed by the Constitution and exposed to danger, threatening their own life or family members or facing serious restrictions of personal freedom.'

5. Decree of the Minister of Foreign Affairs of 9 September 1992.

6. There is no longer a need to demonstrate income and housing requisites, as for family reunion; see article 27 of law 40/98.

7. Another interesting amendment concerns the explicit mention of deserters and draft evaders, to whom the right to enter and to reside is guaranteed anyway (art. 2 bis pf. law no. 390/92).

8. Direttiva della Presidenza del Consiglio dei Ministri, 15 July 1997, *Official Gazette*, 18 August 1997.

9. Direttiva della Presidenza del Consiglio dei Ministri, 2 August 1998, *Official Gazette*, 8 August 1998.

10. Statistics 1998: 2734 asylum seekers from Kosovo, out of a total of 7674. Several thousand Kosovar asylum seekers who arrived in Italy towards the end of 1998 are not yet reflected in this figure.

11. See Appendix 1.

12. 'Closing remarks' by Mrs Sadako Ogata of the UNHCR at a meeting of the Humanitarian Issues Working Group of the Peace Implementation Council, Geneva, 6 April 1999.

13. Official *Gazzetta* of 26 May 1999. Title of the decree: 'Temporary protection measures for humanitarian purposes to be guaranteed on the territory of the State in favour of persons originating from the war-zones in the Balkan area.'

Bibliography

Books and journal articles

Bolaffi, G., 'Redesigning Italy: the new flow of immigration', *Indiana International and Comparative Law Review* 4 (2) (1994), 000–000.

Campani, G., 'Albanians in Italy: asylum–seekers, refugees, immigrants', in M. Appelqvist, J. Blaschke, R. Cohen *et al.* (eds) *Avenues to Integration* (Naples: Ipermedium Divisione Editoria, 1995).

Delle Donne, M., 'Difficulties of refugees towards integration: the Italian case', in M. Appelqvist, J. Blaschke, R. Cohen *et al.* (eds) *Avenues to Integration* (Naples: Ipermedium Divisione Editoria, 1995).

Hein, C., 'Protezione temporanea come definizione complementare di rifugiato', in *Affari Sociali Internazionali* (Milan: FrancoAngeli, 1994).

Hein, C., ' "De Facto" Fluchtlinge und vorlaufiger Rechtsschutz im Volkerrecht und Rechtsvergleich', in K. Barwig, G. Brinkmann *et al.* (eds) *Vom Auslander zum Burger: Festschrift für Fritz Franz und Gert Müller* (Baden-Baden: Nomos, 1994).

Hein, C., 'Zum Stand der Harmonisierung del Asylrechts of europäischer Ebene', in *Neue Regierung – Neue Ausländerpolitik* (Baden-Baden: Nomos, 1999).

Macioti, M.I. and Pugliese, E., *Gli Immigrati italiani* (Rome and Bari: Laterza, 1984).

Nascimbene, B., 'Il contributo alla tutela dei diritti umani: diritto d'asilo e motivi umanitari', in S. Marchisio and F. Raspadori (eds) *L'Italia e i diritti umani* (Padua: CEDAM, 1995).

Ungari, P. and Pietrosanti Malintoppi, M.P., *Verso un tribunale permanente internazionale dei crimini contro l'umanità: precedenti storici e prospettive di istituzione* (Rome: Luiss University, 1998).

UNHCR, *The State of the World's Refugees: A Humanitarian Agenda* (Oxford: Oxford University Press, 1998).

Reports

Camera dei Deputati, 'Lo Spazio Schengen: libertà di circolazione e controlli alle frontiere estere', in *L'Italia e Schengen* (Rome, 1998).

Caritas, di Roma, *Dossier Statistico 1999* (Rome: Anterem, 1999).

Conferenza Nazionale dell'Immigrazione CENSIS, *Immigrati e società italiana* (Rome: Consiglio Nazionale dell'economia e del lavoro, EDITALIA, 1991).

ECRE/ENAR/MPG, *Guarding Standards: Shaping the Agenda* (Brussels, 1999).

Primary sources

Decree of the Minister of Foreign Affairs of 9 September 1992.

CHAPTER EIGHT

France: international norms, European integration and state discretion

SANDRA LAVENEX

Introduction

Notwithstanding its long tradition as an asylum country, France kept a remarkably low profile in the European response to the refugees fleeing former Yugoslavia. Not only was the intake of refugees, especially from Bosnia and Kosovo, very limited, but protection was granted in an informal and *ad hoc* manner rather than on the basis of existing laws and regulations. This chapter identifies two main constraints behind the French government's hesitant response to the Kosovo refugee crisis. With regard to domestic politics, the French reaction was shaped by the paradoxical demands of a highly politicized public opinion on migration on the one hand, spurred by the electoral career of right-wing political parties, and the apparent wave of public support and solidarity with the Kosovo refugees, on the other. From an international perspective the French situation was characterized by the discrepancy between the relatively low importance of the Yugoslav refugee crisis domestically, with a small number of ex-Yugoslavs living in France, and international pressure for cooperation and 'burden sharing' in Europe.

This chapter proceeds in four steps. The first section describes the emergence and the limits of a secondary regime for the protection in France of refugees fleeing war and civil war, focusing particularly on the reception of Bosnian refugees in the first half of the 1990s. In order to highlight the broader political context of these evolving policies, the second section deals with the general political discourse surrounding the question of refugee protection in France and discusses the major changes introduced to French asylum law in the 1990s. The third section then turns again to the actual implementation of these evolving refugee policies and scrutinizes the approach developed with regard to the admission and protection of Kosovar Albanians in the spring of 1999. The question of how far this approach was influenced by the European integration process is addressed in the fourth section, before the chapter concludes with a more general reflection on the significance of temporary protection in the light of the established principles of refugee law.

The hesitant emergence of temporary protection

Among European states, France has the longest tradition of refugee protection. Codification of the right to asylum goes back to the French Revolution and found its first expression in the Constitution Montagnarde of 1793, which declared that the French people 'give asylum to foreigners banned from their countries in the name of liberty'.[1] Republican principles and the devotion to the protection of human rights shaped France's self-perception as *'terre d'asile'* and the overall generous approach to the admission of refugees during most of the nineteenth and twentieth centuries.[2]

For a long time the Geneva Convention of 1951 was the exclusive legal basis for granting protection.[3] A secondary form of temporary protection outside the framework of the Geneva Convention was formally introduced only in 1998 as part of the Jospin government's reforms. Outside formal refugee law, however, secondary forms of protection have always existed in France. During the 1970s, crises in South America and Indochina led the French government to admit significant numbers of refugees on a quota basis. Furthermore, as in most other Western countries, persons fleeing from Eastern Europe were generally admitted even if they did not strictly fulfil the persecution criteria of the Geneva Convention.

The concept of temporary protection, however, which centres around the principle that protection shall be only provisional until the situation in the home country allows for the return of the refugees, began to take shape only in the mid-1980s. In this period, two developments coincided. On the one hand, questions of immigration and integration became increasingly politicized, and France's long tradition as a country of immigration was questioned more and more. On the other hand, a significant increase in the number of asylum seekers, in particular from Third World countries, was accompanied by a dramatic decline in the recognition rates for refugees, thus giving rise to the impression of increasing abuse of asylum procedures.[4] These rising numbers of rejected asylum seekers and the humanitarian constraints on their expulsion gave rise to new, less formal forms of protection in France.

First steps towards temporary protection in the mid-1980s

The first step in the establishment of secondary forms of protection was made with a circular issued by the Prime Minister in 1985 which granted the Interior Ministry the right to suspend expulsions of rejected asylum seekers in cases where the person faced serious risks with regard to his or her security and freedom if returned to the country of origin.[5] This regulation was, however, applied in a limited manner and in the 1980s concerned mainly people from Lebanon and Poland – countries with which France traditionally had close links.[6] The essential differences with the traditional protection regime based on the 1951 Geneva Convention, listed below, can be characterized as signalling informality, variability and executive discretion. The differences between temporary protection and the traditional regime were:

- the absence of a right on the part of the refugee to have his or her case considered;
- the absence of an independent institution in charge of examining the asylum claim (such as the Office Français de Protection des Refugies et Apatrides (OFPRA));
- the absence of need on the part of the prefect to give reasons for his or her decision towards the refugee;
- the absence of legal remedies against negative decisions; and
- the provisional nature of the residence permit, together with the discretionary power of the prefecture to end the protection status whenever this is deemed to be appropriate.[7]

Temporary protection of Bosnian refugees

These three characteristics – informality, variability and executive discretion – continued to shape the French reaction to the arrival of Bosnian refugees in the early 1990s and still mark the approach towards people fleeing ethnic cleansing in Kosovo, as will become clear from this chapter.

With the outbreak of war in former Yugoslavia, no specific law providing temporary protection was envisaged. Instead, the existing possibilities in the general aliens legislation were considered sufficient and, above all, flexible enough to be made applicable through circulars in the specific cases concerned.[8] As a consequence, the French approach towards refugees from former Yugoslavia in the early 1990s was regulated by a complex set of approximately twenty administrative texts – circulars, telegrams, internal notes – which, in order not to develop a pull effect, were not made public.[9] These texts left the grant of temporary protection and its suspension to the full discretion of the prefects – that is, the local branch of the Interior Ministry.

The first measure taken in this respect was a telex from the Interior Ministry to the prefects of 3 August 1992 which generally suspended the execution of expulsion measures and provided for the delivery of renewable temporary residence permits valid for three months to persons from former Yugoslavia.[10] The text concerned only citizens of the republics of former Yugoslavia who arrived in France subsequent to the commencement of hostilities. Persons who had transited for more than a temporary stop in 'safe countries' were excluded from the provisions. The obligation to possess a visa in order to enter France remained in force. Persons coming without a visa could, however, be granted a three-month resident permit provided the prefect was satisfied that the person had come from a conflict zone. This criterion was interpreted in such a way that, for example, Albanians from Kosovo were refused temporary protection on the grounds that their regions of origin were not part of the conflict.[11] In contrast to asylum seekers, beneficiaries of temporary protection had the right to work.

During this period the French government strongly emphasized that it did not want to lend support to the policy of ethnic cleansing by organizing massive and permanent or semi-permanent transfers of the Bosnian population to France. While early return of these people to their country of origin was thus a first priority, people from former Yugoslavia holding temporary residence permits were not excluded from the possibility of being granted a more inclusive and permanent status by applying for formal refugee status. However, as shown in a confidential note by the OFPRA, the administrative agency in charge of examining asylum requests, this status was to be delivered in a limited manner. This note provided that in order to 'evaluate the merits of fears of persecution' it was necessary to 'evaluate the possibilities and conditions in which some of the people belonging to a minority nationality in one republic can make their way to the republic whose nationality they ethnically belong to'.[12] This note was criticized by several humanitarian organizations for implicitly accepting the practices of ethnic cleansing. Nevertheless, while the numbers of refugees from former Yugoslavia remained comparably low, recognition rates for Bosnian refugees have been very high in France, and an overall number of 3033 people were granted refugee status between 1992 and 1998.[13]

Given the informality of reception policies towards citizens of former Yugoslavia in France, no accurate statistics are available regarding the total number of people benefiting from temporary protection mea-sures.[14] It is estimated that between 10,000 and 20,000 people from former Yugoslavia arrived in France between 1992 and 1998. These numbers include people coming to join family members already in France, sometimes illegally, people staying with French families, and people under government programmes.[15]

Table 8.1 Temporary protection in France between 1992 and 1994

Nationality	1992	1993	1994
Bosnians	2259	2290	974
Croatians	93	281	181
Others	736	1899	719
Total	3088	4470	1874

Source: IGC, *Report on Temporary Protection in States in Europe, North America and Australia* (Geneva, 1995), pp. 104ff., numbers for three- and six-month residence permits are merged

The number of persons granted temporary protection in this period is much lower. As Table 8.1 shows, most temporary residence permits were issued in 1993, with a total of 4470 people compared to 3088 people in 1992 and 1874 people in 1994. According to the French government, the decline in numbers of temporary residence permits in 1994 was linked to the fact that more people applied for Convention status, owing to the prolongation of the crisis in former Yugoslavia. After a period during which examination of applications had been frozen, the OFPRA started to examine requests in January 1993.

A review of asylum applications by persons of Yugoslav and ex-Yugoslav origin since 1992 reflects these trends. For the whole period between 1992 and 1998, recognition rates for Bosnian refugees were very high and amount to an average 89.7 per cent. The number of Kosovar Albanians requesting asylum in France increased significantly in 1998. Most of them received formal refugee status.[16]

To sum up, it can be said that France admitted only a limited number of refugees from former Yugoslavia in the first half of the 1990s. The admission of these persons occurred in an *ad hoc* and informal manner and was based on administrative regulations outside the existing legal framework for the protection of refugees. In fact, it appears that a large part of the estimated 10,000–20,000 people from former Yugoslavia who arrived in France between 1992 and 1998 have been granted neither temporary protection nor formal refugee status but entered the country on the basis of family reunification schemes or other government programmes, or illegally. Still, it is important to note that most Bosnian refugees who entered the formal status determination procedure were seen to fulfil the persecution criteria of the 1951 Geneva Convention.

Reflecting on the French approach towards refugees from former Yugoslavia and the hesitant development of temporary protection, one must take into consideration another group of refugees fleeing from situations of generalized violence with whom France has traditionally had much closer ties: the Algerians.

The Algerian case

French debates on secondary forms of protection concentrated on a group of people (besides those fleeing the Yugoslav conflicts) who, although not fulfilling the persecution criteria of the Geneva Convention, nevertheless could not be returned for humanitarian reasons. These were those Algerian citizens who sought asylum in France on the grounds of persecution perpetrated not by their state, but by Islamic movements in their home country. Although the two groups fell under slightly different regulations, the Algerian question played a dominant role in the further development of secondary forms of protection in France and shaped the debates surrounding the admission of Kosovar refugees in 1999.

Given that French jurisprudence does not recognize persecution by non-state actors as satisfying the grounds for the granting of Convention status, only 1 per cent to 4 per cent of Algerian refugees were actually granted Convention status.[17] Recognizing the difficulties of sending these people back, the Interior Ministry issued a telegram in 1993 granting prefects, together with an interministerial commission (Internal, Foreign and Social Affairs), the right to issue temporary residence permits to persons who feared serious risks to their life, liberty or security in Algeria.[18] This procedure was much more cumbersome and protracted than that established for 'refugees' from former Yugoslavia, and also deprived the Algerians of the right to work during the procedure. Given the important presence of Algerians in France and the historical ties binding the two countries, this interministerial procedure soon drew increasing criticism from the public and politicians alike and led, in 1998, to the introduction of a formal law on temporary protection.

Before presenting this law, the next section sets the broader context of immigration policies in France and discusses the domestic dynamics behind the increasing politicization and securitization of the migration question which increasingly constrain the room to manoeuvre in the humanitarian reception of refugees.

Political discourse and the securitization of refugees

Unlike in the Kosovo crisis in 1999, the admission of Bosnian refugees in the early 1990s took place in a climate of intensifying restrictions of the asylum law and an increasingly polarized discourse concerning foreigners. These restrictions started with the introduction of accelerated

Table 8.2 Total number of asylum applications in France, 1980–98

Year	Total asylum applications
1980	18,790
1981	19,863
1982	22,505
1983	22,350
1984	21,714
1985	28,925
1986	26,290
1987	27,672
1988	34,352
1989	61,422
1990	56,053
1991	47,380
1992	28,872
1993	27,524
1994	25,964
1995	20,170
1996	17,153
1997	19,983
1998	22,374

Sources: 1980–93 figures from L. Legoux, *La Crise de l'asile politique en France* (Paris: Centre Français sur la Population et le Développement, 1995), p. 118; 1994–8 figures from IGC, Asylum Statistics: www.igc.ch/frstatistics.htm

procedures in the OFPRA in 1989, continued with the introduction of carrier sanctions and the formalizing of transit zones under the Socialist government in 1992, and culminated in the comprehensive reforms of 1993 launched by the newly appointed conservative Interior Minister, Charles Pasqua. In the light of strongly declining numbers of asylum seekers since 1990 (see Table 8.2), this turnabout in the French asylum tradition is the consequence of a discursive shift in the perception of the refugee question, in which both asylum seekers and European integration have been linked as threats to the French nation and cultural identity. When the Socialists came back to power with Lionel Jospin as Prime Minister in 1997, one of their first priorities was to calm the polemics on immigration and establish the guidelines for a new immigration and asylum policy that could command the support of both the left and the right. However, the restrictive stance implemented in the first half of the 1990s has not been abandoned. In the light of the past debates on immigration, the aim of restriction continues to shape the French government's policies and played a crucial role in the approach developed *vis-à-vis* Kosovo Albanians.

Societal fears and immigration

The strongly politicized nature of the immigration question in France, and the pivotal role played by this issue in the self-positioning of the main political parties since the mid-1980s, is the consequence of shifts in the public and political perception of the immigration 'problem', in which migrants and refugees have been increasingly construed as threats to the cultural identity and national integrity of French society.

The underlying logic behind these processes of securitization is that immigration is seen as a threat to society because it leads to shifts in the composition of a state's population and thereby threatens the basis of this society's very identity.[19] Security and threats are not objective matters, but security is a way to frame and handle an issue which mobilizes particular expectations and institutions. To argue in terms of existential threats is a means to mobilize attention and power by claiming urgent political priority and exceptional political means. In France this securitization of the migration question has been put forward mainly by the right-wing National Front, but has quickly spread to dominate the discourse of the traditional political parties – leading to a shift of the right further to the right and a destabilization of the centre and the left.[20] Its dynamics and effects are thus not merely reduced to the societal sphere, but are an integral part of domestic politics in France and have a profound impact on the political sphere of government and thereby on the organization of the state.[21]

The politicization of immigration in France started during the economic recession of the 1970s and evolved in the 1980s from an initially purely economic question to a threat to national identity and citizenship.[22] The increasing perception of migration as a threat in the mid-1980s (securitization) was significantly promoted by the xenophobic discourse of Le Pen's National Front, which soon occupied centre stage in local and presidential elections.

In terms of securitization, French immigration discourse is based on two axes: a civic and an ethnic one. The civic semantic is linked to the republican understanding of the French nation and problematizes migrants in particular in view of a perceived lack of political loyalty and affiliation to the French political system. Two recurrent motifs are migrant associations and terrorist activities, which are seen as representing a threat to the political independence of the French people and as undermining the civil and secular basis of the French state. The fear of terrorism is directly linked to the relations with Algeria and has played a major role in the restriction of French immigration policies since the terrorist attacks in Paris in 1986. A symbol of the civic semantic is also the Islamic headscarves affair, another recurrent motif in French immigration discourse which vividly expresses the tension between the Muslim immigrant population and the laic and secular understanding of the French state. The second axis of the securitization discourse is of an ethnic nature and problematizes migrants primarily with regard to their cultural background, their traditions and religion. This is the semantic of the 'non-assimilables' – that is, people in particular from the former colonies in Central and North Africa, whose cultural, ethnic or religious differences tend to impede assimilation into French society. These people, mostly of Muslim origin, not only are regarded as an exception to the universal values and homogeneous self-concept of the French nation but are also seen to threaten the identity and existence of the nation through their high fertility rates.[23]

Traditionally, French immigration discourse concentrated on voluntary migrants and questions of integration, citizenship and illegal immigration. In accordance with France's republican self-understanding and its image as a country supporting human rights, refugees were originally kept out of this securitization discourse, and republican ideals continued to shape their perception as 'fighters for liberty' as well as France's role as '*terre d'asile*'.[24] This changed dramatically with the coming to power of the conservative RPR/UDF[25] coalition in 1993 and Charles Pasqua as Interior Minister, and was immediately linked to the discourse on Europeanization and the fear of an '*Europe passoire*'.[26] The connection between internal or societal security, asylum seekers and Europeanization consisted in the prospect of an abolition of internal borders in Europe and the fear of lack of sufficient control over the entry and stay of third-country nationals on French territory.

The consequences of this securitization on the transformation of French refugee policies in the 1990s are developed in the following subsections.

The about-turn in French refugee policies and Europeanization

Immediately after seizing power in 1993, Charles Pasqua, promising to 'reduce immigration to zero', introduced the question of asylum seekers and refugees into the already polarized foreigner discourse and proposed an incisive reform of the asylum law. This reform was part of a more comprehensive reformulation of French immigration policies which included a reform of the nationality code,[27] a law on identity checks,[28] and a new aliens bill[29] that heavily restricted conditions of entry and access to asylum procedures, restricted the social rights of immigrants, and enhanced expulsion measures.

With regard to asylum seekers, Pasqua aimed at implementing the

170

regulations adopted at the European level in the Schengen and Dublin Conventions as well as the 1992 London Resolutions. In order to be passed, these regulations required, as did the German asylum reform of 1993, a limitation of the asylum right contained in the French constitution.[30] According to a ruling of the Constitutional Council in 1993,[31] this right excluded the possibility for the French authorities to deny access to the asylum procedure purely on the grounds that asylum could have been requested elsewhere. As a consequence, a new article[32] was inserted in the French constitution according to which France retains the right to conclude international agreements with other European countries concerning the right of asylum.[33]

These reforms, legitimated in the name of European integration, marked a significant turn in the French republican tradition. For the first time in France's history, the asylum regulations were included in the general ordinance on the entry and stay of foreigners,[34] thus blurring the lines between voluntary and forced migration. Asylum seekers became subject to the general measures of immigration control, and access to asylum procedures was significantly restricted. These reforms had two main impacts: first they excluded whole categories of asylum seekers from access to the asylum procedure, provided either that they fell under the responsibility of another member state according to the Schengen and Dublin Conventions[35] or that they had transited through a so-called 'safe third country' in accordance with the 1992 London Resolution.[36] Furthermore, the notions of 'manifestly unfounded' asylum claims[37] and 'safe countries of origin' were largely approximated to European standards.[38]

In the broader perspective of French immigration discourse, these incisive changes in French refugee policies reflect two main developments. On the one hand, the securitization discourse was extended to the category of refugees and asylum seekers, who, in accordance with the French republican tradition and France's historic self-understanding as '*terre d'asile*', had hitherto been seen mainly in a human rights perspective as persons deserving protection. On the other hand, these developments also document the conjunction of two securitization discourses – that is, the link of the 'threats' of immigration with the fears of Europeanization which found their most visible expression in the discourse on an '*Europe passoire*' and the Maastricht Treaty. Again, these fears had both an ethnic and a civic dimension. The abolition of internal borders in Europe was seen as bringing the risk of losing control over the entry of non-nationals, thus entailing the danger of being 'flooded' by migrants and asylum seekers alike. The Maastricht Treaty in turn was seen as threatening the composition of the political community by incorporating the principle of joint citizenship and introducing the right to municipal elections for third-country nationals.[39]

The 1998 reforms: return to the republican tradition?

After seizing power in 1997, one of the main objectives of the Jospin government was to put an end to the ongoing polemics on immigration and to reinvigorate France's self-understanding as country of human rights and *'terre d'asile'*.[40] This aim was backed by a vast social movement in favour of more liberal immigration policies and against the increasing influence of the extremist National Front on the political discourse. This movement reached its peak in early 1997 as a protest against renewed restrictions of the general immigration laws under the Interior Minister, Jean-Louis Debré.[41]

Reacting to this strong manifestation of public opinion, the new Jospin government announced a comprehensive reformulation of French immigration and asylum policies which would live up to France's republican ideals and, at the same time, ensure the state's capacity to control the borders and fight illegal immigration. In fact, a major motive of these reforms was to find a consensus with the majority parties of the centre and the right, and thereby to put an end to the politicization of the immigration question in French political discourse.

This orientation towards consensus characterizes the asylum reform passed in 1998. Contrary to earlier announcements, this reform did not introduce major changes to the restrictions implemented on the access to asylum procedures and procedural guarantees with the Pasqua law.[42] Instead, the valorization of republican ideals consisted mainly in two innovations. The first was the symbolic confirmation of the constitutional asylum right through the introduction of a second procedure for granting refugee status which is no longer based on the refugee definition of the 1951 Geneva Convention but on the definition of the preamble of the French constitution which speaks of 'everyone persecuted because of his actions on behalf of liberty'. As laid out already in the legislative debates, this right is to be interpreted in a very restrictive manner and to apply only to a small elite of liberal activists.[43]

The second innovation speaks directly to the topic of this book and consists in the introduction of a formal law on temporary protection. This so-called 'territorial asylum' may be granted by the Interior Ministry after consultation with the Foreign Ministry and at the instigation of the prefects or the OFPRA. This status will be given to persons who can establish that their life or liberty are threatened in their country of origin or if they are exposed to inhuman treatment in the sense of article 3 of the European Convention on Human Rights and Fundamental Freedoms.

In practice, these dispositions formalize the already existing practice presented above and confirm the grant of temporary protection as a discretionary right of the state. In the words of the Interior Minister, Chevènement, temporary protection shall be compatible with the 'political, diplomatic, economic, cultural, and strategic'[44] interests of the state. A positive innovation was the introduction of the possibility to have a negative decision reviewed; however, negative decisions need not be justified and legal remedies are not allowed to delay the applicant's expulsion.

The restrictive reading of this new provision is illustrated in a circular of the Interior Ministry dated 25 June 1998, according to which the provision shall be limited to 'threats or risks resulting from persons or groups other than the public authorities of that country'.[45] This limitation excludes substantial numbers of people fearing persecution by non-state actors, be it in Congo, Sri Lanka or, as argued below, Kosovo. In addition, the implementing circulars define temporary protection in such a way that only people who arrive directly from their home country may apply for it.[46]

One year after the coming into force of the new law in May 1998, fewer than 1000 persons had been granted temporary protection.[47] In fact, the introduction both of constitutional asylum and of temporary protection in France reflect the strong foreign policy orientation of its refugee policies: both innovations were predominantly oriented at the situation of Algerian refugees fearing persecution by Islamic groups. They were not, however, an answer to the increasing reality of war and civil war as causes of refugee flows.

The reception of Kosovar refugees

As the preceding discussion on the development of political discourse and refugee policies in the 1990s indicates, the French political context was more favourable towards refugee admission at the time of the Kosovo crisis than during the Bosnian exodus, when significant restrictions were introduced to refugee law under Interior Minister Pasqua. Not only was the French republican tradition given a central place in the political campaign of the newly elected Socialist government, but large social movements had expressed their solidarity with the immigrant population. Furthermore, the influence of the extremist National Front was paralysed, owing to the protracted disputes between its patriarchal leader Jean-Marie Le Pen and his ex-adjunct Bruno Mégret which ultimately split the political party into two camps.[48]

Notwithstanding these differences in the domestic political situation, the reception of Kosovar Albanians fleeing ethnic cleansing in their home country in 1999 was, like the Bosnian case at the beginning of the 1990s, characterized by a high degree of discreetness, informality and *ad hoc* decision-making. Like the preceding governments, Prime Minister Jospin declared that France preferred to help refugees within their broader region of origin rather than support their evacuation to France, which would play into the hands of Serbian endeavours at ethnic cleansing. Joining the voices of the British and Italian governments, France's first reaction to the proposals of the German presidency of the European Union (EU) to establish quotas for the admission of Kosovo refugees in the EU in early April 1999 was negative. Declaring that he refused to 'accept the accomplished fact of deportation perpetuated by the Serbs',[49] Prime Minister Jospin opposed the idea of admitting a large number of Kosovar Albanians to France.

The following subsections set out the factors which, in the end, led to the admission of a certain number of Kosovars and discuss the legal provisions regulating their stay in France.

The pressure of public opinion

For years politicians in France, as in other Western European countries, have based their position with regard to 'third-country' nationals[50] on the assumption of an increasingly xenophobic public opinion and presumed public pressure for more restrictive policies. Yet the popular reaction to the Kosovo crisis in 1999 showed the limits and the equivocal nature of this influential assumption. Immediately after Prime Minister Jospin's statement on 4 April that France was not in favour of admitting Kosovo refugees, a wave of solidarity spread in the French population which eventually led the Prime Minister to review his position. Two days after his negative statement, Jospin was prompted to appease the growing criticisms and assure the National Assembly that France was 'naturally willing to temporarily admit a certain number'[51] of Kosovo refugees to its territory. However, Jospin underlined that this should happen only on a voluntary basis and without leading to the separation of families.[52]

The movement of solidarity in the French population was launched by the appeal of associations for donations but soon developed a dynamic of its own and far exceeded the expectations of its initiators. In the words of the ex-Secretary of State for Health and Social Action Bernard Kouchner,[53] France had not seen such a wave of generosity 'since the arrival of the boat people'.[54] In a few days, the French Red Cross had received more than 6000 tons of donated food; Médecins du Monde collected 4 million francs (610,000 euros), and more than 400,000 people offered to house refugees in their homes.[55] While this mobilization clearly supported the government's relaxation of its initial strictness, it also overtaxed the administrative apparatus, which could not follow through the bureaucracy necessary for these offers of hospitality to be made good. After meticulous examination of the housing offers by the departmental directions of sanitary and social affairs (Ddass), only 2000–2500 offers were taken up. According to public officials, few motivated helpers would actually ensure that there would be enough space and time for the accommodation and care of the refugees, particularly if these arrived with their families.[56] Notwithstanding these difficulties, this wave of solidarity is remarkable, given that the volunteers are expected to bear in full the costs for food and lodging.

As a reaction to this public mobilization, the French government finally agreed to admit between 5000 and 10,000 Kosovo refugees. By August 1999, 6339 people had been evacuated from refugee camps in Macedonia to France. In addition, the Interior Ministry estimated the number of spontaneous arrivals at 1500 Kosovo refugees.[57]

An uncertain legal status

The spontaneous arrival of a small number of Kosovar refugees near the French border with Italy in early April 1999, together with the wave of hospitality expressed by the French population, soon put the government under pressure to regulate the legal framework for the reception of these persons. Uncertainty as to the general approach to take to the problem and the lack of preparation shaped the first weeks following the realization that France could not avoid giving some sort of legal status to the arriving refugees. The confusion was also due to the lack of coordination between the three ministries with competency on this issue (the Ministries of the Interior, Foreign Affairs, and Labour and Solidarity), and the office of the Prime Minister.[58]

As a consequence, the first statements on the legal status for Kosovo refugees were contradictory. In his speech of 6 April to the National Assembly, in which he acknowledged that a certain number of Kosovars would be admitted to France, Jospin declared that these persons would be granted temporary protection according to the new Chevènement law of 1998.[59] However, he strongly underlined that the French government's priority was to help the refugees within their immediate region of origin in order to allow for their speedy return when the situation in their home country made this possible.[60] For this purpose, the government allocated a total of 225 million francs (34.3 million euros) worth of bilateral aid.[61]

More confusion entered the debate a week later, when the newspaper *Le Parisien* published the text of a very restrictive diplomatic telegram which had been circulated out to French consulates in Europe at the beginning of April. According to this telegram, the consulates were requested to 'pay particular attention to public order considerations and a heightened migratory risk' when issuing visas to persons of Yugoslav origin.[62]

It was only after this highly sensitive publication that the French government clarified the legal approach developed towards Kosovar

Albanians. The government immediately denied that this telegram concerned Kosovars. At the same time, it was made clear that contrary to earlier announcements by the Prime Minister, these persons would not be admitted under the temporary protection scheme established with the Chevènement law of 1998. Instead, France resumed the tradition of informal and discretionary provisional residence permits which had been applied to the Bosnian refugees at the beginning of the 1990s. The public authorities thus created an uncertain legal status for Kosovar Albanians, depriving them of the juridical safeguards included in the 1998 law on temporary protection (see above).

The status of Kosovar Albanians was set out in two notes from the Interior Ministry (14 April 1999) and the Foreign Ministry (19 April 1999) which were then merged in a circular of the Interior Ministry (3 May 1999). Accordingly, the following regulations were set in place. In principle, Kosovar refugees willing to travel to France were to register with the UNHCR in the refugee camps in Macedonia and Albania, and were thereby relieved of visa obligations. However, people who reached France on their own without a visa were admitted. Following their entry, the refugees received a provisional authorization to stay for three months, issued by the competent prefecture. After these three months, the authorization could be prolonged for one year for those persons who arrived via the UNHCR and six months for those who arrived spontaneously. This second authorization gave access to the right to work and to social benefits. With regard to social reception, the Kosovars were first given shelter in collective housing, where they received also medical treatment. Thereafter, they could either remain in collective establishments or be lodged with receiving families.[63] As a general rule, priority would be given to vulnerable persons and to persons with existing family links in France. Considering that very few Kosovar Albanians reside in France, this second criterion concerned only a very limited number of persons.[64]

Notwithstanding this hesitation in the formulation of a legal status for Kosovar refugees, French authorities admitted from the beginning that the situation of these persons fell within the scope of the 1951 Geneva Convention. At a meeting with the UNHCR in early April 1999, the director of the OFPRA, the administrative agency in charge of the formal procedure for determining refugee status, assumed that many Kosovars would fulfil the persecution criteria of the Convention.[65] In its note of 14 April the Interior Ministry also admitted that these persons fell under the Convention rather than under the temporary protection scheme, which, as described above, had been defined to apply only to persecution by non-state actors. By this note the French government in fact approved the judgement by the UNHCR, which called upon Western European governments to grant these persons full refugee status according to the

Geneva Convention.[66] However, priority was still given to temporary residence permits.

After the termination of NATO air strikes on Yugoslavia in June 1999, the receiving countries decided, at an intergovernmental conference chaired by the UNHCR in Geneva, to coordinate their return of Kosovo refugees. The participating countries agreed on the principle of voluntary return of these persons, agreed to bear the charges of this return, and agreed to examine the possibility of exploratory returns. France decided to begin organizing returns in August 1999. A procedure was set in place which allowed for explorative travels by the heads of family in view of a future return as well as a programme of voluntary repatriation for those Kosovo Albanians willing to return home. Apart from the travel expenses, financial help of 600 francs was allocated for explorative travels and 3000 francs for definitive returns for adults and 1000 francs for children. On 9 November 1999, 813 explorative travels had been organized, 807 persons returned to France, while 16 chose to stay in their home country. In the same period, 2757 persons were repatriated.[67] A new circular of the Interior Ministry of 12 October 1999 laid out that, after that date, any Kosovar staying irregularly in France would no longer profit from the special status commented above, thus signalling the end of the special temporary protection schemes.

Domestic and international determinants of the French position

The regulations in force for the Kosovar Albanians largely correspond to those established for the admission of Bosnian refugees. The priority of the French government was to help the refugees to move close to their home country in order to allow for their early return after the hostilities had calmed down. However, the regulation of their situation in France bears a certain contradiction: why was the establishment of a secondary set of informal temporary admission procedures necessary, if it is generally acknowledged that most of these persons would qualify for refugee status according to the Geneva Convention? And even if one accepts the principle of temporary protection, why was this not given in the framework of the 1998 law? These contradictions must be interpreted in the light of domestic and international factors: the dynamics of political discourse and the fear of a resurgence of the polemics surrounding immigration and the situation of France in the broader international context, including the political ideology which shapes Western European responses to refugee flows today.

The strong polarization of the French political landscape over the issue of immigration, which goes back to the beginning of the 1980s, and the endeavours of the newly elected Jospin government to calm the polemics on the basis of consensus and establish an enduring immigration and refugee policy, constitute an important factor constraining the political response to the Kosovo crisis. Jospin's initial defensive stance *vis-à-vis* the admission of these refugees can be interpreted as an attempt not to jeopardize the fragile consensus with the political centre and right on the issue of immigration and to avoid rekindling political and public debates. However, the vast mobilization of French public opinion in support of the Kosovars also shows the misperception of public opinion and values by policy-makers. The assumption of a generally xenophobic public opinion which is often invoked for the legitimation of restrictive policies had already been falsified in 1997 with the social movements against the Pasqua and Debré laws; however, it still seems to exert much influence on the positioning of the political elites. An additional domestic factor constraining the government's reaction was differences within the government itself, resulting from a lack of coordination between the competent ministries (Interior, Foreign and Social Affairs) and from differences within the coalition.

The domestic constraints were further influenced by the international context of the French reaction. In comparative perspective, the Yugoslav crisis and the resulting refugee flows have, since the beginning of the conflicts, had only a marginal impact on refugee policy in France. As shown above, only 3033 Bosnians were granted Convention refugee status during the whole period from 1992 to 1998; similarly, the number of persons benefiting from temporary protection was always limited (see Table 8.1). These relatively low numbers, together with the traditional focus on the Algerian case, also play a large part in explaining France's low profile in the reception of these refugees. Finally, the development of secondary and less inclusive forms of temporary protection outside the traditional refugee regime based on the 1951 Geneva Convention corresponds to a more general trend in Western European countries which has been significantly promoted at the EU level. From this perspective, the hesitant development of temporary protection schemes and the parallel maintenance of access to the regular status determination procedure under the Geneva Convention show at the same time the importance and the limits of new European concepts of refugee protection in France. This point is discussed in more detail in the next and final sections.

The ambiguous impact of European integration on French refugee policies[68]

If measured on the basis of the prospect of a common EU approach to refugee flows in general and, more specifically, the Yugoslav crisis, the French reaction seems to be disappointing. The French government did not support the plans of the German, Dutch and Austrian governments for a system of 'burden sharing' in the reception of these refugees. However, while French refugee policies seem to follow rather specific domestic, historical and geographical lines, European integration does have an important impact by providing a forum for the pursuit of predominantly restrictive policies and by shaping the ideational context of refugee protection in Europe.

The Europeanization of refugee policy

The impact in France of European integration on immigration policies has mainly concerned questions relating to the entry of asylum seekers to the territory as well as access to formal status determination procedures. This corresponds to the implementation of the Schengen and Dublin Conventions as well as the 1992 London Resolutions; later (mainly informal) agreements reached under the third pillar of the Maastricht Treaty have had little influence on French refugee policies.[69] This renationalization of refugee policies coincided with a general down-pacing of cooperation at the European level which also found its expression in a weakening engagement of French representatives for a deepening of the European *acquis* in these matters.[70]

The Europeanization of French refugee policies started in 1991 under the Socialist government, when some limited amendments were introduced to the asylum regulations in line with the ratification of the Schengen Agreement.[71] While the Socialist government thus saw the need for timely adaptations as a consequence of Europeanization, the 1993 reforms under the new conservative Interior Minister, Charles Pasqua, went much further. Legitimated as implementation measures of a common European refugee policy, these changes marked an incisive turn in French refugee policies and entailed a limitation of the constitutional asylum right (see above).

The maintenance of sovereignty

Notwithstanding this implementation of the European *acquis*, the French government was at all times careful to uphold its sovereignty *vis-à-vis* the EU. This concern found its expression in the text of the 1993 constitutional revision, which, apart from confirming the implementation of European agreements, explicitly reiterates the exception clause of the Schengen Agreements and Dublin Convention according to which France retains the right to process an asylum claim even if it is not determined under the European provisions as the responsible state.[72]

In addition, France's interest in European integration on asylum and immigration matters weakened significantly after the implementation of the 1993 restrictive reforms. This found its expression not only in the tardy implementation of the other provisions of the Schengen Agreement but also in the position adopted at the 1996-7 Amsterdam intergovernmental conference[73] and in the critical stance adopted with regard to the establishment of a system of burden sharing in the event of massive and unexpected refugee flows.

The Chevènement law of 1998 is also symptomatic of this trend. First, following a ruling of the Council of State, the highest administrative court in France, which limited the application of the 'safe third-country' rule to EU member states,[74] this rule was removed from the exclusion grounds for applications made inside the country.[75] Second, the revaluation of the constitutional right to asylum symbolizes a departure from the earlier asylum practice based on the international refugee definition of the 1951 Geneva Convention and contradicts the efforts to find a common definition of a refugee at the European level on the basis of that convention.[76] Finally, the review presented above of the emergence and the determinants of temporary protection in France has shown that rather than being shaped by common European dynamics, France's approach was very much determined by specific domestic factors, foreign policy considerations *vis-à-vis* Algeria and the fact that France was little affected by the refugee flows produced by the Balkan wars.

Conclusion

The French reaction to the Kosovo refugee crisis, like that of other EU member states, mirrors the dilemmas of refugee protection today. On the one hand, we witness an extension and multiplication of the causes of forced migration which often no longer fit the way EU states interpret the refugee definition of the 1951 Geneva Convention and which have led to the institutionalization of secondary forms of protection. On the other hand, this process of differentiation occurs in the context of intensifying attempts by Western governments to control immigration and to limit the intake of asylum seekers and refugees. As this chapter has shown, the coincidence of these two dynamics leads to ambiguous and sometimes even contradictory responses. Although the Kosovar refugees would, in most cases, fulfil the persecution criteria of the Geneva Convention, they were generally admitted under less inclusive, secondary protection schemes which not only cost less to the admitting state but also grant its authorities almost unlimited discretion over the reception and return of these refugees. In this light, temporary protection offers a way to demonstrate humanitarian concern by opening the borders to refugees while at the same time reassuring the reluctant receiving country that doing so will not necessarily imply granting long-term asylum.

Apart from this more general feature concerning the expansion of temporary protection, however, the French case has also provided two other important insights. The first is the recognition that contrary to the securitization discourse common among politicians and some thinkers, public opinion can be very supportive of the admission of large numbers of refugees. In the case of France, large-scale social mobilization in favour of receiving Kosovar Albanians even led the government to revise its initially defensive position. The second important conclusion concerns the relevance of European integration in asylum and immigration matters and the impact of this integration on domestic refugee policy. Here, the case of France has shown that, so far, the impact of Europeanization has been limited to the adoption of restrictive measures limiting the access of asylum seekers to the territory and to the full status determination procedure, including legal safeguards. More substantive aspects of refugee policy such as the criteria for granting protection or the actual approach to concrete refugee crises, however, still very much follow specific domestic traditions and particular geographic affinities. French interest in establishing a supranational European refugee policy is low. In this light, European cooperation does not challenge the core of national sovereignty; on the contrary, it has rather strengthened state sovereignty by allowing limits to be drawn on traditionally inclusive domestic and international asylum norms. Furthermore, sovereign control as exercised via administrative discretion is being strengthened by the way in which the concept of temporary protection has been adopted. Protection under the Geneva Convention had international standards; the way France has applied temporary protection allows it to take back discretion and let those international norms slip.

Notes

1. The right to asylum was contained in article 120 of this constitution, which never entered into force.
2. G. Noiriel, *La Tyrannie du national: le droit d'asile en Europe 1793–1993* (Paris: Callmann-Lévy, 1991), and P. Weil, *La France et ses étrangers* (2nd edition, Paris: Folio, 1995).
3. D. Norek and F. Doumic-Doublet, *Le Droit d'asile en France* (Paris: Presses Universitaires de France, 1989).
4. L. Legoux, 'La Demande d'asile en France: le pic de 1989 et la théorie de la dissuasion', *Revue Européenne des Migrations Internationales* 9 (2) (1993), 31–65, and L. Legoux, *La Crise de l'asile politique en France* (Paris: Centre Français sur la Population et le Développement, 1995).
5. Circular of the Prime Minister of 17 May 1985 together with the circular of the Interior Ministry to the prefects of 5 August 1987 regulating the implementation procedure (K. Hailbronner, *Die Rechtsstellung der De Facto-Flüchtlinge in*

den EG-Staaten: Rechtsvergleichung und europäische Harmonisierung (Baden-Baden: Nomos, 1993)).

6. Amnesty International and France Terre d'Asile, *Droit d'asile en France: état des lieux* (Paris: Amnesty International, 1997), p. 33.

7. On the evolution of temporary protection schemes in Europe, see K. Hailbronner, *Die Rechtsstellung der De Facto-Flüchtlinge in den EG-Staaten*, K. Kerber, 'Temporary protection: an assessment of the harmonisation policies of European Union Member States', *International Journal of Refugee Law* 9 (3) (1997), 452-75; J. Thorburn, 'Transcending boundaries: temporary protection and burden-sharing in Europe', *International Journal of Refugee Law* 7 (3) (1995), 459-80; J. van Selm-Thorburn, *Refugee Protection in Europe: Lessons from the Yugoslav Crisis* (Dordrecht: Martinus Nijhoff, 1998).

8. IGC (Intergovernmental Consultations on Asylum, Refugee and Migration Policies in Europe, North America and Australia), *Report on Temporary Protection in States in Europe, North America and Australia* (Geneva, 1995).

9. Amnesty International/France Terre d'Asile, *Droit d'asile en France*, p. 33.

10. The possibility of granting such an authorization (*autorisation provisoire de séjour*) already existed in the French Aliens Act (ordinance no. 45-2658 of 2 November 1945) and largely corresponds to the practice of temporary protection during the 1980s (see above).

11. Amnesty International/France Terre d'Asile, *Droit d'asile en France*, p. 33.

12. Note of 10 December 1992, quoted in *Migration News Sheet* of February 1993, p. 7.

13. Numbers from OFPRA, *Demandeurs d'asile d'ex-Yougoslavie 1992-1998*, 12 April 1999.

14. F. Liebaut and J. Hughes (eds), *Legal and Social Conditions for Asylum Seekers and Refugees, France*: www.drc.dk/eng/PUB/legsoc/France.html (Danish Refugee Council, 1997).

15. IGC, *Report on Temporary Protection*.

16. See note 13.

17. In the mid-1990s, the Commission de Recours des Réfugiés (CRR), the second instance in the formal asylum examination procedure, developed a new jurisdiction that recognized in some cases non-state persecution as grounds for granting formal refugee status. According to its *'Théorie de la vanité'* (theory of futility), refugees who were not granted protection by their state from persecution by third parties, although they had sought it, could be recognized as refugees under the 1951 Geneva Convention. Later, this jurisprudence was extended also to persons who had not formally sought for protection by their state, but whose application would anyhow have been futile (C. Saas, 'Die Neuregulung der Einreise und des Aufenhalts von Ausländern in Frankreich: viel Lärm um nichts', *Zeitschrift für Ausländerrecht und Ausländerpolitik* 23 (1) (1999), 10-17).

18. Telegram of the Direction des libertés publiques et des affaires juridiques du ministère de l'Intérieur (DLPAJ) of 22 December 1993.

19. See O. Waever, B. Buzan, M. Kelstrup and P. Lemaitre, *Identity, Migration and*

the New Security Order in Europe (London: Pinter, 1993) and O. Waever, 'Securitization and desecuritization', in R.D. Lipschutz (ed.), *On Security* (New York: Columbia University Press, 1995).

20. M.A. Schain, 'The immigration debate and the National Front', in J.T.S. Keeler and M.A. Schain (eds), *Chirac's Challenge: Liberalization, Europeanization and Malaise in France* (New York: St Martin's Press, 1996), pp. 169–98, and R. Schor, 'L'Extrême Droite française et les immigrés en temps de crise: années 1930–années 1980', *Revue Européenne des Migrations Internationales* 12 (2) (1996), 241–60.

21. This 'statist' dimension of securitization may be read as a criticism of the 'Copenhagen School' cited above (Ole Waever, Barry Buzan *et al.*) and has been expressed with reference to France by D. Bigo, 'Security(s): internal and external, the Möbius ribbon', Paper presented at the ISA Annual Convention in Toronto, 18–22 March 1997).

22. See R. Kastoryano, 'Immigration and identities in France: the war of words', *French Politics and Society* 14 (2) (1996), 58–66; D. Schnapper, *La France de l'intégration: sociologie de la nation en 1990* (Paris: Gallimard, 1991); and M. Silverman, *Deconstructing the Nation: Immigration, Racism and Citizenship in Modern France* (London: Routledge, 1992).

23. See P.-A. Targuieff (ed.), *Face au racisme* (Paris: Éditions la Découverte, 1991), and Silverman, *Deconstructing the Nation*.

24. C. Norek and F. Doumic-Doublet, *Le Droit d'asile en France* (Paris: Presses Universitaires de France, 1989), p. 38; J.Y. Vincent, 'Le Régime juridique des étrangers en droit français', in J.A. Frowein and T. Stein (eds), *Die Rechtsstellung von Ausländern nach staatlichem Recht und Völkerrecht* (Berlin: Springer-Verlag, 1987), p. 485; P. Weil, *La France et ses étrangers* (2nd edition, Paris: Folio 1995), p. 36.

25. The abbreviation RPR stands for the centre-right party Rassemblement pour la République and UDF for the centrist party Union pour la Démocratie Française.

26. The English translation of *Europe passoire* would be 'Europe as a sieve'.

27. Law no. 93–933 of 22 July 1993.

28. Law no. 93–992 of 10 August 1993.

29. Law no. 93–1417 of 30 December 1993.

30. The constitutional right to asylum in France is contained in section 4 of the constitutional preamble, which reads, 'Everyone persecuted because of his actions on behalf of liberty has the right of asylum in the territories of the Republic.'

31. This decision of the Constitutional Council of 12–13 August 1993 (no. 93–325) was the longest ever rendered and censured eight of the 51 articles of the proposed law. This ruling in fact merely reiterated the interpretation of this right in an earlier ruling of the Constitutional Council of 25 July 1991 (no. 91–294 DC). The ruling confirmed the constitutionality of the 1990 Schengen Agreement with explicit reference to the exception clause of article 29IV of that agreement, according to which every state retains the right to examine an asylum claim on the basis of its national provisions, even if the agreement determines a case to be the responsibility of another state.

32. Bill of 19 November 1993 introducing article 53-1 into the French constitution.

33. K. Oellers-Frahm and A. Zimmermann, 'France's and Germany's constitutional changes and their impact on migration law: policy and practice', *German Yearbook of International Law* 38 (1995), 249-83; J.-L. Quermonne, 'Chronique d'une révision constitutionnelle bouleversée: la révision constitutionnelle en France, en régime de "cohabitation"', *French Politics and Society*, 12 (1) (1994), 1-15.

34. Ordinance no. 45-2658 of 2 November 1945 on the entry and stay of foreigners in France.

35. This exclusion procedure is regulated in article 53 of the French constitution together with article 35*quater* of decree of 27 May 1982 for asylum requests which are made at the border and article 31*bis* of the ordinance on the entry and stay of foreigners of 2 November 1945.

36. Although not explicitly spelled out in the law, the safe third country rule was applied in the case of applications at the border by the border officials (see Report of the Interior Ministry, *Zones d'attente des ports, des aéroports et des gares ferroviaires: bilan synthétique de l'année 1996*) as well as in the procedure applying inside the territory according to article 31*bis* of the ordinance of 2 November 1945. On the implications of the 'safe third country' rule with a focus on Central and Eastern Europe, see S. Lavenex, *Safe Third Countries: Extending EU Asylum and Immigration Policies to Central and Eastern Europe* (Budapest: Central European University Press, 1999).

37. Article 31*bis* of the ordinance of 2 November 1945.

38. Although not explicitly mentioned in the 1993 law, the notion of safe countries of origin was included in the status examination procedures in the OFPRA and was later explicitly legalized with the Chevènement law of 8 April 1998 modifying the law of 25 July 1952 (article 10 II).

39. See B. Laffan, 'The politics of identity and political order in Europe', *Journal of Common Market Studies* 34 (1) (1996), 81-102.

40. Lionel Jospin, speech to the National Assembly on 19 June 1997, printed in *Libération*, 20 June 1997.

41. This mobilization effort involved the movement of the '*sans papiers*' and the 'movement of the artists' - that is, well-known French personalities of the cinema, literature and arts who strongly expressed their opposition to the increasing securitization of the immigration question and, more specifically, the proposal of Interior Minister Debré to impose an obligation on residents hosting aliens to declare their departure at the termination of their stay to the competent authorities.

42. F. Julien-Laferrière, 'La "loi Chevènement" sur l'entrée et le séjour des étrangers et sur le droit d'asile', *Regards sur l'Actualité* 242 (1998), 17-39; C. Saas, 'Die Neuregelung der Einreise und des Aufenthalts von Ausländern in Frankreich: Viel Lärm um nichts', *Zeitschrift für Ausländerrecht und Ausländerpolitik* 23 (1) (1999), 10-17.

43. Chevènement in the National Assembly on 15 December 1997. According to an article in *Le Monde* of 9 April 1999, only two people have benefited from this constitutional asylum since its introduction in 1998.

44. Chevènement in the National Assembly on 15 December 1997. See also Amnesty International, *Une année d'application de l'asile territorial: quelques premières observations* (Paris, 11 May 1999).

45. Quoted in Amnesty International, *Une année d'application de l'asile territorial*.

46. Saas, 'Die Neuregelung der Einreise und des Aufenthalts von Ausländern', p. 16.

47. *Le Monde*, 9 April 1999.

48. According to an opinion poll conducted by SOFRES in late April 1999, the National Front has lost nearly half of its supporters compared to 1998 and 1997.

49. Prime Minister Jospin on 4 April 1999, quoted in *Le Monde*, 9 April 1999, p. 12.

50. The term 'third-country nationals' has been coined in the process of European integration and, in the light of an emerging EU citizenship and common immigration control policies, refers to citizens from non-member states.

51. Prime Minister Jospin on 6 April 1999 in the National Assembly, quoted in *Le Monde*, 8 April 1999.

52. He thus confirmed the recommendations made by the UNHCR concerning the reception of Kosovar refugees; see *Le Monde*, 26 May 1999.

53. Bernard Kouchner is now High Representative of the UN in Kosovo.

54. Quoted in *Le Monde*, 13 April 1999.

55. *Le Monde*, of 10 and 13 April 1999 and 21 May 1999; *Libération*, 21 April 1999.

56. *Libération*, 21 May 1999.

57. Information from the UNHCR office in Paris.

58. *Le Monde*, 8 April 1999.

59. Prime Minister Jospin in the National Assembly on 6 April 1999, quoted in *Le Monde*, 8 April 1999.

60. See *Le Monde*, 15 April 1999.

61. Charles Josselin, Minister for Cooperation in the National Assembly, on 7 April 1999.

62. *Le Parisien*, 13 April 1999.

63. See *Fichier des Affaires étrangères*, 19 April 1999: Accueil des Kosovars, and Amnesty International *et al.*, *Accueil des réfugiés du Kosovo*, 19 April 1999.

64. See also note of the Interior Ministry of 14 April 1999: Réfugiés du Kosovo, Note à l'attention de Monsieur le Délegué en France du HCR.

65. Quoted in Amnesty International, Section française, *Les Réfugiés kosovars et la France*, note of 20 April 1999.

66. Philippe Lavanchy, delegate of the UNHCR for France, in *Le Monde*, 26 May 1999.

67. Information from the UNHCR office in Paris.

68. The Europeanization of French refugee policies is analysed in comparative perspective in S. Lavenex, 'The Europeanization of refugee policies: between human rights and internal security', PhD dissertation (Florence: European University Institute, 1999).

69. On the development of a common European asylum and immigration policy, see E. Guild and J. Niessen (eds), *The Developing Immigration and Asylum Policies of the European Union* (The Hague: Kluwer Law International, 1996) and D.G. Papademetriou, *Coming Together or Pulling Apart? The European*

Union's Struggle with Immigration and Asylum (Washington, DC: Carnegie Endowment for International Peace, 1996).

70. This was already reflected in Interior Minister Pasqua's ambiguous stance towards full implementation of the Schengen Agreement between 1993 and 1995 and also characterized the position of his successor, Debré. Finally, the new Interior Minister, Chevènement, under the Jospin government is known for his scepticism *vis-à-vis* European integration, a scepticism which is also characteristic of his party, Mouvement des Citoyens.

71. This concerned the introduction of sanctions on carriers enabling the illegal entry of undocumented migrants, as provided in article 26 of the Schengen Agreement; law of 26 February 1992 introducing article 20*bis* in the ordinance of 2 November 1945 on the entry and stay of foreigners.

72. Article 53-1 of the French constitution.

73. In particular, France opposed an increased role for the European Parliament and the competence of the European Court of Justice in asylum and immigration matters, and did not actively support transfer of these policy fields from the third to the first pillar; see European Parliament, *Summary Position of the Member States of the European Union with a View to the 1996 Intergovernmental Conference* (Brussels: Intergovernmental Conference Task Force, 29 March 1996).

74. Ruling of the Council of State (*Conseil d'État*) in the *Rogers* case of 18 December 1996.

75. However, the procedures applying at the border were not amended, and the importance of these changes is limited if one considers that France, being surrounded by Schengen and EU member states (apart from Switzerland), could in theory return all those asylum seekers who arrive by land to one of these countries.

76. See Joint Position adopted on 4 March 1996 on the harmonized application of the definition of the term 'refugee' in article 1 of the Geneva Convention of 28 July 1951 relating to the status of refugees.

Bibliography

Books and journal articles

Amnesty International, *Une année d'application de l'asile territorial: quelques premières observations* (Paris, 11 May 1999).

Amnesty International and France Terre d'Asile, *Droit d'asile en France: état des lieux* (Paris: Amnesty International, 1997).

Bigo, D., 'Security(s): internal and external, the Möbius ribbon', Paper presented at the ISA Annual Convention in Toronto, 18–22 March 1997.

Guild, E. and Niessen, J. (eds), *The Developing Immigration and Asylum Policies of the European Union* (The Hague: Kluwer Law International, 1996).

Hailbronner, K., *Die Rechtsstellung der De Facto-Flüchtlinge in den EG-Staaten: Rechtsvergleichung und europäische Harmonisierung* (Baden-Baden: Nomos, 1993).

IGC (Intergovernmental Consultations on Asylum, Refugee and Migration Policies in Europe, North America and Australia), *Report on Temporary Protection in States in Europe, North America and Australia* (Geneva, 1995).

Julien-Laferrière, F., 'La "loi Chevènement" sur l'entrée et le séjour des étrangers et sur le droit d'asile', *Regards sur l'Actualité* 242 (1998), 17-39.

Kastoryano, R., 'Immigration and identities in France: the war of words', *French Politics and Society* 14 (2) (1996), 58-66.

Kerber, K., 'Temporary protection: an assessment of the harmonisation policies of European Union Member States', *International Journal of Refugee Law* 9 (3) (1997), 452-75.

Laffan, B., 'The politics of identity and political order in Europe', *Journal of Common Market Studies* 34 (1) (1996), 81-102.

Lavenex, S., 'The Europeanization of refugee policies: between human rights and internal security', PhD dissertation (Florence: European University Institute, 1999).

Lavenex, S., *Safe Third Countries: Extending EU Asylum and Immigration Policies to Central and Eastern Europe* (Budapest: Central European University Press, 1999).

Legoux, L., 'La demande d'asile en France: le pic de 1989 et la théorie de la dissuasion', *Revue Européenne des Migrations Internationales* 9 (2) (1993), 31-65.

Legoux, L., *La Crise de l'asile politique en France* (Paris: Centre Français sur la Population et le Développement, 1995).

Liebaut, F. and Hughes, J. (eds), *Legal and Social Conditions for Asylum Seekers and Refugees, France*, Danish Refugee Council (1997): www.drc.dk/eng/PUB/legsoc/France.html.

Noiriel, G. *La Tyrannie du national: le droit d'asile en Europe 1793-1993* (Paris: Callmann-Lévy, 1991).

Norek, C. and Doumic-Doublet, F., *Le Droit d'asile en France* (Paris: Presses Universitaires de France, 1989).

Oellers-Frahm, K. and A. Zimmermann, 'France's and Germany's constitutional changes and their impact on migration law: policy and practice', *German Yearbook of International Law* 38 (1995), 249-83.

Papademetriou, D.G., *Coming Together or Pulling Apart? The European Union's Struggle with Immigration and Asylum* (Washington, DC: Carnegie Endowment for International Peace, 1996).

Perotti, A. and Thépaut, F., 'Le Président de la République et les immigrés', *Migrations Société* (1989), 41-58.

Quermonne, J.-L., 'Chronique d'une révision constitutionnelle bouleversée: la révision constitutionnelle en France, en régime de "cohabitation"', *French Politics and Society* 12 (1) (1994), 1-15.

Saas, C., 'Die Neuregelung der Einreise und des Aufenthalts von Ausländern in Frankreich: Viel Lärm um nichts', *Zeitschrift für Ausländerrecht und Ausländerpolitik* 23 (1) (1999), 10-17.

Schain, M.A., 'The immigration debate and the National Front', in J.T.S. Keeler and M.A. Schain (eds) *Chirac's Challenge: Liberalization, Europeanization and Malaise in France* (New York: St Martin's Press, 1996), pp. 169-98.

Schnapper, D., *La France de l'intégration: sociologie de la nation en 1990* (Paris: Gallimard, 1991).

Schnapper, D., 'The significance of French immigration and integration policy', in F. Heckmann and W. Bosswick (eds) *Migration Policies: A Comparative Perspective* (Stuttgart: Enke, 1995).

Schor, Ralph, 'L'Extrême Droite française et les immigrés en temps de crise: années 1930–années 1980', *Revue Européenne des Migrations Internationales* 12 (2) (1996), 241–60.

Selm-Thorburn, J. van, *Refugee Protection in Europe: Lessons from the Yugoslav Crisis* (Dordrecht: Martinus Nijhoff, 1998).

Silverman, M., *Deconstructing the Nation: Immigration, Racism and Citizenship in Modern France* (London: Routledge, 1992).

Targuieff, P.-A., (ed.), *Face au racisme* (Paris: Éditions La Découverte, 1991).

Thorburn, J., 'Transcending boundaries: temporary protection and burden-sharing in Europe', *International Journal of Refugee Law* 7 (3) (1995), 459–80.

Tuppen, J., *Chirac's France, 1986–1988: Contemporary Issues in French Society* (London: Macmillan, 1991).

Vincent, J.Y., 'Le Régime juridique des étrangers en droit français', in J.A. Frowein and T. Stein (eds) *Die Rechtsstellung von Ausländern nach staatlichem Recht und Völkerrecht* (Berlin: Springer-Verlag, 1987).

Waever, O., 'Securitization and desecuritization', in R.D. Lipschutz (ed.) *On Security* (New York: Columbia University Press, 1995).

Waever, O., Buzan, B., Kelstrup, M. and Lemaitre, P., *Identity, Migration and the New Security Order in Europe* (London: Pinter, 1993).

Weil, P., *La France et ses étrangers* (2nd edition, Paris: Folio 1995).

Wihtol de Wenden, C., 'The French debate: legal and political instruments to promote integration', in H. Fassmann and R. Münz (eds) *European Migration in the Late Twentieth Century: Historical Patterns, Actual Trends, and Social Implications* (Aldershot: Elgar, 1994).

Primary sources

Ministère des Affaires étrangères, Fichier du 19 April 1999 sur l' Acceuil des Kosovars.

Ministère de l'Intérieur, note du 14 April 1999 à l'attention de Monsieur le Délégué en France du HCR.

Web sites

IGC, Asylum Statistics: www.igc.ch/frstatistics.htm

CHAPTER 9

Conclusion

JOANNE VAN SELM

Introduction

The aim of this concluding chapter is to pull together some of the points made in the preceding case studies and, to the extent that it is possible at this relatively early stage, to draw some of the lessons which could be learned from the handling of the Kosovo refugee crisis and highlight some of the emerging areas worthy of further reflection.

The four themes set out in Chapter 1, the Introduction to this volume, and carried through the case studies will be returned to. Woven through those themes will be some discussion of emergent areas for potential further research and thought. The sections below will thus deal with:

1 the lessons of the reception and statuses accorded to Bosnians drawn on in dealing with the displacements of Kosovars, including a comparative European Union (EU) perspective. What did the EU member states think they should expect of one another, and of the potential for collective action? What were the lessons drawn from the national level?
2 the national debates on asylum and immigration within which this crisis took place and which influenced policy-making, including the national debates on EU integration on this area;
3 the wider theoretical issues, most particularly on questions of 'societal security' and xenophobia;
4 the way EU integration (or lack of it) on the subject affected policy-making in the different states, encouraging notions of a comprehensive approach centring on protection, but linked to foreign policy and security approaches to conflict resolution and intervention, and leading to more lasting solutions which highlight return;
5 the lessons learned, and emerging areas for reflection.

JOANNE VAN SELM

Lessons learned from the reception of the Bosnian displaced

The lessons learned from the experience of dealing with the protection of post-Cold War refugees fleeing conflict presented in the cases studied fall into two categories: the lessons expressed in measures taken at national level and those expressed by debate and rhetoric concerning the EU level, whether expressed in European fora or for a domestic audience.

At the national level all EU states studied here had introduced restrictive measures making the spontaneous arrival of Bosnians (and other refugees and asylum seekers) more difficult, and putting procedural obstacles at least in the way of their effective legal protection, even if the individuals concerned were in effect safe from *refoulement*. Visas, carrier sanctions and 'safe third country' rules have all been mentioned in the above chapters as restrictive measures employed in this context. Also at the national level, many states introduced new statuses as a direct result of the perceived need for a non-Convention, temporary protection category. The Netherlands introduced such a new legal status while Bosnians were still arriving, although of total arrivals, many more received a Convention status than the new short-term permit. Austria also adapted its legislation granting short-term residence during the Bosnian crisis. Italy introduced *ad hoc* measures of temporary protection, but they were not of a format which could be used in any new crisis situation arising: further *ad hoc* measures would be needed for that. Germany, Sweden and France all changed their legislation as a result of the Bosnian crisis, even if the new statuses created were not directly used, or available on time in some cases, for the Bosnian displaced. The UK adopted an *ad hoc* quota programme based on the existing status contained in the policy of 'exceptional leave to remain', rather than creating an entirely new status.

These temporary protection approaches have been introduced at the national level in many EU states in spite of the fact that only Germany has seen anything like what could be termed significant returns of Bosnians. Return following the signing of the Dayton Accords was to be doubted. As I have written previously (1998):

> One concern for the broader picture of the development of temporary protection has to be that if the agreement reached in Dayton holds, and the violence ceases, but refugees do not return, governments will be persuaded that their scepticism was well placed, and the evolution of temporary protection policies as contingency planning for future crises will be halted.[1]

The lack of massive returns did not prevent the development of temporary protection statuses as part of governments' array of measures at the national level, although it did, as all authors have shown here, stand in the way of generous approaches, in terms of numbers, towards the actual arrival and admission of Kosovars. This motivated the search for so-

190

called 'reception in the region' options, but a further lesson learned, as suggested in the chapter on The Netherlands, seems to have been not to attempt the 'safe area' approach within Serbia itself.

The development of statuses of temporary protection in the laws and policies of many member states thus does not show that scepticism surrounding the possible length of stay of protected persons has been removed. It perhaps rather shows that governments believe that their electorates want to think that the refugees will only be staying a short time. By the time potential departure, and especially forced returns, come about, and especially if there is a time lag of years rather than months, there can be just as much public discontent. As Morten Kjærum has eloquently said, 'those global fears then turn to local tears'.[2]

One level on which the Bosnian experience has not been sufficient to motivate the development of a temporary protection approach, however, is the EU level. All states considered used the Bosnian case as the example needed to seek, or at least claim to seek, an EU-level solution for the next crisis. However, when the next (or continuation of the) Balkan crisis came along in the form of the exoduses from Kosovo at the time of the NATO intervention, no EU system involving a uniform or harmonized status was in place. There was no agreement on the type of reception to be offered and there was certainly no preconceived agreement on solidarity in the face of a large-scale exodus from a European state which could turn into a large-scale influx to the EU states. Indeed, discussions on the temporary protection joint action proposed by the European Commission had virtually collapsed precisely because it did not contain measures for spreading the responsibility of protection around the member states to which key states could agree.

Expectations with regard to solidarity when the mass displacements from Kosovo occurred without an enforceable or effective 'responsibility-sharing' measure in place varied, and did not always reflect in a logical way, the lessons perceived to have been learned from Bosnia. Germany, Koser indicates, expected other EU states to do nothing as a result of the experience with receiving Bosnian refugees. However, while this anticipation may have been correct, it did expect more to be done this time around, or at least seek a way of not being the only bearer of the humanitarian burden in the form of sheltering refugees within its own territory. The German government accepted 10,000 refugees on the evacuation programme, and then waited until other states had shown willing in a reasonable measure. The Netherlands, on the other hand, which also felt it had done more than its fair share in the Bosnia case, tried to do nothing until it had proof that its partners were also going to act. It was one of the states which filled its initial quota a few weeks into the conflict, giving part of the sufficient proof Germany required to reopen its doors. Sweden also, as Abiri shows above, took the position that it had done more than its fair share in managing the Balkan refugee crisis by accepting and maintaining the presence of Bosnians.

Interestingly, in the UK's case Guild points out that where numbers were concerned, it was not so much that the UK had learned lessons which it could effectively use to reduce its role, but rather that the other EU states had learned lessons in how to handle the UK. As she puts it, 'the immediate pressure brought to bear by European Union partners may have contributed to' the UK coming closer to its numerical target in the Kosovo case than in the Bosnian case. The lesson the other member states may have learned was 'to put immediate and continued pressure on the UK to accept refugees for resettlement and not to accept vague indications'.

Austria's experience prior to the Bosnian case where mass movements of conflict refugees were concerned was that other Western states were the final destination of people transiting Austria. In the Bosnian case, Austria learned that its days as a transit state for conflict refugees were over, and the Kosovo case proved this to be correct: geopolitical changes, as well as technological changes meaning that transportation for refugees is not primarily overland, have caused Austria to become, like its northern and western neighbours, a host country to asylum seekers and refugees. This lesson is one which, in immigration terms generally, Italy is only just learning, and one which has been reinforced in the Kosovo case. Although many of those fleeing spontaneously, rather than on evacuation programmes, did still only transit Italy, those evacuated to Italy in general remained there until they returned to Kosovo in July and August 1999.

National debates

Although the need for an EU-level approach seems to figure in the political context in which protection of the Kosovars in all states took place, it is one of the few common features. Perhaps one of the most striking conclusions to be drawn here is how different the national debates surrounding asylum remain in each of the member states, at least in their details. However, one should not forget that many of the debates surrounding this issue are almost cyclical in nature, and the more so when one adds the perceived knock-on effects of policy changes in neighbouring and partner EU states.

In Germany the debates around asylum and immigration at the time of the Kosovo crisis focused on the costs of protection, the internal distribution (or burden-sharing) system and the changes to citizenship legislation which were progressing towards the introduction of *jus soli*.

The Netherlands and the UK were both also going through domestic debates on legislation, but in their cases the legislation was that precisely on asylum and immigration. The context in The Netherlands was also one of a recent rise in the numbers of asylum seekers (which have since decreased below the forecast levels, and below the levels of previous years). This had led to an increase in the manifestation of anti-asylum seeker sentiment, as more reception centres were needed, involving local information and discussion meetings at each new location. In the UK the numbers of asylum seekers were also increasing, and there was general management chaos, with the entire computer and filing system in disarray for a variety of reasons which Guild explains in Chapter 4.

Sweden, meanwhile, had seen legislative changes, and was in the process of political discussions surrounding the nature of its 'comprehensive approach' to the asylum issue, including the use of foreign policy and various internal security-oriented policies. As in France, following legislative changes and wide-ranging, generally restriction-oriented debate in the early 1990s, public opinion was more strongly for, rather than against, the reception of conflict-fleeing refugees than had been the case during the Bosnian displacements, even if politicians appeared either slow to pick up on this, or wary that the mood might change. Austria had also seen legislative changes, and, in the midst of an election campaign, was experiencing an apparent, and internationally publicized, rise in anti-immigrant sentiment. However, Stacher characterizes (Chapter 6) a quite clear distinction between a real and present anti-immigration mood and the warm-hearted reception Austrians remain very prepared to give to conflict refugees. Developments and debate surrounding Italian asylum practices had also been in the international spotlight with the asylum request made by PKK (Kurdish Workers' Party) leader Abdullah Ocalan.

Societal security, xenophobia and 'good refugees'

In all the countries described in this volume there may have been reason for concern as to xenophobic sentiment with regard to immigrants and asylum seekers generally, based often on empirical evidence of, for example, presumed reasons for voting patterns and violent attacks carried out by a very small minority of the population. Such perception of real sentiment is logically at the root of the theories on 'societal security' that have been described in the introductory chapter (Chapter 1) and several other chapters. They are also at the root of much political debate on this subject. However, in all EU states studied here, public opinion on the reception of and assistance to Kosovar refugees during the conflict proved very accepting and welcoming. All the authors in this volume have demonstrated how political action and policy-making much under-estimated the public shows of solidarity; one could indeed strongly suggest that while state-level solidarity seemed to be absent, individual solidarity for fellow human beings was very much present.

Society, in the form of public opinion, 'spoke' in favour of the displaced persons from Kosovo. Waever *et al.* point out the problems their concept of 'societal security' bring in the matter of who speaks for society.[3] They acknowledge that the voices heard may sometimes not be ones which necessarily have to be taken seriously. However, they appear, as governments do, to take the loud shouts of those favouring exclusion to be closer to some form of empirical truth than the views of silent, perhaps more tolerant, majority. As Waever *et al.* indicate, society is not a unitary actor; there is a hierarchy. One could add that that notion of a hierarchy is not necessarily based on rectitude or magnitude, but perhaps rather on decibels and effects. In this case, humanitarian sentiment appeared to speak the loudest, even if governmental attention was still focused on other voices and other pragmatic reasoning with regard to refugee and 'societal' protection. One question is that of whether Kosovo was an exception, or a precedent; and whichever it was, what created that positive reaction.

Of course, much of this reaction was generated by media coverage of the exodus from Kosovo and conditions in the camps close to the border (what one could call the CNN factor). As Matthew Gibney has noted, 'amazingly, in March when Kosovan Albanians began to flee in large numbers, it was as if [the] river of hostility [towards asylum seekers] started to flow backwards'.[4] Gibney explains the popularity of the Kosovar refugees, unprecedented in recent history in that it had no clear ideological underpinning, as was the case of the Hungarians, Czechs and Vietnamese in the Cold War era, by highlighting three features: regionality, implicatedness and relatedness. In essence, the refugees were nearby; the same states, under the NATO flag, were involved in the crisis which directly or indirectly was causing the plight of the refugees; and the people seen on the TV screens were white Europeans, as Gibney says, not only dressed like the EU public watching them in horror, but also often stuck in traffic jams even during their escape.

However, those same features, and most especially the regional location of the displacements, provided reasons for which EU govern-ments were reluctant to remove many of the refugees for protection purposes. The regionality feature meant that wherever the displaced were located, this crisis was going to have financial costs for the EU states. The air campaign aimed at protecting the Kosovars from a humanitarian catastrophe had obvious implications, including, directly or indirectly, for the ultimate timing of flight. A facet of implicatedness which Gibney does not refer to, but which is clear from the chapters on Italy and Austria in this volume, is that having established their own camps in the 'region of origin', EU governments were implicated in the 'smooth running' of reception and the safety of the refugees, not only on their own territory, but also on the territory of Albania and Macedonia.[5] However, the feature of relatedness is perhaps the one which drew the most public attention and sympathy. That relatedness has, of course, connections to the feature of regionality. But implicated in the sense of relatedness which Gibney describes are not only clothes and traffic jams: whether one wishes to recognize it or not, race clearly also struck a chord here. However, if the factor of relatedness was really so strong, then further questions about the importance of religion, so often portrayed as the basis of potential existential clashes in Europe, must also be open to new analysis.

Something more complex than racism, xenophobia or even 'societal selfishness' – the sense of having it so good that any newcomer is not welcome as they are likely only to change the situation and want a part of the existing pie – seems to have been at work.[6] And something more complex, or at least more nuanced, seems to be more widely at work, both in policy creation and in public and political debate on asylum in the EU states. As Abiri noted concerning Sweden (Chapter 5), the notions of threats to identity and other societal insecurities do not appear to be explicitly at play in the bases of new policy thinking, and even if they are implicitly observable, they are not so distinct as to allow such positivist theoretical reasoning to take place uncritically. There is no single truth in migration discussions, whether linked to security issues or not, only perceptions on all sides (policy-makers, public, host state/society, immigrants, asylum seekers, states of origin) which together construct a complex human debate.

As indicated in the Introduction to this volume (Chapter 1), we do not seek actively to engage in theory-making, but rather to lay open questions for further, theoretically and conceptually oriented, debate. One such question has to be the locus or nature of a (perceived) threat to 'identity' or the society which identifies itself with certain characteristics. The rather simplistic notion picked up in the presentation of 'societal security' has been that immigrants, or the phenomenon of migration, present some kind of existential threat to societies and their identities. The chapters in this book seem rather to suggest that, where asylum seekers are concerned at least, and in the case of Kosovo in particular, the migrants or their migration do not cause the threat which European societies or public opinion perceives; rather, the challenge to people which forces them to flee is perceived as a challenge to what might be called 'human identity'.[7] In other words, the 'refugees' themselves, as individuals, do not threaten the stability of receiving states, although their numbers may be perceived by some as destabilizing. The more concrete threat comes from the state of origin which ceased to protect the people concerned. What is more, a further threat to the public perception of its identity comes from the wider community of states (of which their own state forms a part) which refuses to live up to its obligations to grant protection and a status to those who are denied the normal protection of their state of origin. This is reinforced in more traditional security terms when policies aimed at keeping the 'refugees' close to the state of origin only encourage a geographic widening of the conflict, either when fighters among the refugees (in the Kosovars' case, the UCK – Kosovo Liberation Army) continue to fight across the border, or at least use the border 'refugee' camps as bases, or when the forces in the state of origin continue their attacks on the fleeing population even once they are across an internationally recognized frontier. In either case this security threat would clearly be avoided if the 'refugees' were not only permitted, but also encouraged, to move to protection further away. Under the circumstances, it was convenient that Kosovar Albanians were often heard claiming that they did not want to move far from home. However, many more might well have turned to smugglers to buy their escape if the crisis had continued for much longer, and as Hein describes (Chapter 7), considerable numbers were in fact doing so. Our understandings of the nature of, and reasons for, people-smuggling, particularly of those people who in fact have a declared right to seek protection in another state, will be supported by further reflection on these complex security issues.[8] Some of the displaced may have been people who would seek (or seem to seek) to abuse the hospitality of a protecting state. But the vast majority, rather than being threats, were the victims of threats and the victims of intolerance, and that seems to have been their lot almost everywhere they turned. It seems also to be the lot of many Serbs and Roma, some innocent, some not, in their turn displaced from their homes in Kosovo, with little protection and nowhere to go. By November 1999 there were estimated to be between 120,000 and 200,000 Serbs displaced from Kosovo, the majority in Serbia.[9]

Kosovo has thrown open many significant issues for theorizing and for the conceptualization of the nature of post-Cold War security. Security remains an essentially contested concept, whose understanding is only, apparently, becoming more complex with the removal of what for forty years was *the* major concern: nuclear war between ideologically opposed superpowers. Reflection on the interlinked notions of security and insecurity (military, societal and human, to name but three) is certainly needed, and the ethical dimensions of this area of international relations must surely not be left aside.[10] The chapters in this volume have all demonstrated the value of norms in consideration of approaches to refugee protection, and impressions of public perception of the Kosovar refugees are one demonstration of the role of ethical decisions and debates in day-to-day life which Frost so usefully describes.

EU integration and the comprehensive approach

The most prevalent feature of all EU decision-making concerning displaced Kosovars, both collective and nationally, as is apparent from the descriptions in this book, was vacillation. Questions of status played a significant role, at least theoretically: whether the 'refugees' were 'Convention refugees' or not was a matter of discussion, and often politicians, including those in government, agreed with the United Nations High Commissioner for Refugees (UNHCR) and non-governmental organizations (NGOs) that the Kosovars fitted the bill presented in the Convention definition. However, all states granted their own form of temporary protection to those arriving on the Humanitarian Evacuation Programme (where such a status category existed), and at least did not return those arriving spontaneously or those who had previously arrived, even if Convention status was not, in fact, granted.

Many of the major players in the EU sought an EU-level approach in this policy field from the earliest days of the crisis. However, not having agreed in advance to contingency planning and criteria, they could not agree in the face of a major displacement crisis about where, when and how the refugees should be protected. Agreement on the essence of 'reception in the region' was challenged by the realities of public opinion and Macedonian reluctance to bear a protection responsibility which could threaten its own political stability. There was clearly no agreement on EU solidarity, whether in the share of responsibility for the EU part of the Humanitarian Evacuation Programme or in sharing the costs of reception. There was also no agreement on other areas of financial interest, such as return. In considering here the portrayal Kosovo gives of the state of European integration where asylum is concerned, I will focus on three features: 'solidarity', return incentives and the 'comprehensive approach'.

Solidarity

All the chapters in this volume have referred to questions labelled 'solidarity' referring to interstate systems of support and distribution with regard to protection issues. Where solidarity in numbers is concerned, the authors have shown how these seven states entered negotiations and perceived their own role, in what effectively was similar to a game of poker. There is no binding 'burden-sharing' principle agreed at EU level. Discussions between states, as well as the rights-based views of the UNHCR, NGOs and many academics, indicate strongly that the distribution of refugees, as individuals, cannot work in theory, or (particularly given other EU developing rights to freedom of movement) in practice. If any form of 'physical burden sharing' could have a remote possibility of being operationally possible, it would have to be according to a quota evacuation programme. In that sense, Kosovo gives an interesting basis for analysing how close states came to a balanced form of distribution, even without a model in place. The only models which are in place are the domestic ones in two of the countries studied here, Germany and Austria. These rely on population figures per state or province alone (not density, or relative economic performance, for example). In such a model one would find that EU states should share responsibility in the proportions set out in Table 9 of Appendix 2. Table 2 in the same appendix shows the distribution of arrivals on the evacuation programme from Macedonia. Comparing these percentages, one sees that *if* such a simple model of distribution had been in place, the spread of refugees under a quota would have been rather different. Only Luxembourg accepted, under the quota programme, a number of 'refugees' close to what these proportions indicated might be its 'fair share'. Austria, Denmark, Finland, Germany, Ireland, Italy, The Netherlands and Sweden took 'more than their fair share', while the UK, France and Spain were furthest 'below target'. The quota figures which were in fact established (Appendix 2, Table 3) show a different story as to 'preparedness' to accept refugees. However, there were big differences between actual arrivals and the quota established. Meanwhile, comparison of the total numbers of asylum applications from citizens of Yugoslavia in 1999 (Appendix 2, Table 4) and the programme arrivals shows further differences: the programme arrivals in Austria, Belgium, France, Germany, Luxembourg and the UK were proportionally lower than their share of the total arrivals of asylum applicants.

One question for future reflection is whether or not temporary protection at the EU level has per se to include a measure of 'burden sharing' or 'responsibility sharing' or solidarity, or whether the two are separable; and indeed whether different measures and linkages are possible and useful or appropriate depending on whether protection is granted under a quota programme with numerical divisions or on an individualized basis for spontaneous arrivals.

Return

Lavenex states in Chapter 8 on France that EU states seem to be able to agree more readily on return than on original reception. In many ways she has a point; however, it is interesting to note what could be called a new element of divergence for the 'asylum shopping catalogue'. In efforts to 'encourage' return, EU states give allowances – often, as is the case for Kosovars, under a programme managed by the International Organization for Migration. For Kosovars the repatriation allowances offered were very divergent, as can be seen from Table 9.1.

It might be tempting to try to draw conclusions relating to a

Table 9.1 Repatriation allowances for Kosovars (EU member states)

Member state	Amount (euros)	Additional information
Austria	218	Allowance can go up to 654 euros, dependent on damage to home in Kosovo. Travel expenses covered.
Belgium	247	Go and see permitted, but at refugees' own expense
Denmark	2418	806 euros per child. Max. 1344 additional allowance for expenses on building equipment.
Finland	670	or 1350 euros per family. Travel expenses covered.
France	495	153 euros per child. 92 euros travel expense assistance offered for 'go and see'.
Germany	153	76.5 euros per child. Max. 765 euros per family. Additional 230 euros per adult and 115 euros per child once in Kosovo, to a maximum of 690 euros.
Greece	N/A	
Ireland	—	
Italy	0	Military flights used for voluntary return.
Luxembourg	275	150 euros per child. Travel expenses covered.
Netherlands	567	794 euros for a family with two children and 95 euros per additional child. For those not on the HEP 227 euros per person and 322 Euro for a family with 2 children. No 'go and see'.
Portugal	0	No 'go and see'. Only entire families.
Spain	—	Financial aid given once in Kosovo. Priority given to those refugees/returnees with useful skills for rebuilding Kosovo.
Sweden	566	Max. 3400 euros per family. No 'go and see'. If return to Sweden, do so at own expense, within validity of permit, but do not need to reimburse assistance.
UK	375	No 'go and see'.

Source: Various NGO documents (October 1999)

Note: A dash (—) means that no clear information is available, including no information indicating that the amount is zero.

government's desire to return protection seekers on the basis of this information, or the relative wealth and generosity of states, but the heart of the matter in the context of this volume is rather how EU member states have again created details which distinguish them, and which, given their own voiced concern for how smugglers select destinations for the displaced, asylum seekers and other migrants they transport, seem paradoxical in a Union which is claiming to seek a common approach. One would not suggest that states should be less humane or generous in their channelled attempts to improve the wider economic situation in Kosovo via returnees, or their assistance to those who have temporarily sought their protection and depended on them. Nevertheless, coordination in relatively new areas, and the details of those new areas, or the whole protection package would seem essential – otherwise there are only ever more areas for later negotiation and bargaining around the Council of Ministers' table.

Comprehensive approach

One way in which the effects of a so-called comprehensive approach have been demonstrated in this volume is in the vision Guild gives (Chapter 4) of the token protection of refugees as a means of making a foreign policy expression: showing action and humanitarianism as part of the external image of a country for the purposes of its foreign policy. This tokenism as an expression of foreign policy is directed not only at fellow host states (e.g. in the EU context) but also at the regimes one is opposing. Just as in the Cold War, the granting of asylum by Western states to those fleeing communism was seen as a way of showing political and ideological opposition to the Soviet bloc, so in the 1990s the token protection of refugees from conflict has become an expressive element of foreign policy. The significant difference lies once again in numbers: the communist states blocked much exit, whereas in the Kosovo case at least, expulsion of potential refugees was a goal of the Milošević regime.

Policy linkage in the post-Cold War period is clearly different from that pre-1989. The notion of a comprehensive approach to migration emerged in the late 1980s, and the discussion has been very policy oriented. However, future thought in this area could usefully engage theoretical discussion, for example on the range of security concepts with this policy debate.

One argument for suggesting that Kosovo's 'refugees' should not have been seen as unacceptable or unwelcome in large numbers in EU states is that those very states had intervened in the crisis prior to the cross-border movement of most of the displaced – the implicatedness referred to above. Logically, this is part of the chain of the comprehensive approach to protection described in Chapter 1 at the causality end. Whether the displacement of ethnic Albanians from Kosovo was directly or indirectly caused by the NATO bombs is not at issue. Rather, an ethical approach to the chain of events would suggest that the intervention by NATO states, proclaimed as being motivated by humanitarian concerns, pure and simple, set in motion a morally unavoidable duty to protect those humans whose suffering the outside states were already seeking to avoid or alleviate by their use of force in what they called a just cause.[11] The confusion and changing motivational claims as a result of the effects of 'implicatedness' can be seen in the narrowing of the goals guiding the NATO action as that went on, as expressed by Susan Woodward:

> Once the bombing began ... the number of dead and injured – estimated at 2,000 soldiers and civilians in the 13 months from February 1998 to March 1999 – began to skyrocket. And as residents streamed out of the province ... the goal of the campaign seemed to narrow from forcing compliance with the Rambouillet Accords, including insistence on a NATO-led international security force, to putting a stop to the 'ethnic cleansing', 'violence', and 'repression'. When the refugee toll surpassed the 100,000 that NATO and UNHCR planners had apparently considered the maximum and moved towards its eventual 750–800,000, the goal narrowed further, to reversing the refugee flow.[12]

This picture of narrowing goals raises questions about the relevance of a comprehensive approach if that is conceived in the relatively simplistic terms of employing a combination of foreign, security, trade and development policies, in conjunction with immigration and asylum policies, to uphold both human rights and sovereign rights over membership of the host state or residence there.

Events have an encompassing, or knock-on, effect. It is impossible to understand one element in the chain without understanding others; hence for an analyst, the conflict and displacements in and from Kosovo necessitate a comprehensive approach for comprehension. However, policy appears often to be made without those links in mind, and without institutional discussion or what could be called collective thinking. Although, as Abiri shows, some states are looking towards reform and an 'integrated refugee and immigration policy' implying close coordination between traditional refugee and immigration policy-making and policy-making in the fields of foreign affairs and international aid, making 'support for the struggle for human rights, measures to manage the economic and demographic imbalances, and promotion of trade with the developing countries' part of the refugee policy, this chain of thought is obviously not always present in policy-making, In particular, it is not always present when it comes to major crises and conflict (including the use of military security forces and policies) or decision-making by states involved in various organizations (NATO and the EU, but also NATO and the UNHCR as institutional apparatuses).

An area in which reflection could be inspired by the consideration of the comprehensive approach in this volume is that of the 'knock-on' effects which policies inevitably have. Not only could states, organizations and ministries usefully further consider the multiple impacts of policies and communicate better in advance of implementation, but also analysts and theorists could usefully consider what 'comprehensiveness' really implies. Above all, when engaging in theorizing on the widening of the security debate, consideration needs to be given to the place of human rights and protection issues, not only as migration and refugee matters, but also as an integral part of our developing notions of security.

If one picks up the questions of human rights and protection, matters of state sovereignty are never far away. This is, as implied in discussion of institutional organizing of various interlinking approaches, a key issue in refugee protection. Sovereignty enters the debate in more than one area, but one issue of sovereign concern is that of membership and entry to the territory, and society, of a given state. Another area is in the realm of foreign policy, and particularly security policy. Although there is a willingness, on paper at least, to give attention to integration on asylum and immigration policies, it is not clear how far EU states might be prepared to go in surrendering, or perhaps rather pooling or sharing, sovereignty on these matters. The sovereign hand remains, in practice, very much at the tiller. That is even more the case where foreign and security policies are concerned; there is no political will to go beyond an alliance on foreign and security policies, in spite of the appointment of a Monsieur PESC (EU representative on the Common Foreign and Security Policy). Where both the practical logistics and academic consideration of a comprehensive approach are concerned, this is of supreme importance. The chain of policies which form a comprehensive approach begin and end with foreign and security policies: dealing with the causes of migration and protection outside one's own territory (in the 'region' of origin'), as is both increasingly practised and discussed, is a matter of foreign policy concern. Seeking either the repatriation/return or the resettlement of refugees or the temporarily protected is also, in either case, a matter which affects the international relations of states, and thus of foreign policy concern. The matter of solidarity likewise falls in this area of sovereign management: how much will a state give, and how much can it take? How far EU states are prepared to go in altering their conception of sovereignty in this chain of policy areas is an important question.

Preliminary lessons learned and areas for reflection

In the previous four sections several areas have been mentioned on which further reflection is needed in the light of the presentation made here of the reception of Kosovo's refugees in the EU. From the point of view of analysing and understanding international relations, more thought needs to be given to the nature of 'security', be it conceived of as traditional, national, international, military or societal or human, and the links between these conceptualizations, and indeed their contradictions. With regard to the process of European integration on this subject, there clearly needs to be more reflection not only on the ways and means of coordination, harmonization and creation of a common policy, but also on the goals of such cooperation. Those goals should not be exclusively the member states' goals or the goals focused on individuals as set out in international norms, and championed by NGOs. Rather, consideration needs to be given to the reasons for cooperating on protection issues from all points of view.

Three final areas for reflection will be briefly described here: the differentiation (or discrimination) between quota arrivals and spontaneous arrivals from the same displacement situation; the use and meaning of temporary protection; and the role of images and perceptions in state-level approaches to protection of refugees.

Typology: quota – spontaneous

Attention needs to be drawn to the distinctions which are increasingly being made in the typology of migrants. Recent debates have concentrated on immigration *and* asylum. Immigrants and asylum seekers are seen as two separate categories, although all asylum seekers are, from the point of view of transferring their presence and residence from one state to another, also immigrants. Meanwhile many EU states use asylum as a major category for immigration, further confusing this distinction.

However, the distinction is not so simple, and the complexities do not lie only at the definitional end once people have arrived (who is a refugee; who is a long-term economic immigrant, who temporary; whose primary purpose is family reunification; etc.). There are also complexities which, to this author's knowledge, have thus far been less clearly distinguished or handled in analytical literature or policy-making, at the arrival or pre-arrival end of the spectrum. Clear distinctions were made by EU member states, as all authors have demonstrated, between quota arrivals and spontaneous arrivals, both in their actual treatment (access to status, housing, other entitlements) and in the portrayal made of them. The distinctions were not always equivalent from one state to another: the UK seems to have been more favourable towards spontaneous arrivals, The Netherlands towards quota arrivals, for example. And further distinctions were made between sub-groups of spontaneous arrivals: whether they arrived before, during or after the NATO bombing campaign, and of course how they arrived. Koser refers, for example, to three categories in the German context: asylum seekers, 'quota refugees' and clandestine migrants. And the differences (or discrimination?) seems to end in all cases when return or repatriation is at issue: whether one is a quota refugee with a temporary status, an asylum seeker with no status determined as yet or a 'clandestine' immigrant, return became more or less expected as of July 1999.

As has been pointed out above, quota programmes might be one of the limited ways in which EU states could influence distribution of 'refugees' or implement some form of solidarity. However, spontaneous arrivals will always reach EU states, and as Hein points out, the proportions of these arrivals will very often be linked to communities already resident in a given state as a result of previous migrations (e.g. for Kosovar Albanians, in Switzerland and Germany). The question is how notions of quotas and unpredictable spontaneous arrivals interplay, or can interplay, in both analysis of major displacements and policies aimed at managing those flows, particularly where those policies might also aim (usefully or otherwise) at some form of distribution.

Temporary protection

A further matter for reflection, already very much on the EU agenda, but given new light and new empirical data for analysis, is the question of what temporary protection is and how it can be used. Understandings of this already varied from state to state, and analysts have often confused the issue further by employing the same terminology of 'temporary protection' to talk about different concepts and approaches which perhaps have only the notion of short-term expectation as a common feature. The UK, as Guild demonstrates, used almost the US type of approach of making temporary protection grants have the effect of an amnesty for people who previously had been either illegally resident, or considered non-returnable even if they were not granted a status.[13] Italy also uses amnesties, though not necessarily in the form of temporary protection; rather, the protection of non-return (albeit without status) and administrative 'non-concern' is used by refugees who choose not to seek asylum while awaiting a general amnesty. In The Netherlands, meanwhile, although all protection is likely to become temporary in the first instance under new legislation as described in Chapter 3, temporary protection in the case of Kosovars was applied in different ways for spontaneous arrivals present for years before the 1999 intervention, those arriving spontaneously during the intervention period and those arriving on the Humanitarian Evacuation Programme – even though their status and criteria were formally the same.

What is more, as has often been pointed out in discussion surrounding conflict refugees, particularly in the early 1990s, there is often great confusion about where the line may be, should be or can be drawn between Convention refugees and temporary protection.[14] In many of the chapters in this volume it has been pointed out that the public and many politicians felt that Kosovars matched the Convention criteria, in that they were individually fleeing the fear of persecution on the grounds of race and religion. This is an area which highlights the tension between law and politics in refugee protection – linking thus to our thoughts on the comprehensive approach, as well as to questions of imagery, public opinion, and often to the matter referred to above of spontaneous or quota arrival. Politicians have created laws (and sometimes policies which have judicial effects on status) undermining the rights associated with Convention protection and limiting its extension on a national basis. Lavenex clearly pointed to this in her discussion of how temporary protection extended on a national basis can result in a government finding a political escape route between the Convention, or universal norms, on the one side, and maybe, in the future, European norms on the other. The EU, as a result of the conclusions of the Tampere summit meeting (15–16 October 1999), will be reopening discussions on temporary protection on the basis of a proposal to come from the European Commission. One matter still open to question and consideration is how an EU-level temporary protection measure might relate to the Convention. A further issue is that of the space which may still be left open for national discretion, either through late implementation of an EU measure in a particular crisis if it has been agreed upon in advance, or through disagreement over the nature of such a measure, as has been the record to date.

Images

Finally, ending the book as it began, the question of perceptions and images is one which analysts of displacement, international relations and European integration could usefully explore in the context of Kosovo. The chapters in this volume have shown widespread positive public perception of Kosovars as conflict refugees during the actual intervention. The implication of their own states seems indeed to have added to the sense of these being 'good refugees', so long as active military intervention was being undertaken in the sense of military strikes. Once the military became 'peacekeepers' and civilian ground staff moved in under K-FOR, UNMIK (United Nations Interim Administration Mission in Kosovo) and other flags, the perceptions seemed to change: implication was still the case, but in a different, seemingly peaceable and reconstruction oriented context. The conflict refugees, as Guild and Stacher in particular show in this book, were welcomed; once the conflict was, as far as the outside world was concerned, over, the positive assumptions altered.

For some people the memory of those 'poor Kosovar refugees' had already faded by August 1999, when media reports of 'large' groups of illegal Kosovar Albanian immigrants were appearing. The confusion had already begun for some in May, when the same newspaper or TV news bulletin included stories of the displaced and refugees in Albania, Macedonia, Montenegro and Kosovo itself in need of humanitarian assistance, and illegal migrants being smuggled into Italy. All involve people from the same general situation, all were Kosovars, but the former were portrayed as victims needing food parcels and military support to regain their homeland, the latter as a problem which the Western European authorities would have to deal with. The paradoxical labelling falls into the same category of mixed perceptions: the same individual who was a 'poor, helpless Kosovar refugee' when in Albania could be redefined as an 'illegal scrounging immigrant' on arrival via smuggling networks in EU states.[15]

By including the excluded, states and societies can demonstrate and reinforce their nature, or identity, as humane and dynamic. They can also provide a force for rejecting racism and xenophobia. However, EU (and other) states often voice and demonstrate a reluctance to integrate newcomers. Where those fleeing conflict are concerned, one must of course raise questions about the need for integration, in the fullest sense of the word, since return might be held to be a strong possibility, as was indeed the case for many Kosovars in 1999. Nevertheless, where fears about potential integration of newcomers, including conflict refugees, are concerned, there is cause for deep questioning of the nature of society and inter-state relations if a threat-oriented perception becomes a key feature in political decision-making about all facets of protection (status, location, rights, etc.). A key area for future consideration is how the norms established during the ideological confrontation of the Cold War era can adapt to, or withstand the tests of, the post-Cold War world. If 'ethnic cleansing', or group-targeted persecution on the grounds of race, religion, nationality, political opinion or social group, is the post-Cold War version of the individual persecution from which the West was prepared to shelter victims of communism in the Cold War era, then those same Western societies need to face up to pressing questions, including, as this book has demonstrated, whether the apparent reluctance of some to welcome and integrate foreigners is sufficient reason to exclude the victims of persecution and conflict.

Notes

1. J. van Selm-Thorburn, *Refugee Protection in Europe: Lessons of the Yugoslav Crisis* (Dordrecht: Martinus Nijhoff, 1998), p. 154.

2. M. Kjærum, 'Challenges facing the asylum policy of the European Union and its member states, in particular in relation to temporary protection', Paper presented at the workshop on Freedom of Movement and the Treaty of Amsterdam, Åbo Akademi, Turku, Finland (15 September 1999).

3. O. Waever, B. Buzan, M. Kelstrup and P. Lemaitre, *Identity, Migration and the New Security Agenda in Europe* (London: Pinter, 1993), pp. 188-9.

4. Matthew J. Gibney, 'Kosovos and beyond: popular and unpopular refugees', *Forced Migration Review* 5 (August 1999), 29.

5. The evaluation of UNHCR activities in the Kosovo crisis explains how these bi-laterally established camps stood in the way of an effective UNHCR presence. This point should also be considered when evaluating EU states' attempts to formulate a 'comprehensive-approach'. See A. Suhrke, M. Barutciski, P. Sandison and R. Garlock, *The Kosovo Crisis: An Evaluation of UNHCR's Emergency Preparedness and Response* (February 2000), www.unhcr.ch.

6. I am indebted to my colleague Meindert Fennema for a discussion on this notion of 'societal selfishness' and his raising of this point as distinct from xenophobia and of interest in this context.

7. In this way, the security concepts covered here also involve what is called 'human security', as Astri Suhrke has described it. Trying to bring a fundamental conceptual basis to the notion which the Canadian and Norwegian governments in particular have been pushing as an ethically oriented, rights-based, but indeterminate notion of 'human security', Suhrke suggests basing the understanding on vulnerability. Vulnerable individuals need protecting. In this one can see the beginnings of something which could be a link with societal security, a useful alternative to it, or even a contradiction of it. If those supporting human security seek to protect vulnerable individuals, and those offering the understanding of societal security seek the support of identity, even at the expense of vulnerable individuals (or indeed while making some individuals more vulnerable), then there are obvious areas for further reflection. See A. Suhrke, 'Human security and the interests of states', *Security Dialogue* 30 (3) (1999), 265-76.

8. The right to seek and enjoy asylum from persecution is enshrined as article 14 of the Universal Declaration of Human Rights.

9. UNHCR, *Refugees Daily*, 5 November 1999.

10. See M. Frost, 'A turn not taken: ethics in IR at the millennium', *Review of International Studies* 24 (4) (1998), 119-32, for a very useful overview of mainstream international relations, and the appropriateness of developing normative theory in that context.

11. See M. Walzer, *Spheres of Justice: A Defence of Pluralism and Equality* (Oxford: Blackwell, 1985) and M. Walzer, *Just and Unjust Wars: A Moral Argument with Historical Illustrations* (2nd edition, New York: Basic Books, 1992) for strong ethical reasoning for this position.

12. S.L. Woodward, 'Should we think before we leap?', *Security Dialogue* 30 (3) (1999), 278.

13. The American TPS (temporary protected status) is described, for example in S. Martin, A. Schoenholtz and D. Waller Meyers, 'Temporary protection: towards a new regional and domestic framework', *Georgetown Immigration Law Journal* 12 (4) (1998), 543-87, and M. Krikorian, 'Here to stay: there's nothing

as permanent as a temporary refuge': www.cis.org/back899.pdf, 17 August 1999, describes the way in which the USA uses TPS as a form virtually of amnesty, e.g. for Nicaraguans at the time of Hurricane Mitch in 1998.

14. See, for example, Selm-Thorburn, *Refuge Protection in Europe*, chapter 1; W. Kalin, 'Refugees and civil wars: only a matter of interpretation?', *International Journal of Refugee Law* 3 (3) (1991), 435–52.

15. An article in a Dutch newspaper showed precisely this point, with a confused Kosovar detained for illegal entry asking in the title, 'Why am I being imprisoned? I haven't killed anyone': 'Waarom zit ik vast? Ik heb niemand gedood', *NRC Handelsblad*, 12 May 1999, p. 5.

Bibliography

Books and journal articles

Frost, M., 'A turn not taken: ethics in IR at the millennium', *Review of International Studies* 24 (4) (1998), 119–32.

Gibney, M.J., 'Kosovos and beyond: popular and unpopular refugees', *Forced Migration Review* 5 (August 1999), 28–30.

Kalin, W., 'Refugees and civil wars: only a matter of interpretation?', *International Journal of Refugee Law* 3 (3) (1991), 435–52.

Kjaerum, M., 'Challenges facing the asylum policy of the European Union and its member states, in particular in relation to temporary protection', paper presented at the workshop on Freedom of Movement and the Treaty of Amsterdam, Åbo Akademi, Turku, Finland, 15 September 1999.

Krikorian, M., 'Here to stay: there's nothing as permanent as a temporary refuge': www.cis.org/back899.pdf 17 August 1999.

Martin, S., Schoenholtz, A. and Waller Meyers, D., 'Temporary protection: towards a new regional and domestic framework', *Georgetown Immigration Law Journal* 12 (4) (1998), 543–87.

Selm-Thorburn, J. van, *Refugee Protection in Europe: Lessons of the Yugoslav Crisis* (Dordrecht: Martinus Nijhoff, 1998).

Suhrke, A., 'Human security and the interests of states', *Security Dialogue* 30 (3) (1999), 265–76.

Walzer, M., *Spheres of Justice: A Defence of Pluralism and Equality* (Oxford: Blackwell, 1985).

Walzer, M., *Just and Unjust Wars: A Moral Argument with Historical Illustrations* (2nd edition, New York: Basic Books, 1992).

Woodward, S.L., 'Should we think before we leap?', *Security Dialogue* 30 (3) (1999), 277–82.

Primary sources

Universal Declaration of Human Rights.

Reports

Suhrke, A., Barutciski, M., Sandison, P. and Garlock, R., *The Kosovo Crisis: An Evaluation of UNHCR's Emergency Preparedness and Response* (February 2000): www.unhcr.ch

Web sites

UNHCR Refugees Daily, 5 November 1999: www.unhcr.ch/news/media/daily.htm

APPENDIX 1

Reception in other states: information relating to other key states involved in the reception of Kosovars

JOANNE VAN SELM

Protection of Kosovo's displaced in countries other than the seven selected European Union states has been referred to in this volume. The intention in providing this appendix is to offer a convenient source of supporting information, rather than additional analysis. The circumstances of protection of Kosovars arriving between March and June 1999 in a range of states will be described here. These are: Albania; the former Yugoslav republic of Macedonia; Montenegro; Bosnia; Turkey; the eight EU states not covered in the main body of this book; Norway; Switzerland; the United States; and Australia.[1]

Albania

By 6 April 1999, twelve days into the NATO bombing campaign and Serb reactions to that, at least 262,000 Kosovars had arrived in neighbouring Albania. These were in addition to the 18,500 Kosovar refugees who had arrived between 1 March and 24 March, more than half the estimated exodus in those twelve days, and more than double the number of Kosovars to be found in Macedonia. The daily arrival rate was exceeding the total arrivals in the 24 days prior to the NATO campaign. Those arriving were reporting atrocities including summary executions and torture of ethnic Albanians by Serb forces. Almost all displaced Kosovars crossing at Qafe Prushit were arriving on foot; those arriving at Morini came mostly by car or by train or bus. Reports, throughout the exodus, suggested that very few men of 'fighting age' were among the groups crossing the frontier.

210

By 20 April there were more than 350,000 Kosovars seeking refuge in Albania. At that point arrivals suddenly petered out: only 50 people crossed the Morini border on 19 April. Security in the Kukës area was giving rise to grave concerns. Efforts were under way to try to move the refugees away from the border area into southern Albania. However, as would be the case throughout the two and a half month crisis, the refugees themselves were very reluctant to move. By 21 April 212,200 refugees had been moved southwards by the authorities, and some more may have followed the flow by their own means: one of the biggest problems in the early days was that tractors (often the refugees' only remaining possession) had to be left behind. By 5 May the figure had reached some 260,000. NATO played a significant logistical role in the removals. Work was undertaken to construct some 29 new camps, and by 2 June two-thirds of these were completed, with the capacity to take a total of 78,000 refugees. The situation became more acute as more fighting, including NATO shelling, took place closer to the border: on 26 May some shells fell on Albanian villages in the area. This fighting in the area, and shelling straying across the border, continued into early June. However, as time went on, security was not the only problem in the Kukës camps, which were intended to be purely transitory. The increase in population in the area was putting incredible strains on, for example, the water supply. Efforts were undertaken to increase per capita access to drinking water.

The United Nations High Commissioner for Refugees (UNHCR) and non-governmental organizations (NGOs) were providing assistance, and one month into the refugee crisis in Albania, provisions in the form of clothing, hygiene kits and mattresses were being distributed. The UNHCR was taking over management of tent camps in Albania which had previously been in Italian hands, and NGOs such as the Cooperative for American Relief Everywhere (CARE) were acting as implementing partners. The UNHCR gradually took over most camps which had been set up bilaterally by governments in agreement with Albanian authorities. Many refugees were in fact staying with Albanian families, and the UNHCR and the Red Cross were seeking to provide them with some of the necessary assistance. The UNHCR at the end of May was also coordinating the sponsorship being offered to families under the Swiss 'cash for shelter' programme.

At the end of April the number of daily crossings into Albania rose into the thousands again: many were people who had been internally displaced in Kosovo, but had now decided, or had been forced, to make the move across the international border. On 7 May the UNHCR Special Envoy, Dennis McNamara, announced that the Albanian government had agreed to take up to 1 million refugees if necessary. This would include people resettled from neighbouring Macedonia. Although Albania asked for substantial and necessary financial and humanitarian assistance, it undertook to accept very significant numbers of ethnic Albanians from Kosovo, in spite of the precarious political and economic condition in which the state and its society found themselves. On 26 May it was announced by the EU that Albania was to be awarded 'preferential trade terms' in return for its solidarity in refugee protection.

The first day since the start of the exodus on which refugees did not cross the Morini border into Albania, which had been the busiest exodus point, was 17 May. The following day only one person crossed; on 19 May nineteen people crossed. It was unclear whether Serb forces were blocking the exodus, or the Kosovars themselves had decided to stay put for the time being. By 24 May the daily crossings were back up into the thousands; and released prisoners were joining the exodus.

With optimism surrounding the signing of a peace accord, although it had not been implemented, the refugees were, by 8 June, even more reluctant to relocate southwards to Albania. The first date after the announcement of the peace agreement on which no arrivals were reported in Albania was 10 June. The UNHCR distributed information in Albania trying to avoid an over-quick return by the refugees. As NATO troops entered Kosovo under the K-FOR banner, ethnic Albanians from Kosovo started to return to the northern areas around Kukës, hoping to be able to go home soon. Around 5000 refugees crossed the Morini border back into Kosovo on 16 June; the following day some 15,000 made the same journey. In the first week of K-FOR presence, some 50,000 returnees made the journey from Albania back into Kosovo. Only the Morini border crossing was judged safe for passage; other (unofficial) border posts were heavily mined. Four of the nine tent camps in Kukës were closed down by 20 June. In just seven days the number of refugees in Kukës dropped from some 112,000 to less than 35,000. By 1 September only some 10,000 of the 450,000 Kosovar refugees who had been in Albania were still there. The rest had returned to Kosovo, and a few had probably gone, by their own means, to EU states.

Macedonia

By 6 April 1999 there were 120,000 ethnic Albanian refugees from Kosovo in Macedonia, in addition to the 16,000 who had arrived between 1 and 24 March. Macedonia was also still hosting some 1250 refugees from Bosnia. An estimated 14,000 people were moved away from the border area to transit centres.

On 7 April the no man's land, which had held 40,000 stranded Kosovar Albanians prevented from moving on, was suddenly empty. Some of the missing were those who had been moved on (some might say 'expelled') to Norway and Turkey. Others were later rediscovered in Albania. Some of the people were also thought to have moved on to Greece.

The security situation in Macedonia was by this time already tense. Macedonia had a substantial ethnic Albanian minority already, and the political balance was already somewhat worrisome, as witnessed by the ongoing involvement of the High Commissioner on National Minorities of the Organization for Security and Co-operation in Europe (OSCE) in situations such as the establishment of an Albanian university in Tetovo. The UNHCR was having difficulty obtaining registration information on the refugees, and both its officials and those of other assistance organizations had experienced serious harassment from government officials, requiring intervention by NATO troops in the area. There were protests and demonstrations against NATO, whose troops had been stationed (as a protective force) in Macedonia since the break-up of former Yugoslavia. The Macedonian Prime Minister, Ljubco Georgievski, was quoted (by Reuters) as saying that his country was in danger of political and economic collapse. 'How many do we have to take to satisfy Europe and for the Kosovo people to say thank you? All this time we have been trying to get the UNHCR to take care of the refugees. The problem is they are not doing anything.' Macedonia questioned why it was expected to take endless refugees while Greece had agreed to take only 6000 and Bulgaria refused to open its borders. The anger with the West was compounded by the accusation that the NATO states had, through their bombing, caused the arrival of the Kosovars in the first place.

As was the case in Albania, there were sudden, worrying lulls in refugee arrivals. Some of the first evacuations from Macedonia to Norway and Turkey also presented scenes of chaos, with family members being separated and people being unaware of their destinations. After that the evacuation programme from Macedonia, organized by the UNHCR and the International Organization for Migration (IOM) proceeded, apparently, more smoothly. The two organizations registered refugees in the camps in Macedonia, identifying vulnerable cases and those with family connections in the receiving countries. As of 20 April the registration of those present in the camps was complete: 55,000 refugees were registered. By 18 May the UNHCR had registered a camp population of 76,400, while the Red Cross had registered some 120,432 people as staying with host families. Approximately 30,000 non-registered refugees from Kosovo were estimated to be in Macedonia.

Eerie scenes of massive deportations by train were played out on the Kosovo–Macedonia border. As arrivals continued to increase, the Macedonian government agreed to the opening of new camps and enlargement of existing ones, but also sought the resettlement of the refugees via the Humanitarian Evacuation Programme and to neighbouring Albania.

On 8 May UNHCR staff witnessed an estimated 1000 refugees being refused entry from Kosovo. They were forced to go back into Kosovo. The next day Macedonian officials gave assurances that the country would continue to admit refugees. There were few arrivals for a week or so, as rumours spread within Kosovo, according to reports, that the border had been closed. Once arrivals started again, major influxes were the order of the day. Between 21 and 25 May some 30,600 people crossed the border. The following week arrivals dropped dramatically again, as the Serbs reportedly started allowing only those people with papers to leave. Prior to that they had been destroying identification documents and requiring people to sign papers saying they were leaving voluntarily and surrendering all property. The requirement of possession of documentation was again lifted, so reports indicated, by 6 June.

By 27 May, one person in ten in Macedonia was a refugee. Reports in the first days of June suggested that many refugees in Macedonia were starting to give up ideas of return and looking to go abroad. Within two weeks the situation was changing dramatically.

Conditions in the camps were often appalling, and efforts were being made to improve sanitation and inoculate against diseases. However, as in Albania, various Western states established 'national camps' as part of the 'reception in the region' effort. These camps varied in their standards of hygiene, comfort and luxury, inspiring one writer at least to suggest that maximum standards be developed alongside minimum ones. They also took up a large amount of national aid budgets which might otherwise have gone into central, UNHCR-coordinated funds for more balanced relief operations.[2] Many of the necessary supplies, such as blankets, were being ordered locally by the UNHCR. Again, as in Albania, the chief concern was for the hygiene problems summer brought with it, but preparations for a potential winter of misery were also not far from the minds of agency officials. NATO set up a camp for 25,000 Kosovars – the Macedonian government had planned one for 100,000, but the UNHCR insisted on trying to meeting internationally accepted standards, meaning a capacity of 10,000 refugees per camp.

On 8 June a Macedonian village was for the first time the target of rifle-fired grenade attacks from Kosovo.

Independent returns from Macedonia to Kosovo began on 15 June. In some instances one or two family members went on ahead, returning to Macedonia to collect the rest of the family. In order for such 'look and see' visits to take place, the UNHCR again had to become involved in negotiations with the Macedonian authorities about keeping the border open. Some 1000 Serbs also crossed the border, coming out of Serbia in the first ten days after K-FOR's and UNHCR's entry into Kosovo. Aid workers suggested their departure was primarily due to the worsening economic situation.

By the time organized repatriations started on 27 June, 155,000 ethnic Albanians had returned to Kosovo from Macedonia, and 67,200 were left in the country. The first camp (Radusa) was closed on 30 June. By 1 September, 217,600 people holding registration documents had returned, and probably many of those who had been staying unregistered with families in Macedonia had likewise left. Some 5000 people remained in camps.

Montenegro

Between 1 March and 24 March, 25,000 people from Kosovo had arrived in Montenegro. Between 24 March and 6 April there were 36,700 arrivals in Montenegro. On 6 April 1000 people arrived on foot, in Rozaje, from Istok, a thirteen-hour walk. Bridges which could have been used by refugees had been blown up by NATO bombs, for example on the road from Mitrovica to Montenegro.

In Rozaje there was much harassment of displaced persons and those assisting them, and thus concerns for safety. Many of the earliest arrivals moved to the coast, and some people moved from Montenegro into Albania. Local Muslims and people of Albanian origin in Rozaje were starting to leave either for Albania or for Bosnia. From 5 April to 1 May an estimated 7000 Kosovars left the coastal town of Ulcinj for Albania and other destinations. The UNHCR throughout May and early June was transporting people from the border town of Rozaje to the coastal town of Ulcinj. Even so, by 7 May every eighth person in Montenegro was a refugee.

As a partner in the new Yugoslavia with Serbia, Montenegro's security situation was precarious. What is more, it was receiving displaced persons, not refugees, as no international border had been crossed by the Kosovar Albanians, or later Serbs. This made a difference in the assistance which could be anticipated. On 21 April it was reported that the Yugoslavs had brought heavy weaponry into Montenegro both to shell Kosovo and to attack Kosovar displaced persons in Montenegro. Six people were killed on the border by uniformed, but unidentified, forces. On 17 May it was reported that the Yugoslav army had moved to take control of the border crossing between Montenegro and Albania. Men were being arrested and taken back into Kosovo. Two days later the UNHCR was assisting in the release of many of the 106 who had been detained.

As in Albania and Macedonia, the influx of Kosovars came with peaks and lulls. By 19 May it was increasing again: there were 1000 arrivals in four days. Then there were no arrivals for a few days, from 21 to 25 May, before a few people came across the border reporting that Yugoslav soldiers had been separating women and men. Tension was high from the time the border was taken by the Yugoslav army. By 30 May bus loads were arriving again.

With the end of the NATO bombings on 10 June, Montenegrin officials said they would allow Montenegro to be used as a logistical base for the provision of relief supplies to Kosovo, and as a route for refugees returning from Albania. For Montenegro, the end of the bombing campaign did not mean only the return of displaced persons, but also new Serbian arrivals.

On 14 June 126 people, including 119 Serbs, arrived – the first large group of Serbs reported to have moved to Montenegro from Kosovo. That inflow increased over the following days; Montenegro said assistance to them would be offered on the same basis as it was to Kosovar Albanians. By 17 June more than 17,500 were reported to have arrived over a five-day period. Serbian civilians were also reported to be leaving Montenegro in convoys, heading for Serbia proper. Some of the new arrivals only transited Montenegro on the way to Serbia; others stayed, and yet others returned to Kosovo after a brief period.

On 21 June the UNHCR was reporting that returns to Kosovo were still being deterred by Yugoslav army checkpoints on the road from Montenegro to Kosovo. Meanwhile, Kosovo Liberation Army (KLA) members on the Kosovo side were harassing Serb civilians who were trying to leave. As Serbs from Kosovo made arrangements with Italian K-FOR troops regarding their return, the UNHCR was concerned at what could happen if the two returning groups were travelling on the same road at the same time.

Eight hundred Kosovar Albanian displaced persons returned to Kosovo on 22 June, two-thirds on a 'look and see' basis, the other third with definite plans to remain.

Statistics on 22 June showed 69,500 Kosovar Albanians still in Montenegro – only 250 having returned. Meanwhile, 19,300 Serbs had been in Montenegro, 8700 or so of them had moved on into Serbia proper. The return of Kosovar Albanians, once started, seemed fairly rapid: 2800 returned on 23 June: by 27 June, 21,500 had returned; by 30 June 37,000. But more and more Serbs were arriving and/or asking for assistance: by 30 June 21,400 had been in Montenegro, of whom 8800 were estimated to have gone on into Serbia. By 3 July the returns totalled 45,300; more than two-thirds of the displaced persons had returned within twelve days.

The UNHCR's organized repatriation programme began on 7 July. All returns up to that point had been spontaneous; they totalled some 48,300. Four hundred and seven Kosovars used the UNHCR's assistance to return on the first day of the programme.

By 31 August a total of 56,400 people were reported to have returned from Montenegro to Kosovo. At their peak, statistics had indicated that some 65,000 Kosovars were present in Montenegro.

Bosnia

By 21 April Bosnia was reported to be struggling under the influx of 40,000 refugees who had fled Yugoslavia since the explosion of the Kosovo conflict. Most were ethnic Albanians (15,000) or Yugoslav Muslims, but there were also some 2000–3000 Serbs and Montenegrins. Bosnia appealed, via a speech by the vice-chairman of the Council of Ministers (Neven Tomic) to the annual meeting of the European Bank for Reconstruction and Development (EBRD), for international help to support the refugees. They were being sheltered in transit centres which were in fact intended to help resettle displaced Bosnians.

By early May the number arriving from the Sanjak region declined sharply. The number of Serbs arriving had been increasing, however. On 17 May, the head of the Bosnian Serb refugee agency said that it did not have enough money to take care of the 30,000 Serb refugees who had fled Yugoslavia since 24 March; many of them were seeking to avoid conscription.

Carlos Westendorp, High Representative in Bosnia, said that the conflict in Kosovo, and influx of some 40,000 refugees, were hampering implementation of the Dayton Peace Accords.

At the peak, government sources indicated some 70,000 refugees in Bosnia as a result of the Kosovo war: 20,000 Kosovars, 21,000 from Sandjak, plus 30,750 Serbs, Croatians and Montenegrins from the Federal Republic of Yugoslavia (FRY).

Returns from Bosnia got under way on 26 June, and some refugees from previous crises apparently also took this opportunity to return to Kosovo and Serbia. The first airlift from Bosnia to Kosovo took place on 26 August. By 31 August a total of 11,500 people had left Bosnia.

Turkey

Turkey, like Norway, was a recipient of some of the first evacuees on 6 April 1999. These 1360 people were not registered; many were separated from family members, and did not know where they were going. These brought the total number of arrivals from Kosovo in Turkey since 24 March to 6000. By July a total of 5765 evacuees had arrived. Evacuees were accommodated in reception centres throughout the country and considered 'guests of the Turkish Republic'. Voluntary repatriation began in July, with assistance available to those who had arrived before 21 June 1999. Assistance included travel costs and US$50 per person (47 euros). By 27 July 652 assisted returns had taken place. This number had risen to 1764 by 11 August.

Greece[3]

As a neighbour of both Albania and the former Yugoslav republic of Macedonia (FYROM), Greece would be the EU state most likely to be affected by any spillover of the refugees and displaced persons from Kosovo, one would imagine. However, there are two notable facts about Kosovo's refugees, both Albanian and Serb, in Greece. The first is that no one was newly registered as a refugee or asylum seeker from Kosovo in Greece between January and August 1999. The second is that, although no one is registered as such, during July and August groups of Albanian 'illegal aliens' rounded up in Athens included some ten people who claimed to be from Kosovo, and to have joined Albanians in crossing the border seeking seasonal employment.

On 5 April the Greek government had pledged a quota of 5000 Kosovars as a result of EU negotiations. Those 5000 would receive temporary protection. However, the 5000 people were not evacuated to Greece. Instead, the Greeks, like many other EU states, opted for a policy of keeping the refugees close to home, in their 'first country of asylum': Albania and FYROM – one could say the 'buffer zone' between Greece and the source of the displacements. The Greek government provided humanitarian assistance to the refugees in the camps in those two states. It officially ran one refugee camp in Pogredatz, through the Greek Army Forces in Albania, which was dismantled at the end of June 1999. But much aid was sent through less official channels via the Greek church in southern Albania, that is metropolitan Anastasios.

Humanitarian aid to Skopje was facilitated by diplomatic channels, while the coordination and delivery of food and medical aid was done by the Skopje-based Greek humanitarian NGO European Perspective, responsible for aid to refugees living with families (some 200,000) in the region. Material assistance collected by most Greek organizations, professional groups and municipalities was sent to Serbian internally displaced persons and refugees in Kosovo and Serbia through the Orthodox Church channels and other professional organizations (e.g. medics and pharmacists).

As there were officially no refugees or temporarily protected persons from Kosovo in Greece, there was no repatriation programme.

Belgium

The total number of arrivals under the Humanitarian Evacuation Programme was 1223. Temporary protection was granted (to ethnic Albanians only) for six months. This permit was renewable, and offered the right to work and to family reunification. The processing of asylum applications was frozen. Accommodation was provided in reception centres for the duration of the protection. While people could find their own housing if they wished, this is rather difficult in Belgium. Returning refugees receive BFr 10,000 per person (247 euros). Return is carried out on an IOM programme. 'Go and see' is permitted at the refugees' own expense. Special authorization to return must be obtained by those with an outstanding asylum application, otherwise the right to have the claim examined would be lost. One hundred and forty-two assisted returns had taken place by 11 August 1999.

Denmark

The number of arrivals under the Humanitarian Evacuation Programme was 2823. Like spontaneous arrivals, they received a temporary residence permit, renewable every six months for a maximum of two years. Those benefiting from this temporary status could apply for a work permit. Accommodation in reception centres was provided, with equal treatment with asylum seekers. An assisted return programme was being run with IOM. Travel expenses would be covered together with financial assistance of Dkr 18,000 (2418 euros) per adult and Dkr 6000 (806 euros) per child. A further maximum of Dkr 10,000 (1344 euros) would be given for expenses connected with rebuilding work on property in Kosovo. Health insurance and medical expenses would be covered for one year following return. Those taking advantage of the 'go and see' provisions would have to return to Denmark within three months, and cover their own travel expenses. By 11 August 1999, 159 people had returned, and 400 expressions of interest in return had been lodged.

Finland

The 960 people who arrived on the Humanitarian Evacuation Programme and other Kosovar Albanians received an eleven-month residence permit, renewable for up to three years, with the right to work. They were accommodated in ten reception centres around the country, where they received the same services as asylum seekers, although they did not participate in regular integration programmes. By 12 August 1999, 216 people had taken advantage of the assisted return programme. This was voluntary, with travel costs covered and an allowance of 670 euros per person or 1350 euros per family. The returnees may decide to return to Finland, at their own expense, within the period of validity of their residence permit.

Ireland

The 1033 people who arrived on the Humanitarian Evacuation Pro-gramme were granted a one-year residence permit with the right to work. Accommodation was provided in reception centres around the country, and an integration programme including English-language tuition and vocational training was offered. By 11 August 1999, 102 people had returned on an IOM-assisted repatriation programme.

Luxembourg

No temporary protection regime was on offer to the 101 arrivals, who were mainly medical evacuation or family reunification cases. Asylum requests could be lodged at any time. The right to work was granted to those arriving before 14 April regardless of their legal status. Accom-modation was provided in reception centres and other facilities. Assisted, voluntary return could take place with travel costs covered and an allowance of 275 euros per adult and 150 euros per child. No returns had taken place by 11 August 1999.

Portugal

One thousand two hundred and seventy-one Kosovars were evacuated to Portugal under the Humanitarian Evacuation Programme. They were granted humanitarian protection for a six-month period, and accommo-dated in some thirty reception centres across the country, with meals and pocket money provided. No financial support is made available for returns on the IOM-operated programme. For families, only the entire family is allowed to return on the programme, not one or two members, and no 'look and see' visits are permitted. After return on this assisted programme, legal status in Portugal is lost. By 11 August 985 people had returned.

Spain

Those 1426 Kosovo Albanians arriving under the Humanitarian Evacua-tion Programme (HEP) were granted residence on exceptional grounds and the right to work. They and spontaneous arrivals could all apply for asylum. Those under the HEP were accommodated in large reception centres for one month, and then transferred to smaller centres. Spontaneous arrivals who had lodged an application also had access to these facilities and the accompanying language and vocational training courses. Priority in the return programme was given to those with skills essential for rebuilding. Financial aid was given after return. By 11 August 1999, 622 people had returned on the assisted programme.

Norway

As noted above, Norway received some of the first people chaotically evacuated from Macedonia: 90 people on 6 April 1999, who were not properly registered, did not know where they were going and, often, were separated from their families. The total number of Kosovars evacuated to Norway by 5 July was 6072.

The processing of asylum applications was frozen: Kosovar Albanians, whether arriving on the evacuation programme, arriving spontaneously or already in Norway after an asylum application had been rejected, would be given 'collective protection' for four years. Under this form of protection they would enjoy rights almost equivalent to those of Convention refugees, including the right to work and family reunification. Accommodation was provided in reception centres around the country, and, together with a basic monetary allowance, would be available as long as the people in question benefited from 'collective protection'.

By 15 July repatriation had already started. This was on a voluntary basis and in cooperation with the IOM. Those wishing to repatriate were given Nkr 15,000 (1800 euros) per person with no upper limit per family. Those wishing to return would have their travel documents returned, or, if they did not have any, be issued with a Norwegian Alien's Passport, valid for travel to Kosovo. 'Go and see' is permitted, with return to Norway and resumption of 'collective protection' allowed as long as the residence permit has not expired. In this case the refugee in question also has to pay for the flight to Norway and reimburse any financial aid received. By 11 August 1999, 1397 assisted returns had taken place.

Switzerland

On 7 April 1999 the Swiss idea of 'cash for shelter' was suggested and presented at a UNHCR emergency humanitarian conference. This would involve payments to hosts (families) sheltering refugees in Kosovo's neighbouring states.

President Ruth Dreifuss scored a public relations coup by flying into Macedonia by helicopter and taking a symbolic twenty Kosovars back with her. Switzerland, which hosted more Kosovars than any European state other than Germany, agreed both to grant temporary protection on a group basis to spontaneous arrivals and to take evacuated groups. Asylum application processing was not frozen, and both spontaneous arrivals and those arriving on the evacuation programme were allowed to apply for asylum, although those arriving via Italy could be returned there on the basis of a readmission agreement. In general, Kosovar Albanians were given temporary admission as long as the situation in Kosovo remained dangerous. As of 30 April special provisions on family reunification would also be applied.

The total number of asylum seekers from Kosovo in Switzerland as of 27 July was 60,000. Of these, 1800 had arrived on the Humanitarian Evacuation Programme, 29,860 had arrived spontaneously between January and June 1999, and 8000 had arrived under special visa regulations. As of 11 August 1999, 16,618 Kosovars had temporary protection.

Registration of arrivals was carried out in reception centres near the borders. After registration, 'refugees' were transferred to reception centres dispersed around the country. Meals and 'pocket money' were provided. Those arriving on the special visa regulation were permitted to stay with family members already present in the country.

No more temporary protection statuses were being granted after 16 August 1999. The temporarily frozen asylum applications of Kosovar Albanians were reopened on 1 July 1999. The application of cessation clauses for those refugees granted Convention status was likely to come under consideration by the Justice Minister in August 1999.

Repatriation on a voluntary basis in cooperation with the IOM had started in July. Returning refugees could obtain financial assistance, provided they had been included in the temporary protection programme (which would end on 1 October 1999) and had entered Switzerland before 1 July 1999. Sums of SFr 2000 (1260 euros) per adult and SFr 1000 (630 euros) per child were available. Reconstruction kits including plastic sheets, wood and tools would be provided after arrival in Kosovo. To receive this assistance, refugees had to withdraw their applications for legal residence in Switzerland. By 11 August 1999, 1227 assisted returns had taken place.

USA

On 6 April 1999 the 'Guantánamo option' was raised, but by 9 April (when the first arrivals had been planned to take place) it had been abandoned. The idea, to shelter Kosovars at the US base in Guantánamo, Cuba, was opposed by the UNHCR. The Washington representative of UNHCR, Karen Abu Zayd, said, 'The whole idea of moving the refugees out of asylum near their homes is bad, moving out of the region is worse and

Guantánamo is the worst of all.' There was also opposition from academics – voiced by Alexander Aleinikoff and Kathleen Newland of the Carnegie Endowment in a *Washington Post* opinion article. The prospect of putting 20,000 refugees behind barbed wire in Guantánamo should be chilling, they said. Those sheltered there would not be able to apply for asylum because they would not be in the United States. The USA decided instead to establish barracks in Macedonia. By the end of the bombing campaign some 6000 Kosovar Albanians had been evacuated to the USA. As happened elsewhere, many of these people returned to Kosovo during July and August 1999.

Australia

The Australian government announced a quota for 4000 Kosovos under the Humanitarian Evacuation Programme, on 6 April 1999, even before many EU states had decided on co-operating with evacuations.

Notes

1. This appendix presents basic information, primarily gathered from the UNHCR's Daily News service (based on media reports) and the UNHCR's Kosovo Update, produced daily from April to July 1999, and thereafter phased out gradually by mid-September 1999. Neither of these sources contains official United Nations material; they are services provided for public information. Further information used comes from various NGO reports.
2. See T. Porter, 'Coordination in the midst of chaos: the refugee crisis in Albania', *Forced Migration Review* 5 (August 1999), 20–3.
3. Many thanks to Dr Eftixia Voutira of the University of Thessalonika, Greece, for supplying information used in this section.

APPENDIX 2

Tables relevant to all chapters

Table 1 Total arrivals in EU member states of persons evacuated on the UNHCR/IOM Humanitarian Evacuation Programme between 5 April and 6 July 1999

Country	Arrivals
Austria	5,080
Belgium	1,223
Denmark	2,823
Finland	958
France	6,339
Germany	14,689
Greece	0
Ireland	1,033
Italy	5,829
Luxembourg	101
Netherlands	4,060
Portugal	1,271
Spain	1,426
Sweden	3,675
UK	4,346
Total	52,853

Source: UNHCR Kosovo Crisis Update, 9 July 1999: www.unhcr.ch/news/media/kosovo.htm

Notes:
Total evacuations: 91,057
Percentage of total to EU: 58%

Statistics suggest that approximately 900,000 Kosovar Albanians (half of the total population) fled Kosovo between March and June 1999. Many of the other 900,000 were displaced within Kosovo. Up to 90 per cent of the 900,000 who left remained in the neighbouring states and Montenegro (some of these persons probably sought asylum in EU or other European states, or at least entered those states via means other than the evacuation programme). 10 per cent were evacuated, of whom 60 per cent were evacuated to EU states. The influx to the EU was 6 per cent of the Kosovars who left Kosovo, or 3 per cent of the entire Kosovar population.

Table 2 Humanitarian evacuations of Kosovars to EU member states from the former Yugoslav republic of Macedonia (FYROM) (cumulative totals), 5 April–1 July 1999

	AUST.	BELG.	DK	FIN.	FR.	GER.	GR.	IRE.	ITALY	LUX.	NETH.	PORT.	SPAIN	SWE.	UK
20 April	324	517			348	9,974								287	161
27 April	811	676		334	1,185	9,974							103	595	330
2 May	1,145	1,205	156	481	2,354	9,974					854		208	758	330
5 May	1,299	1,205	324	481	2,354	9,974					1,311		208	1,078	330
8 May	1,890	1,205	486	481	2,662	9,974			279		1,626	192	443	1,537	330
17 May	2,635	1,205	1,021	962	3,137	11,602		300	1,825		2,014	506	683	2,133	782
25 May	3,388	1,223	1,513	958	3,717	12,627		449	3,758		2,014	808	900	2,606	1,465
2 June	4,552	1,223	1,997	958	4,543	13,378		603	5,829		2,594	952	1,124	3,089	2,176
8 June	5,080	1,223	2,507	958	5,175	14,013		749	5,829		3,568	1,112	1,240	3,396	3,119
14 June	5,080	1,223	2,670	958	5,614	14,372		893	5,829		4,067	1,271	1,316	3,539	3,756
16 June	5,080	1,223	2,670	958	5,711	14,608		893	5,829	101	4,067	1,271	1,316	3,675	4,056
17 June	5,080	1,223	2,823	958	5,875	14,726		893	5,829	101	4,067	1,271	1,426	3,675	4,056
19 June	5,080	1,223	2,823	958	5,965	14,726		893	5,829	101	4,067	1,271	1,426	3,675	4,191
1 July	5,080	1,223	2,823	958	6,339	14,689		1,033	5,829	101	4,060	1,271	1,426	3,675	4,346

Notes:

Figures are taken from UNHCR Kosovo Crisis Updates: www.unhcr.ch/news/media/kosovo.htm

Statistics are for information purposes only: the web site specifies that it is not an official UN document.

Dates refer to the date of the report, so generally evacuations are up to the preceding day.

Dates are selected to give a weekly overview and show significant increases in shorter periods of time.

Where the 1 July figure is lower than the previous figures, the 1 July figure is the 'corrected total'.

Total evacuations from FYROM to EU member states 5 April–1 July 1999: 52,853

As a percentage of that total:

	AUST.	BELG.	DK	FIN.	FR.	GER.	GR.	IRE.	ITALY	LUX.	NETH.	PORT.	SPAIN	SWE.	UK
	9.6%	2.3%	5.3%	1.8%	12.0%	27.8%	0%	2.0%	11.0%	0.2%	7.7%	2.4%	2.7%	7.0%	8.2%

Table 3 Quotas and arrivals per EU member state to 5 May 1999

Country	Quota	Total arrivals
Austria	Up to 5,000	1,455
Belgium	1,200	1,205
Denmark	1,200–1,400	324
Finland	1,000	481
France	none	2,354
Germany	10,000	9,974
Greece	5,000	0
Ireland	1,000	0
Italy	10,000	0
Luxembourg		
Netherlands	2,000	1,909
Portugal	1,500	0
Spain	Several thousand	208
Sweden	5,000	918
UK	Several thousand	330

Source: UNHCR Statistical Unit (1999)

Table 4 Asylum applications from citizens of Yugoslavia, 1998–9

	AUST.	BELG.	DK	FIN.	FR.	GER.	GR.	IRE.	ITALY	LUX.	NETH.	PORT.	SPAIN	SWE.	UK
1998 total	6,600	6,100	370	360	1,300	35,000	10	140	2,600	1,400	4,300	10	170	3,500	9,500
1998 share	9.25%	8.55%	0.52%	0.50%	1.82%	49.05%	0.01%	0.20%	3.64%	1.96%	6.03%	0.01%	0.24%	4.90%	13.32%
(EU) 1999[a] total	3,736	3,752	524	59	466	13,023	–	87	–	1,590	1,540	–	98	1,024	3,469
(EU) 1999[a] share	12.72%	12.78%	1.78%	0.20%	1.59%	44.34%	–	0.30%	–	5.41%	5.24%	–	0.33%	3.50%	11.81%

Notes:
[a] 1999 = January to May.
UK figures are UNHCR estimates.
A dash (–) means 'figure not available': 1999 share is the share of the total for which information is available.

Total applications from former Yugoslavs in the EU: 1998, 71,360; Jan.-May 1999, 29,368.
In 1998 the EU received 72.53 per cent of the total of 98,390 former Yugoslav asylum applications registered in European states by UNHCR. Switzerland received 20.73 per cent. In the first five months of 1999, 61.22 per cent of the 47,968 requests in Europe were made in the EU, and 26.78 per cent in Switzerland.

Table 5 Estimated Bosnian populations in the EU, start of 1997

Country	Recorded populations
Austria	88,609
Belgium	6,000
Denmark	21,458
Finland	1,350
France	15,000
Germany	342,500
Greece	4,000
Ireland	886
Italy	8,827
Luxembourg	1,816
Netherlands	25,000
Portugal	N/A
Spain	1,900
Sweden	60,671
United Kingdom	6,000
Total	584,017

Source: UNHCR (1997)

Table 6 Returns from EU member states to Bosnia, end of 1997

Country	Recorded returns
Austria	1,601
Belgium	104
Denmark	886
Finland	9
France	180
Germany	70,000
Greece	3
Ireland	87
Italy	494
Luxembourg	0
Netherlands	118
Portugal	7
Spain	16
Sweden	285
United Kingdom	460
Total	74,250

Sources: UNHCR (1997); IOM (1997)

Table 7 Total asylum applications in (current) EU member states, 1988–98

	1988	1989	1990	1991	1992	1993	1994	1995	1996	1997	1998	1988–98
Austria	15,800	21,900	22,800	27,300	16,200	4,700	5,100	5,900	7,000	6,700	12,210	145,610
Belgium	5,100	8,100	13,000	15,200	17,600	26,900	14,400	11,400	12,400	11,800	19,410	155,310
Denmark	4,700	4,600	5,300	4,600	13,900	14,300	6,700	5,100	5,900	5,100	5,190	75,390
Finland	100	200	2,700	2,100	3,600	2,000	800	900	700	1,000	1,000	15,100
France	34,400	61,400	54,800	47,400	28,900	27,600	26,000	20,200	17,400	21,400	15,970	355,470
Germany[a]	103,100	121,300	193,100	256,100	438,200	322,600	127,200	167,000	149,200	151,700	90,350	2,119,850
Greece	8,400	3,000	6,200	2,700	1,900	800	1,300	1,300	1,600	4,400	2,240	33,840
Ireland	–	–	–	–	–	100	400	400	1,200	3,900	4,320	10,320
Italy	1,300	2,300	4,800	26,500	6,000	1,600	1,800	1,700	700	1,900	3,950[b]	52,550
Luxembourg	–	–	–	–	–	–	–	–	200	400	1,490	2,090
Netherlands	7,500	13,900	21,200	21,600	17,500	35,400	52,600	29,300	22,200	34,400	40,800[c]	296,400
Portugal	400	200	100	300	700	2,100	800	500	300	300	300	6,000
Spain	4,500	4,100	8,600	8,100	11,700	12,200	12,000	5,700	4,700	4,900	5,480	81,980
Sweden	19,600	30,300	29,400	27,400	84,000	37,600	18,600	9,000	5,800	9,700	11,980	283,380
UK	5,700	16,800	38,200	73,400	32,300	28,000	42,200	55,000	37,000	41,500	46,890	416,990
Total	210,600	288,100	400,200	512,700	672,500	515,900	309,900	313,400	266,300	299,100	261,580	4,050,280

Sources: UNHCR Statistics (1998, table 17): Annual number of asylum applications submitted in selected countries, 1988–97, and UNHCR Statistics: Asylum seekers in Europe during 1998

Notes:

[a] Germany: 1988–97 figures include new and reopened cases; 1998 is new cases only.

[b] +1000 FRY not registered

[c] Excluding waiting list

A dash (–) indicates that the value is zero, rounded to zero, not available or not applicable.

Table 8 Percentage of asylum seekers per EU member state in 1998 and over the period 1988–98

Member state	1998 (%)	1988–98 (%)
Austria	5	4
Belgium	7	4
Denmark	2	2
Finland	–	–
France	6	9
Germany	34	53
Greece	1	1
Ireland	2	–
Italy	2	1
Luxembourg	1	–
Netherlands	16	7
Portugal	–	–
Spain	2	2
Sweden	5	7
UK	17	10

Notes:
A dash (–) means the percentage rounded down to zero, not that were no asylum seekers

APPENDIX 2

Table 9 Population of the European Union, 1995

State	Population (millions)	Percentage of EU total (rounded)
Austria	8.0	2
Belgium	10.1	3
Denmark	5.2	1
Finland	5.0	1
France	58.0	16
Germany	81.5	22
Greece	10.4	3
Ireland	3.5	1
Italy	57.2	15
Luxembourg	0.4	0
Netherlands	15.4	4
Portugal	9.9	3
Spain	39.1	11
Sweden	8.8	2
UK	58.4	16
Total	370.9	100

Source: Eurostat, *The European Union: Key Figures* (Luxembourg: Official Publications, 1995)

Index